HOT CARS OF THE '50s

HOT CARS OF THE
'50s

THE BEST CARS FROM AROUND THE WORLD

GENERAL EDITOR: CRAIG CHEETHAM

THUNDER BAY
P·R·E·S·S

San Diego, California

Thunder Bay Press
An imprint of the Advantage Publishers Group
5880 Oberlin Drive, San Diego, CA 92121-4794
www.thunderbaybooks.com

All notations of errors or omissions should be addressed to Thunder Bay Press, Editorial
Department, at the above address. All other correspondence (author inquiries, permissions)
concerning the content of this book should be addressed to Amber Books Ltd.,
Bradley's Close, 74–77 White Lion Street, London N1 9PF, England.

ISBN 1-59223-189-6

Library of Congress Cataloging-in-Publication Data available upon request.

Produced by
Amber Books Ltd
Bradley's Close
74–77 White Lion Street
London N1 9PF
England
www.amberbooks.co.uk

Printed in Singapore

1 2 3 4 5 08 07 06 05 04

All photographs © 2004 International Masters Publishers AB,
except pages 6–9 © TRH Pictures

Contents

Introduction

The automobile is a lot more than just a means of transport. Today, many of us take our cars, and the convenience they offer, for granted. We jump in, turn the key and drive off without thinking of the years of development, refinement, and engineering expertise that have gone into making our cars—perhaps the most incredible labor-saving devices of the 20th century—the air-conditioned, safe, comfortable and attractive machines that they are. Even in the late 19th century, the automobile was starting to make its presence felt, but it was not until much later that it became accessible to all.

Ever since the industrial revolution, technology and manufacturing have developed at an incredible rate. Machinery that was originally designed to relieve pressure on manual workers was consistently refined and reduced in size, and the discoveries made by early pioneers of engineering have been continually modified to create inventions to make life easier. It was in the middle of the 20th century, immediately after World War II, that we really started to discover how technology could be made to serve leisure just as much as it had industry.

The 1950s saw many new inventions that made life easier. The sliding door elevator, network television, the polio vaccine, parking meters, and solar panel heating were just some of the decade's many inventions that we now take for granted. While rock-and-roll rocked on and the silver screen became all the more star studded, the 1950s also saw some major news stories unfold. The Korean War started and ended, the King of England died and Queen Elizabeth II—still the head of state today—took over the throne, Joseph Stalin died of a brain haemorrhage, and Nikita Khrushchev ordered Russian tanks into Hungary to stamp out a democratic revolution.

In the car world the 1950s was a golden age. Buyers in North America entered a spirit of prosperity unseen since before the depression of

The late 1950s Chevrolet Corvette revised the original 1953 model by adding twin headlamps and increasing the engine power to 230 bhp.

The 1957 Chevrolet Bel Air was the original '57 Chevy of legend, shown here parked in a suburban American street.

the 1930s, and consumer spending hit an all-time high. By the dawn of the decade, 52 million households in the United States owned a car. Ten years later, that number had increased more than three-fold after one of the most productive periods in American industrial history. Detroit was at its peak, cars became fashion objects as much as they were a means of transport, and other social influences, such as television and rock 'n' roll music, made the automobile the most aspired-after product on the American domestic market. Henry Ford's dream of motoring for the masses at last became large scale reality.

REVOLUTIONARY DESIGN
But it was not just in the United States where car design was revolutionized. All across Europe the car was also having a profound effect on the way people lived their lives. In the early part of the decade, economically, Britain was on its knees. Struggling in the aftermath of World War II, British industry was forced to export or die. Fortunately, Britain was home to some of the finest automotive engineers in the world and some of the finest classic cars ever made were produced in the 1950s. By the end of the decade Britain, too, would be undergoing a period of prosperity. Imports and exports grew, and all of a sudden the car market

was a free trading environment. Buyers could choose any of a large number of domestically-produced vehicles, or a whole raft of machines built and designed overseas.

Each car had its own identity. In America, fins and chrome were the order of the day. Every year saw a new model from each of the big manufacturers—and they are all featured in *Hot Cars of the '50s*. Classics such as the 1953 Chevy Corvette, the 1955 Oldsmobile 88, the stunning 1956 Plymouth Fury, and the 1957 Chevy Bel Air are brought together in this spectacular celebration of 1950s motoring legends. Proof, if it were needed, that they just don't build cars like they used to. *Hot Cars of the '50s* is so well detailed and stunningly photographed that it brings you as close as possible to touching these wonderful machines in the metal, smelling their leather, and running your fingers across the chrome, just as many American families did on the day that Pop brought the all-new '57 Buick back from the dealership.

But away from the chrome-plated excesses of North America, European manufacturers were doing things differently. In Britain, wealthy buyers could choose from a whole host of understated

Produced the year after the Bel Air, the Chevy Impala is perhaps one of the most stylish Chevrolets of the decade, with prominent tail fins and bags of chrome.

Jaguars, such as the Mk V and XK120, the elegant Daimler Majestic, and the Traditional Riley RM.

These cars were not covered in glitzy adornments or swamped in chrome. They were finished in traditional British fashion, with rich leather seats, burr walnut dashboards, and intricate ivory-colored clocks and dials that recalled the days when motoring was strictly reserved for the wealthy. Those with more cash could even get behind the wheel of the truly beautiful Bentley Continental R, considered by many to be one of the seminal classic cars.

Today, these cars are highly collectable and realize serious prices among classic car enthusiasts. But if you cannot afford to put one in your garage, then fear not. *Hot Cars of the '50s* is the next best thing. Our expert analyses, detailed descriptions, and passionate driving impressions do their best to put you behind the wheel—and some of the most desirable British cars ever made are featured here.

AFFORDABLE SPORTS CARS
If luxury was not your thing, Britain could also offer a new breed of affordable sports cars. The Austin Healey 100, MG TF, Triumph TR3, and Aston Martin DB4 were all huge hits in the United States,

where it was widely acknowledged that—Chevy Corvette aside—only Britain could build a proper sports car. With its rich motor sports heritage and legion of world-class drivers, Britain was very much at the top of the tree when it came to building cars with the driver in mind. Who could forget those legendary 24-hour races at the French circuit of Le Mans, where man and machine did battle in cars such as the Jaguar C-Type, Jaguar D-Type, and the MGA, racing side-by-side through the night in a quest to win the ultimate prize? Such was their determination that in 1955 the event claimed the lives of 85 spectators and Mercedes-Benz racing driver Pierre Levegh, after a 150-mph collision with Lance Macklin's Austin-Healey caused his Mercedes to fly off the track and into a grandstand.

In the 1950s, motor sport was serious business for car manufacturers. Not only did winning a trophy offer great publicity and exposure, but it also proved the reliability of the successful cars. Dealers used to say "win on Sunday, sell on Monday," such was the importance attached to a particular model's sporting success.

Unlike today, where racing teams have their own individual pit crews, computer telemetry takes care of the engine and chassis set-ups, and drivers sign multi-million dollar contracts and sponsorship deals, the racing drivers of the 1950s did all of the work themselves. With little more than a leather helmet and string backed gloves, racing drivers of the day would take their life in their hands in the quest for the ultimate prize. And if they broke down en route, they would get their tools out and club together to keep their cars on the road. Motor Racing was big business—and it quickly won British manufacturers the accolade of building the finest performance machines on the road.

EUROPEAN STYLE

But don't tell that to the Italians. Their own Ferraris were already becoming widely regarded as the greatest drivers' cars in the world—a description that still rings true today—and we practically guarantee you will drool over the stunning images of the 250GT California featured here. A car that would command well over six figures at auction today, our stunning photographs and lively prose put you so close you can almost smell the leather in the cabin and the feel the heat emanating from the beautifully-sculpted bonnet. Other gorgeous classics featured include the Porsche 356—the first, original and some argue the best car to wear the hallowed German

marque's badge, while lesser-known but nonetheless important models include the Czechoslovakian Tatra and French Renault Dauphine. We also feature one of the most original cars ever to burn rubber—the Mercedes-Benz 330SL, with its classic "gullwing" sideways opening doors, commonly considered as the world's first post-war supercar.

The criteria for selecting the vehicles that feature in this book is simple: they are either cars that were on the roads in the 1950s, or were produced in that innovative decade. Each and every one of them is a classic and is described here in glorious detail. And if you enjoy this trip down Memory Lane, look out for two other books in this series. *Hot Cars of the '60s* and *Hot Cars of the '70s* will help bring you slowly back to the present day with classics from those decades.

The powerful twin-cam six engine first used in the Jaguar XK120 went on to be a standard feature in the C- and D-type racers, as well all Jaguar sedans up to the XJ6.

AC ACECA

The legendary AC Cobra was derived from the AC Ace which spawned a coupe version called the Aceca. The Aceca combined exceptionally handsome lines with outstanding handling and road manners.

"...poised for high top speeds"

"AC's Ace rocked the sports car establishment—a real sporty, race-bred new-comer. The Aceca is more subtle, but retains a few of the Ace's performance nuances. It's heavier, so acceleration isn't as brisk, but because its aerodynamics are superior it is poised for high top speeds. One of the Aceca's greatest delights is its composed and responsive handling balance: The ride is hard, but in its preferred role as a touring machine, it is impressively effective."

Large steering wheels and neat detailing were normal in the 1950s. The Aceca has both.

Milestones

1953 AC launches its first post-war sports car—the Ace roadster, which uses an AC 2.0-liter engine.

Before the Aceca, AC had already demonstrated its flair for a sleek sports car design with the Ace.

1954 By getting a fixed roof, larger doors and a curved windshield, the Ace is transformed into the Aceca.

1956 Bristol's potent 2.0-liter engine is offered as an alternative to the AC powerplant and overdrive is offered as an option.

AC plans to run the Aceca into the 21st century with this new model, the first Aceca since 1963.

1961 A Ruddspeed-tuned Ford 2.6-liter engine, offering power up to 170 bhp, is offered by the factory.

1963 Production of the Ace and Aceca ends.

UNDER THE SKIN

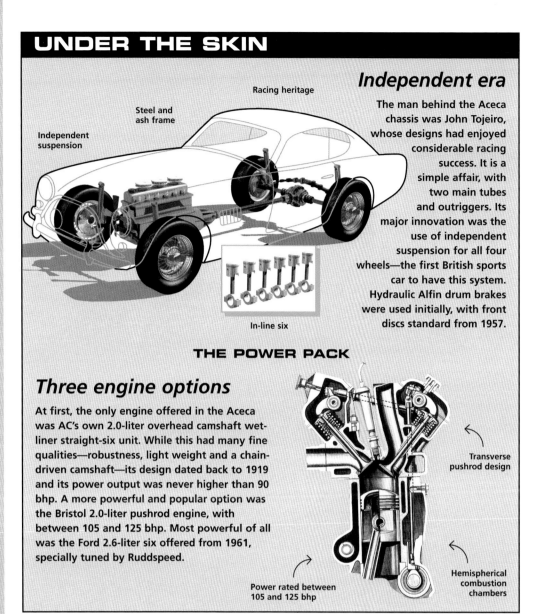

Racing heritage

Steel and ash frame

Independent suspension

In-line six

Independent era

The man behind the Aceca chassis was John Tojeiro, whose designs had enjoyed considerable racing success. It is a simple affair, with two main tubes and outriggers. Its major innovation was the use of independent suspension for all four wheels—the first British sports car to have this system. Hydraulic Alfin drum brakes were used initially, with front discs standard from 1957.

THE POWER PACK

Three engine options

At first, the only engine offered in the Aceca was AC's own 2.0-liter overhead camshaft wet-liner straight-six unit. While this had many fine qualities—robustness, light weight and a chain-driven camshaft—its design dated back to 1919 and its power output was never higher than 90 bhp. A more powerful and popular option was the Bristol 2.0-liter pushrod engine, with between 105 and 125 bhp. Most powerful of all was the Ford 2.6-liter six offered from 1961, specially tuned by Ruddspeed.

Transverse pushrod design

Hemispherical combustion chambers

Power rated between 105 and 125 bhp

Buy Bristol

Of the engines offered, by far the more sought after is the more powerful and more modern Bristol unit. A Bristol-engined car is worth up to 40 percent more than the AC-engined version. The ultra-rare Ford 2.6 version (just eight were made) is highly desirable.

The Bristol-engined cars offer the best combination of power and value.

11

AC **ACECA** 🇬🇧

AC is undoubtedly one of the great British sports car names and the Aceca's all-around quality balanced the company's reputation. It boasted a design and build quality of great integrity.

AC, Bristol or Ford engines

The overhead-camshaft AC engine was a highly advanced unit when it was designed in 1919 but by the 1950s its low-revving nature was a hindrance. The smoother Bristol engine, like the tuned Ford unit, was well received.

Simple but effective chassis

Tojeiro's chassis is a very simple twin-tube affair, combining light weight with clever suspension. Its efficiency and simple design made it ideal for competition use.

Wooden frame

The bodywork is made of aluminum panels but underneath it lies a complex framework composed partly of steel tubes and partly of ash—strong but light.

Practical cabin

Unlike the basic roadster form of the Ace, the Aceca was designed to be a practical GT car. As such, it has a large luggage platform behind the seats that can be accessed from inside the cabin or the tailgate.

Italian-inspired styling

For the Aceca, AC closely examined the Touring body on the Ferrari 195 coupe. Most pundits recognized the Aceca as superbly proportioned and correctly styled.

All-independent suspension

The Ace/Aceca was the first British sports car to gain independent suspension on all four wheels. Its handling is much superior to that of rivals with rigid rear-axles.

Dunlop wire wheels

Elegant and classically sporty Dunlop center-lock wire wheels are standard. Their generous diameter (at 16 inches) is typical of the time.

Specifications

1955 AC Aceca

ENGINE
Type: In-line six-cylinder

Construction: Aluminum cylinder block and head

Valve gear: Two valves per cylinder operated by a single chain-driven overhead camshaft

Bore and stroke: 2.56 in. x 3.94 in.

Displacement: 1,991 cc

Compression ratio: 8.0:1

Induction system: Three SU carburetors

Maximum power: 90 bhp at 4,500 rpm

Maximum torque: 110 lb-ft at 2,500 rpm

Top speed: 104 mph

0-60 mph: 9.4 sec.

TRANSMISSION
Four-speed manual

BODY/CHASSIS
Separate chassis with aluminum two-door coupe body

SPECIAL FEATURES

While the Ace roadster has a flat windshield, the Aceca benefits from curved glass.

The Aceca's rear tailgate enhances GT practicality considerably.

RUNNING GEAR
Steering: Cam gear

Front suspension: Dual wishbones with transverse leaf spring and telescopic shock absorbers

Rear suspension: Dual wishbones with transverse leaf spring and telescopic shock absorbers

Brakes: Drums (front and rear)

Wheels: Wire, 16-in. dia.

Tires: 5.50 x 16 in.

DIMENSIONS
Length: 153.5 in.   **Width:** 61.0 in.

Height: 52.0 in.   **Wheelbase:** 90.0 in.

Track: 50.0 in. (front and rear)

Weight: 2,156 lbs.

Allard **J2**

Stark, crude and antiquated, the Allard J2 remains a true legend for one simple reason: its V8 engine makes it amazingly fast. It's a hairy machine and it proved popular as a circuit racer.

"...remarkable performance"

"This is a car that you approach with awe. Like most successful British sports cars, the J2 uses an American V8 engine and lightweight chassis. With a Mercury 239 V8, it's no surprise that the engine gives remarkable torque and effortless power delivery. The huge steering wheel, widely-spaced pedals and gear shifter require a great deal of effort. Sitting high up, you feel tremendously exposed, with little in the way of protection."

With few creature comforts, driving the J2 can be hard work.

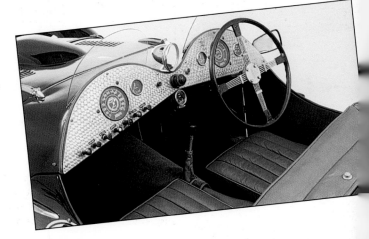

Milestones

1949 Allard's new short-chassis J2 is launched. It is crude in the extreme with split-axle front suspension and separate cycle-type fenders. Standard power is a 239-cubic inch flathead Mercury V8.

J1s are powered by either 239-cubic inch Ford or 239-cubic inch Mercury V8 engines.

1951 An improved model, designated J2X, supplants the original J2. It has a longer nose, leading arm front suspension, and an engine mounted 7.5 inches further forward. It is highly successful in competition.

The Allard K2 is quite civilized with doors and four seats.

1954 Production switches to the more streamlined JR competition model, which has Cadillac suspension and the chassis from the Allard Palm Beach sports car.

UNDER THE SKIN

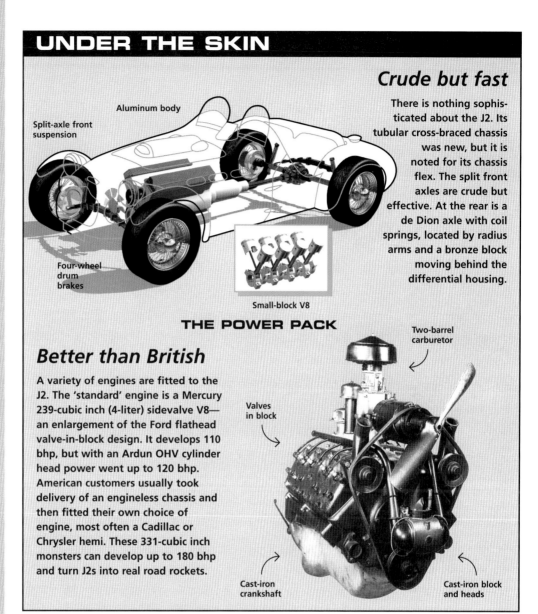

Crude but fast

There is nothing sophisticated about the J2. Its tubular cross-braced chassis was new, but it is noted for its chassis flex. The split front axles are crude but effective. At the rear is a de Dion axle with coil springs, located by radius arms and a bronze block moving behind the differential housing.

Aluminum body

Split-axle front suspension

Four-wheel drum brakes

Small-block V8

THE POWER PACK

Better than British

A variety of engines are fitted to the J2. The 'standard' engine is a Mercury 239-cubic inch (4-liter) sidevalve V8—an enlargement of the Ford flathead valve-in-block design. It develops 110 bhp, but with an Ardun OHV cylinder head power went up to 120 bhp. American customers usually took delivery of an engineless chassis and then fitted their own choice of engine, most often a Cadillac or Chrysler hemi. These 331-cubic inch monsters can develop up to 180 bhp and turn J2s into real road rockets.

Two-barrel carburetor

Valves in block

Cast-iron crankshaft

Cast-iron block and heads

Improved J2X

The most fondly regarded member of the J2 family is the 1951-1954 J2X. The X designation refers to the extended nose (it is 6 inches longer), which is necessary to cover a revised leading arm front suspension which replaced the old trailing arm set up.

Externally, the J2X differed slightly from the short-nosed J2.

Allard J2

The J2 was conceived after Sydney Allard visited the U.S. and saw the benefits of an American V8 engine combined with a lightweight chassis.

Split-axle suspension

To produce an independently sprung set up, Allard chopped a Ford beam axle in half and located each piece by long radius arms.

Stark style

The interior is spartan, with driver protection limited to a small aero windshield.

Three-speed transmission

The transmission is taken straight from the Mercury. The sheer torque from the V8 engine in such a light frame makes extra ratios completely redundant.

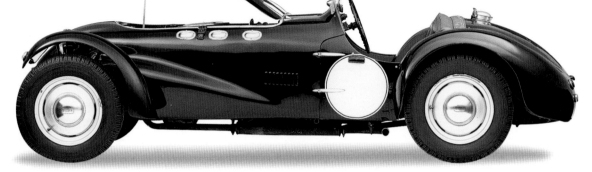

Ford-based rear end

To reduce unsprung weight a de Dion type rear suspension, with a quick-change center section, is used. Radius arms and a bronze block provides location.

Classic dashboard

The engine-turned aluminum dash follows the contours of the 'double-bubble' cowl. The fascia contains a 5-inch speedometer and tachometer, oil and temperature gauge, fuel gauge and a fuel switch.

American V8

The standard J2 engine is a sidevalve Mercury V8, but for more power an overhead-valve Cadillac or Chrysler V8 was commonly installed.

Specifications

1952 Allard J2

ENGINE
Type: V8

Construction: Cast-iron cylinder block and heads

Valve gear: Two valves per cylinder operated by single camshaft via pushrods and rockers

Bore and stroke: 3.81 in. x 3.62 in.

Displacement: 4,375 cc

Compression ratio: 7.5:1

Induction system: Twin carburetors

Maximum power: 140 bhp at 4,000 rpm

Maximum torque: 225 lb-ft at 2,500 rpm

Top speed: 110 mph

0-60 mph: 8.0 sec.

TRANSMISSION
Three-speed manual

BODY/CHASSIS
Separate chassis with two-door aluminum sports body

SPECIAL FEATURES

The shape of the grill is distinctively Allard, and is a feature of all models.

Six functional ventiports on either side of the hood allow hot air to escape from the cramped engine compartment.

RUNNING GEAR
Steering: Marles recirculating ball

Front suspension: Split Ford axle with radius arms, coil springs and shock absorbers

Rear suspension: De Dion tube with radius arms and coil springs

Brakes: Drums (front and rear)

Wheels: Wires, 16-in. dia.

Tires: 6.00 x 16 in.

DIMENSIONS
Length: 148.0 in.   **Width:** 63.0 in.

Height: 44.5 in.   **Wheelbase:** 100.0 in.

Track: 56.0 in. (front), 52.0 in. (rear)

Weight: 2,072 lbs.

Alvis **TD21**

In the late 1950s, if you couldn't afford a Bentley or a Rolls-Royce and thought Jaguars were too common and cheap, the perfect alternative was an Alvis. It had outstanding quality, a famous name and exclusivity.

"...excellent ride and handling"

"Alvis TD21 buyers wanted a driving experience rather than outright speed or acceleration, although both of these were perfectly adequate. The experience comes from a luxury interior, good looks and an excellent combination of ride and handling. Steering is sensitive and accurate and the whole car responds more like a 1960s' sports car than an elegant carriage. The ride is supple and relaxing, and the disc brakes are very effective."

Plenty of wood and leather gives the Alvis a really classy atmosphere inside.

Milestones

1955 Swiss coachbuilder
Graber shows a sport sedan based on the Alvis TC21 chassis. It inspires Alvis to build a similar model in England, but only 16 are made.

The TC21 was a much more traditional, upright car.

1958 The Graber styling
is used for the TD21. It is built as a two-door hardtop and a convertible.

The TD21 was replaced by the TE21 with stacked headlights.

1962 Substantial changes result
in the Mk II. It has Dunlop four-wheel disc brakes rather than front discs and rear drums, the rear lights are restyled and a ZF five-speed manual transmission is added.

1964 The TD21 is replaced
by the new and restyled TE21.

UNDER THE SKIN

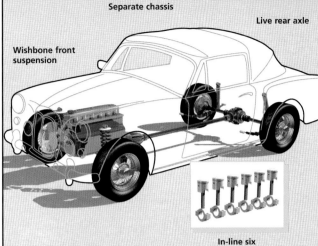

Separate chassis — Live rear axle — Wishbone front suspension — In-line six

Traditional layout

All Alvis cars of this era are front-engined, driving the rear wheels through a four-speed and then a five-speed manual transmission or three-speed automatic. They are built on a separate chassis which is attached to a double wishbone and coil-sprung front suspension, with an anti-roll bar. The rear is a traditional live axle sprung by semi-elliptic leaf springs. Initially, the brakes were front discs and rear drums, but this was changed to four-wheel discs.

THE POWER PACK

Simple six

Alvis' in-line six-cylinder engine dates back to 1950, when the Alvis TA21 was launched. It is a simple design with a cast-iron block and head. There are only two overhead valves per cylinder operated by a single camshaft in the block via pushrods and rockers. It is not a cross-flow design, and so the inlet and exhaust manifolds are on the same side of the engine, compromising the engine's breathing and efficiency. It is, however, very strong and smooth and produces masses of torque.

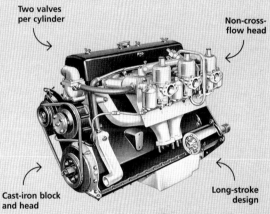

Two valves per cylinder — Non-cross-flow head — Cast-iron block and head — Long-stroke design

Swiss styling

Perhaps the most elegant of the TC to TF21 variants are the original Graber-bodied cars. The Swiss coachbuilder had been building sedans on the TC21 chassis for some time before Alvis took up the gauntlet. The first of the Alvis-commissioned cars had bodies built by the English firm Willowbrook, although Park Ward took over almost immediately.

Swiss-built Graber cars are the rarest and purest.

Alvis **TD21**

The elegant look of the TD21 was all thanks to the Swiss coachbuilder Hermann Graber, who had been building his own design on an Alvis chassis since the early 1950s.

Recirculating-ball steering

You might expect a car of the Alvis' class to have rack-and-pinion steering, but it used an unassisted recirculating-ball system. By 1965, the car could be ordered with ZF power steering.

In-line six-cylinder

Alvis steadily increased the power of its conventional in-line six-cylinder all-iron engine from just 90 bhp in 1950. By the time the TD21 was made, the output had risen to 115 bhp, thanks to a higher compression and twin carburetors.

Separate chassis

There is nothing particularly complicated about the Alvis chassis; it is a conventional ladder-type frame with crossmembers. Because the car had a separate chassis, it was easier to make a convertible version.

Alloy bodywork

The Alvis bodies were coachbuilt and very labor intensive. They are made from a mixture of aluminum and steel. The trunk and hood are alloy, and the first TD21s had steel doors. For the Mk II, they were changed to alloy frames and skins.

Wooden frame

Until 1963, Alvis still used a lot of wooden framing in the old-fashioned way to make the bodies. The windshield pillars are made of solid ash, as are the door posts and the door frames.

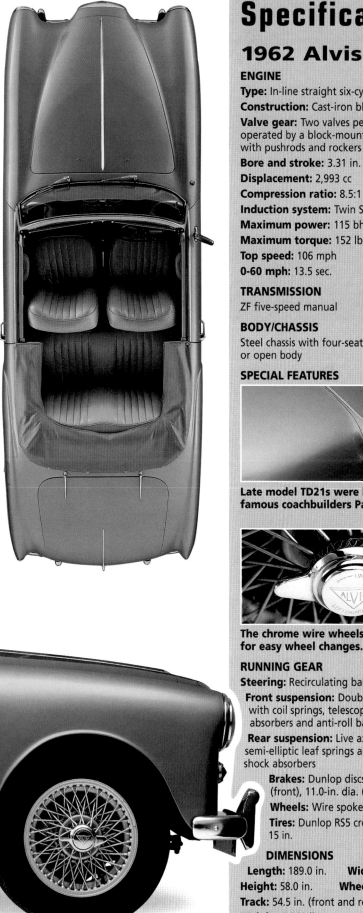

Live axle
The conventional live rear axle is sprung by semi-elliptic leaf springs.

1962 Alvis TD21

ENGINE
Type: In-line straight six-cylinder
Construction: Cast-iron block and head
Valve gear: Two valves per cylinder operated by a block-mounted camshaft with pushrods and rockers
Bore and stroke: 3.31 in. x 3.54 in.
Displacement: 2,993 cc
Compression ratio: 8.5:1
Induction system: Twin SU carburetors
Maximum power: 115 bhp at 4,000 rpm
Maximum torque: 152 lb-ft at 2,500 rpm
Top speed: 106 mph
0-60 mph: 13.5 sec.

TRANSMISSION
ZF five-speed manual

BODY/CHASSIS
Steel chassis with four-seater closed or open body

SPECIAL FEATURES

Late model TD21s were bodied by famous coachbuilders Park Ward.

The chrome wire wheels are knock-on for easy wheel changes.

RUNNING GEAR
Steering: Recirculating ball
Front suspension: Double wishbones with coil springs, telescopic shock absorbers and anti-roll bar
Rear suspension: Live axle with semi-elliptic leaf springs and telescopic shock absorbers
Brakes: Dunlop discs, 11.5-in. dia. (front), 11.0-in. dia. (rear)
Wheels: Wire spoke, 4.5 x 15 in.
Tires: Dunlop RS5 crossply, 600 x 15 in.

DIMENSIONS
Length: 189.0 in.   **Width:** 66.0 in.
Height: 58.0 in.   **Wheelbase:** 111.5 in.
Track: 54.5 in. (front and rear)
Weight: 3,360 lbs.

Aston Martin **DB4 GT ZAGATO**

Aston Martin's DB4 GT was too heavy to be competitive, so it was given lightweight and aerodynamic Italian Zagato bodywork. With its 3.7-liter, six-cylinder engine tuned to 314 bhp, a 150 mph supercar was born.

"...fast and exciting road car"

"The DB4 GT Zagato is a racer that doubles as a fast and exciting road car. Given its high state of tune, the engine doesn't behave too badly. It has a lumpy idle, but when the revs are up it becomes obvious that this noisy powerplant means business. The gearshifter can be obstructive, however, it becomes much easier with familiarity. The Zagato's performance is astounding, with a top speed of 152 mph and hitting 100 mph in less than 14 seconds."

The leather trimmed interior is attractive and all the gauges are easy to read.

Milestones

1958 Aston Martin

launches the DB4. Its 3.7-liter, 240-bhp engine gives astounding performance figures. It is sold alongside its predecessor, the DB Mark III.

Aston Martin's racer from the mid-1950s was the DB3S.

1959 The DB4 GT

debuts at the London Motor Show. Gianni Zagato meets John Wyer, Aston Martin's general manager.

1960 A chassis is

sent to the Zagato factory on the outskirts of Milan, where it is given a new skin. Power is now up to 314 bhp.

The standard DB4 is longer and heavier than the DB4 GT.

1961 Two factory

cars enter the Le Mans 24 Hours race. Unfortunately, both of them retire early.

1963 Production

ends and Aston Martin now has a more specialized racer.

UNDER THE SKIN

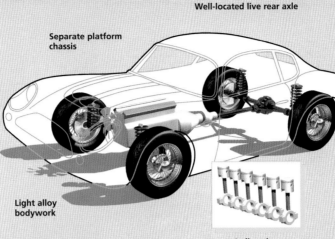

Well-located live rear axle

Separate platform chassis

Light alloy bodywork

In-line six

Short and sweet

Built on the same basic chassis as the DB4 GT, the Zagato has wishbone front suspension and a coil-sprung live rear axle. A limited-slip differential is fitted as standard. The platform was hand-built in England then shipped to Milan for its alloy body. It incorporates light steel tubes that help support the bodywork.

THE POWER PACK

Highly tuned

The starting point for the Zagato engine was the DB4 GT unit, which was in turn derived from the DB4's new in-line twin-cam six. It has a capacity of 3,670 cc from the square bore and stroke dimensions of 3.62 inches x 3.62 inches. The all-alloy engine has chain-driven camshafts operating two valves per cylinder in the cross-flow head with hemispherical combustion chambers. The GT unit has an increased compression ratio, higher-lift cams, three carburetors and two spark plugs per cylinder.

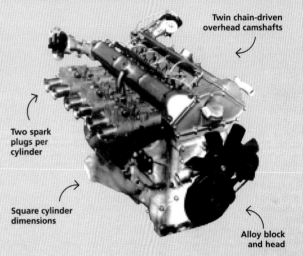

Twin chain-driven overhead camshafts

Two spark plugs per cylinder

Square cylinder dimensions

Alloy block and head

Racer returns

When the original run of 19 Zagatos had been completed, four chassis numbers allocated to the model were left over. In 1991, these remaining chassis numbers were used on near-exact replicas, known as Sanction II cars, which were approved by Aston Martin and built with the help of Zagato.

The Sanction II DB4 GT Zagatos are more powerful than the original cars.

Aston Martin **DB4 GT ZAGATO**

When Aston Martin wanted to beat Ferrari's 250 GT SWB, the company needed something even more special than its 302-bhp DB4 GT. The result was the sensational-looking DB4 GT Zagato.

Independent front suspension

The DB4 GT has a double wishbone assembly with a particularly wide lower link. An anti-roll bar improves the car's cornering.

Thoroughbred six-cylinder engine

The highly-tuned, all-alloy, 3,670-cc straight-six engine has twin overhead camshafts and two spark plugs per cylinder.

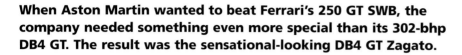

Alloy-rim wire wheels

Center-lock Borrani wire wheels are fitted as standard, with alloy rims to reduce weight. The wheels have 72 spokes—a larger number than usual—to cope with the engine's 278 lb-ft of torque.

Lightweight Perspex windows

To keep weight to a minimum, the Zagato has Perspex side and rear windows.

Specifications

Aston Martin DB4 GT Zagato

ENGINE
Type: In-line six-cylinder
Construction: Alloy block and head
Valve gear: Two valves per cylinder operated by twin overhead camshafts
Bore and stroke: 3.62 in. x 3.62 in.
Displacement: 3,670 cc
Compression ratio: 9.7:1
Induction system: Three twin-choke sidedraft carburetors
Maximum power: 314 bhp at 6,000 rpm
Maximum torque: 278 lb-ft at 5,400 rpm
Top speed: 152 mph
0-60 mph: 6.1 sec.

TRANSMISSION
Four-speed manual

BODY/CHASSIS
Separate box-section chassis with alloy two-door coupe body

SPECIAL FEATURES

A quick-release fuel filler allowed faster refuelling during endurance races.

Twin exhausts help to expel combustion gases as efficiently as possible.

RUNNING GEAR
Steering: Rack-and-pinion
Front suspension: Double wishbones with coil springs and telescopic shocks
Rear suspension: Live axle with radius arms, Watt's link, coil springs and telescopic shocks
Brakes: Discs, 12 in. dia. (front), 11 in. dia. (rear)
Wheels: Borrani center-lock wire wheels
Tires: Avon Turbospeed Mk II, 6.00 x 16 in.

DIMENSIONS
Length: 168 in.   **Width:** 65.3 in.
Height: 50 in.   **Wheelbase:** 93 in.
Track: 54.4 in. (front), 54.5 in. (rear)
Weight: 2,765 lbs.

Short wheelbase
The DB4 GT Zagato (and DB4 GT) has a wheelbase that is 5 inches shorter than the standard four-seater DB4, thus reducing weight.

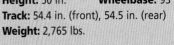

Austin Healey **100M**

In 1952, a stunning open sports car was displayed at the London Motor Show by the Donald Healey Motor Company. The Austin-Healey 100 became Austin's answer to Triumph's TR2 and proved incredibly popular in the U.S.

"...the car is easy to control."

"You sit close to the big steering wheel in the Austin-Healey, but that doesn't mean that the steering requires a lot of effort. It is a bit dead, but very direct and precise. Excellent seats make up for the bouncy and stiff suspension, and it's impossible not to enjoy the torquey engine and precise gearshift. It's not quiet or smooth, but the bellow says there's plenty of power. There is always enough torque to swing the narrow rear tires out, but the car is easy to control."

It's a classic British sports car driving position with the steering wheel at your chest.

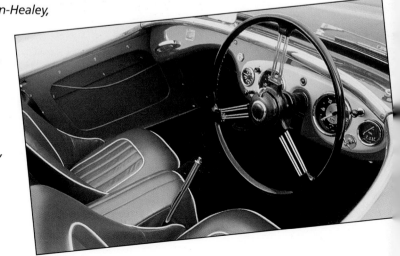

Milestones

1952 The Healey 100

(which is quickly adopted by Austin to become the Austin-Healey 100) is launched. Production begins the following year.

The 100 of 1953 was the first Austin-Healey.

1953 Competition 100s, called Special Test cars, compete in the Liege-Charbonnieres-Liege rally, the Mille Miglia and at Le Mans.

Perhaps the best-known Austin-Healey is the 3000.

1954 A competition version of the 100 finishes third in the Sebring 12 Hours. A batch of similar cars, called the 100S (S for Sebring), follows.

1955 A 100S is sixth at Sebring and five others finish. The 100M is launched.

1956 Production of the four-cylinder 100 comes to an end.

UNDER THE SKIN

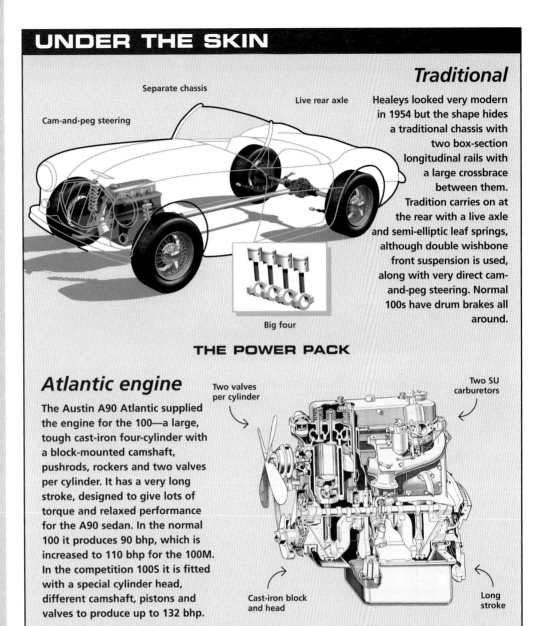

Separate chassis

Cam-and-peg steering

Live rear axle

Big four

Traditional

Healeys looked very modern in 1954 but the shape hides a traditional chassis with two box-section longitudinal rails with a large crossbrace between them. Tradition carries on at the rear with a live axle and semi-elliptic leaf springs, although double wishbone front suspension is used, along with very direct cam-and-peg steering. Normal 100s have drum brakes all around.

THE POWER PACK

Atlantic engine

The Austin A90 Atlantic supplied the engine for the 100—a large, tough cast-iron four-cylinder with a block-mounted camshaft, pushrods, rockers and two valves per cylinder. It has a very long stroke, designed to give lots of torque and relaxed performance for the A90 sedan. In the normal 100 it produces 90 bhp, which is increased to 110 bhp for the 100M. In the competition 100S it is fitted with a special cylinder head, different camshaft, pistons and valves to produce up to 132 bhp.

Two valves per cylinder

Two SU carburetors

Cast-iron block and head

Long stroke

Le Mans 100

The best of the ordinary 100s is the 100M (M for Le Mans). Although it retains the all-iron engine, it is tuned for 110 bhp and there is an excellent 143 lb-ft of torque to guarantee performance. It can reach 110 mph and has a 0-60 time of 9.6 seconds.

The 100M is not as rare as the 100S but is almost as fun and much cheaper.

Austin Healey 100M

One of the most famous and perfect sports car shapes ever created was produced in-house by the small Healey Motor Company, with no input from any of the world's great stylists.

Alloy bodywork

For a simple car the bodywork is very complex, with a main understructure of a substantial front bulkhead, rear bulkhead and inner fenders. The outer panels are mounted on this and are all-alloy in the 100S to save weight.

Tuned engine

The cylinder head of the standard Austin engine is poor, with restricted breathing and inlet and exhaust ports on the same side. The 100M features a higher compression ratio and the 100S had a completely new head, with individual ports and different cam timing.

Underslung chassis

One reason all the big Healeys sit so low is that the chassis rails actually run under the live axle at the rear. This is in total contrast to most designs where the chassis rails kick up at the back to clear the axle.

Two-tone bodywork

The contour of the body lent itself to a two-tone paint scheme. The natural body line started from the top of the front fender and ran the length of the car through the rear wheel well to the rear bumper.

Distinctive grill

The 100 and the 100M have this distinctive curved triangular grill. The 100S uses a different oval grill like that used on the later Austin-Healey 3000.

Separate chassis

The chassis consists of two main box-section longitudinal rails with 'X' cross braces near the center of the car, a single crossmember at the rear and a bigger, stronger crossmember at the front. Outriggers are fitted to carry the inner sills.

Specifications

1955 Austin-Healey 100M

ENGINE
Type: In-line four

Construction: Cast-iron block and cylinder head

Valve gear: Two valves per cylinder operated by single block-mounted camshafts via pushrods and rockers

Bore and stroke: 3.44 in. x 4.37 in.

Displacement: 2,660 cc

Compression ratio: 8.1:1

Induction system: Twin SU carburetors

Maximum power: 110 bhp at 4,500 rpm

Maximum torque: 143 lb-ft at 2,000 rpm

Top speed: 110 mph

0-60 mph: 9.6 sec.

TRANSMISSION
Four-speed manual; optional overdrive

BODY/CHASSIS
Separate chassis with alloy and steel two-seater roadster body

SPECIAL FEATURES

Powerful headlights are a must on a sports car.

The 100M has a leather hood-retaining strap that wasn't fitted to standard 100s.

RUNNING GEAR
Steering: Cam-and-peg

Front suspension: Double wishbones with coil springs, lever-arm shock absorbers and anti-roll bar

Rear suspension: Live axle with leaf springs, lever-arm shock absorbers and Panhard rod

Brakes: Drums (front and rear)

Wheels: 72-spoke wires, 4 x 15 in.

Tires: Crossply, 5.90-15

DIMENSIONS
Length: 147.5 in.   **Width:** 60.5 in.

Height: 47.0 in.   **Wheelbase:** 90.0 in.

Track: 49.0 in. (front), 50.8 in. (rear)

Weight: 2,385 lbs.

Bentley **MK VI**

Moustaches twitched and eyebrows were raised in London clubs at the sight of the first post-war Bentley. The MKVI was a huge departure from the pre-war sports cars, but it succeeded in increasing Bentley's sales.

"...dignified and refined."

"The whole point of driving a Bentley is to sit back and appreciate the quality of your surroundings. The straight-six engine is all but silent and so torquey that you never need to rev it. The ride quality is magic-carpet smooth for a car from this era, and so is the gearshift, although the handling is not sporty. Ettore Bugatti once said that the Bentley was 'the world's fastest lorry,' but no truck was ever this dignified or refined."

A huge steering wheel and upright seats require a dignified driving posture.

Milestones

1933 Due to financial problems, W.O. Bentley sells his company to rival Rolls-Royce.

1946 Bentley launches its first steel-bodied sedan, the MKVI.

A long time after they went out of production, some specialists turned MKVIs into sports cars.

1949 A sister Rolls-Royce model, the Silver Dawn, joins the Bentley.

The Rolls-Royce Silver Dawn has the same chassis as the MKVI.

1951 A larger 4.6-liter engine is introduced in place of the previous 4.3-liter powerplant.

1952 The MKVI is replaced by the new, long-tail R-Type, which lasts for another three years.

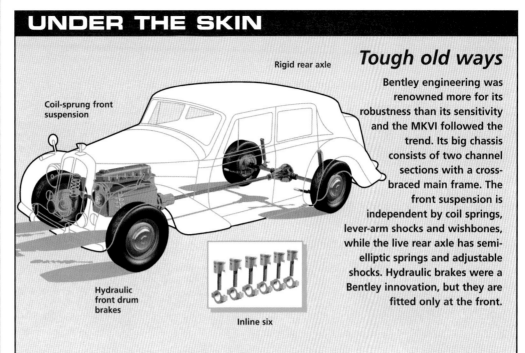

Rigid rear axle

Coil-sprung front suspension

Hydraulic front drum brakes

Inline six

Tough old ways

Bentley engineering was renowned more for its robustness than its sensitivity and the MKVI followed the trend. Its big chassis consists of two channel sections with a cross-braced main frame. The front suspension is independent by coil springs, lever-arm shocks and wishbones, while the live rear axle has semi-elliptic springs and adjustable shocks. Hydraulic brakes were a Bentley innovation, but they are fitted only at the front.

THE POWER PACK

Pre-war straight-six

Despite sharing its internal dimensions with the old MKV engine, the so-called B60 engine in the MKVI was in fact all new. Part of a range of engines designed in 1937 by William Robotham—all with interchangeable pistons—the 4,257-cc engine's chief innovation is its unusual valve layout. The intake valve is mounted overhead, while the exhaust valve is located to the side of the pistons. In postwar years, Bentley fought shy of revealing power outputs, but it was estimated that the engine developed 137 bhp. In 1951, the bore was expanded to give a 4,566-cc displacement, with an estimated 150 bhp on tap.

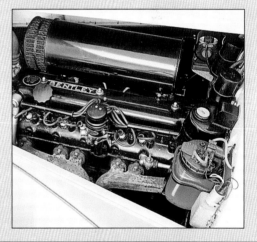

Coachbuilt

A large number of coachbuilt alloy bodies were offered by independent concerns. Particularly sought after are the drophead coupes of companies such as H.J. Mulliner and Park Ward and the sedan coupes of Hooper and Gurney Nutting.

Cars with Mulliner Park Ward coachwork are particularly desirable.

Bentley **MK VI**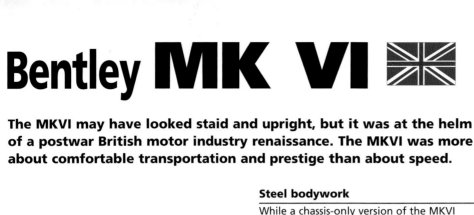

The MKVI may have looked staid and upright, but it was at the helm of a postwar British motor industry renaissance. The MKVI was more about comfortable transportation and prestige than about speed.

Steel bodywork

While a chassis-only version of the MKVI was listed, for the first time ever Bentley fitted its own bodywork (built by the Pressed Steel Company).

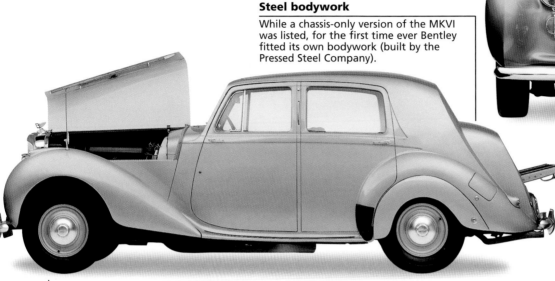

Tiny trun

The major criticism
the MKVI was its tir
luggage area, accesse
by a drop-down trun
lid. The deficiency wa
not rectified until th
1952 R-Type, which ha
an extended trunk wit
a lift-up li

Hydraulic brakes

Bentley was at the forefront of technology in 1946, when it fitted a hydraulic servo for its braking system. However, it operates only on the front drums; the rear ones have a mechanical linkage.

Manual transmission

The MKVI was only ever offered with four-speed manual transmission, unlike later models, which were also available with automatic. Righthand-drive cars had a floor-mounted lever, but lefthand-drive cars for export had a column shift.

Chassis lubrication

A centralized system of chassis lubrication means easier maintenance. Stepping on a pedal delivers lubricant to the steering and suspension systems. There is also a side jacking system.

Specifications

Bentley MKVI

ENGINE

Type: Inline six-cylinder

Construction: Cast-iron block and aluminum head

Valve gear: Two valves per cylinder, one overhead/one side, operated by a single camshaft with pushrods and rockers

Bore and stroke: 3.56 in. x 4.57 in.

Displacement: 4,257 cc

Compression ratio: 6.4:1

Induction system: Twin SU carburetors

Maximum power: Not quoted

Maximum torque: Not quoted

Top speed: 94 mph

0-60 mph: 15.2 sec.

TRANSMISSION

Four-speed manual

BODY/CHASSIS

Separate chassis with steel four-door sedan body

SPECIAL FEATURES

Most British home market MKVIs had floor-mounted shifters on the right of the steering wheel. Export cars came with column shift.

Picnic tables were quaint features that could be folded out from the backs of the front seats.

RUNNING GEAR

Steering: Cam-and-roller

Front suspension: Wishbones with coil springs, shock absorbers and anti-roll bar

Rear suspension: Live axle with semi-elliptic leaf springs and shock absorbers

Brakes: Drums (front and rear)

Wheels: Steel, 16-in. dia.

Tires: 6.50 x 16

DIMENSIONS

Length: 192.0 in. **Width:** 70.0 in.

Height: 68.0 in.

Wheelbase: 120.0 in.

Track: 56.0 in. (front), 58.5 in. (rear)

Weight: 4,075 lbs.

Bentley CONTINENTAL R

In the early 1950s, the Continental must have seemed like a vision from another world. It was a Bentley that remained true to the company ideals of sporty driving reserved for the more affluent enthusiast. It remains one of the most beautiful cars of all time.

"...profoundly impressive."

"Even today, the experience of driving a Continental R is profoundly impressive. From the moment you step into the cockpit, with its tailored leather seats and rich wood ambience, you know you're in for a treat. You sit up high with a fabulous view over the long hood. The engine likes to be pressed hard and delivers a fair turn of speed with an impressive silence. The shifter has a smooth, well-oiled action that betrays the high-quality engineering behind it."

Despite the austerity of the period, the Bentley has an incredibly luxurious interior.

Milestones

1950 Rolls-Royce signals the go-ahead for a fast touring Bentley model and asks coachbuilder H.J. Mulliner to build the prototype (nicknamed 'Olga') on the Bentley Mk VI sedan chassis.

Italian styling house Pininfarina also bodied Continental Rs.

1952 At the London Motor Show, the Continental R enraptures press and public alike.

1954 A larger 4.9-liter engine becomes standard and an automatic transmission is offered as an option.

A new Continental R debuted as the 1990s unfolded.

1955 Production is suspended as the model is replaced by a new Bentley-based Continental coupe.

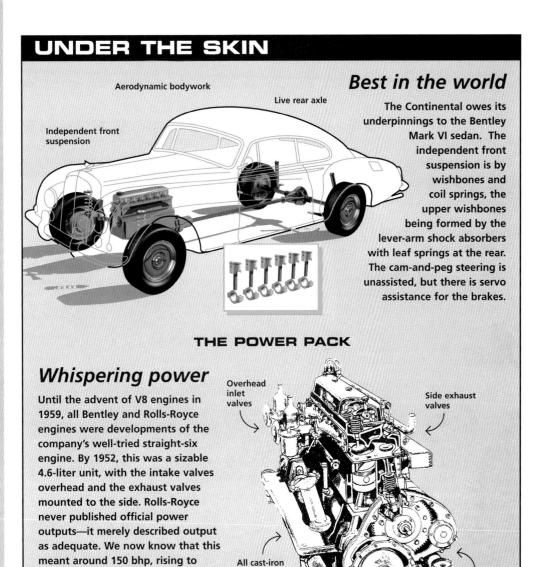

UNDER THE SKIN

Aerodynamic bodywork

Live rear axle

Independent front suspension

Best in the world

The Continental owes its underpinnings to the Bentley Mark VI sedan. The independent front suspension is by wishbones and coil springs, the upper wishbones being formed by the lever-arm shock absorbers with leaf springs at the rear. The cam-and-peg steering is unassisted, but there is servo assistance for the brakes.

THE POWER PACK

Whispering power

Until the advent of V8 engines in 1959, all Bentley and Rolls-Royce engines were developments of the company's well-tried straight-six engine. By 1952, this was a sizable 4.6-liter unit, with the intake valves overhead and the exhaust valves mounted to the side. Rolls-Royce never published official power outputs—it merely described output as adequate. We now know that this meant around 150 bhp, rising to approximately 175 bhp with the 4.9-liter engine. Torque for the 4.6-liter engine is estimated at 147 lb-ft.

Overhead inlet valves

Side exhaust valves

All cast-iron construction

Long-stroke design

Classic style

Of all post-war Bentleys, the Continental R is the most coveted. Its body is among the most handsome of all automobiles and its rarity adds to the mystique. The original Continental has a style and class that later cars with the same name never seemed to match.

The Continental R has handsome fastback styling.

Bentley CONTINENTAL R

This was the world's most expensive car in 1952, and was also a strong contender as the world's fastest four-seater road car. This pinnacle of the touring car tradition was also one of the most handsome cars ever made.

Straight-six engine

The intake-over-exhaust straight-six engine could easily get the hefty Continental R moving along at more than 100 mph.

Choice of transmission

The four-speed manual transmission was a model of slick operation and has a higher final drive ratio for relaxed high-speed cruising. A four-speed automatic transmission was also available.

Classic Bentley grill

To distinguish Bentley from Rolls-Royce, the grill is very different. The profile is more rounded and the 'Flying Lady' mascot is replaced by Bentley's winged 'B.' In the interest of cutting frontal area, and hence drag, the height of the grill is reduced by 1.5 inches.

Comfortable suspension

To achieve the optimum ride quality, there is an independent coil-sprung wishbone front end and a semi-elliptic leaf-sprung rear axle.

Elegant coachwork

To true automotive enthusiasts, the Continental R remains one of the greatest all-time body designs. The aluminum body was hand-crafted by H.J. Mulliner.

Aerodynamic shape

The body was shaped by the wind, literally, as it was developed in the Rolls-Royce wind tunnel. The fastback shape certainly helped airflow, as did the curved windshield. An uncanny lack of wind noise was one important fringe benefit.

Sporty interior

The Continental has a wooden dashboard, deep-pile carpeting, front bucket seats and leather upholstery. The prominent tachometer's redline is set at 4,250 rpm.

Specifications

1952 Bentley Continental R

ENGINE

Type: In-line six-cylinder

Construction: Cast-iron block and aluminum head

Valve gear: Two valves per cylinder, (overhead inlet/side exhaust) operated by a single camshaft via pushrods and rockers

Bore and stroke: 3.62 in. x 4.50 in.

Displacement: 4,566 cc

Compression ratio: 7.0:1

Induction system: Two SU carburetors

Maximum power: Not quoted

Maximum torque: Not quoted

Top speed: 117 mph

0-60 mph: 13.5 sec.

TRANSMISSION

Four-speed manual

BODY/CHASSIS

Separate chassis with aluminum two-door coupe body

SPECIAL FEATURES

The high-quality engineering even extends to the alloy gas filler cap.

The lowered radiator grill carries the traditional Bentley winged 'B' mascot.

RUNNING GEAR

Steering: Cam-and-roller

Front suspension: Wishbones with coil springs and lever-arm shock absorbers

Rear suspension: Live axle with semi-elliptic leaf springs and adjustable telescopic shock absorbers

Brakes: Drums (front and rear)

Wheels: Steel, 16-in. dia.

Tires: 6.50 x 16

DIMENSIONS

Length: 206.4 in.   **Width:** 71.5 in.

Height: 63.0 in.   **Wheelbase:** 120.0 in.

Track: 56.7 in. (front), 58.5 in. (rear)

Weight: 3,543 lbs.

BMW 507

Sublimely handsome, impressive in action and exquisitely rare, the 507 is one of the most desirable BMWs ever made. It was so expensive to build, however, that it was forced to compete with the Mercedes-Benz 300SL.

"...controlled oversteer."

"The 507's V8 engine is not really typical of the breed, having little low-down torque to offer but a fair amount of mid-range power above 3,500 rpm. The car's cornering abilities are excellent once you're into a turn, exhibiting stability and even allowing controlled oversteer. The 507 is really at home sweeping along country roads at high touring speeds, where its solidity, balance and good road manners become quite evident."

The uncluttered dashboard of the 507 is both elegant and functional.

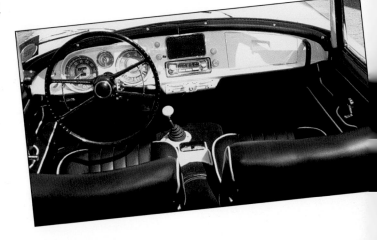

Milestones

1955 The 507 makes its debut at the Frankfurt show alongside another new sporty BMW, the four-seater 503. It has taken just 18 months to get it into production and uses the V8 engine first seen in the big 502 sedan in 1954.

Like the 507, the 1955 503 was styled by Count Albrecht Goertz.

1958 Front discs

become available. They are a welcome innovation, giving improved stopping distances and better fade resistance.

The modern Z07 uses many of the 507's styling cues.

1959 Production of the 507 ends

because the BMW company is at the verge of bankruptcy. One of the reasons for this is the 507 was never been profitable to produce.

UNDER THE SKIN

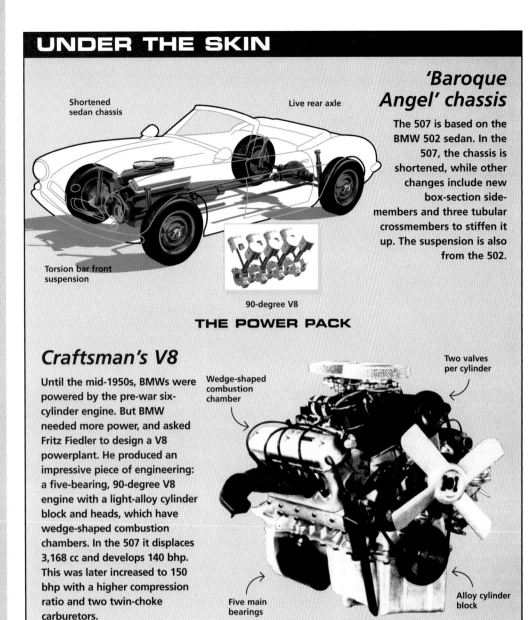

Shortened sedan chassis

Live rear axle

Torsion bar front suspension

90-degree V8

THE POWER PACK

'Baroque Angel' chassis

The 507 is based on the BMW 502 sedan. In the 507, the chassis is shortened, while other changes include new box-section side-members and three tubular crossmembers to stiffen it up. The suspension is also from the 502.

Craftsman's V8

Until the mid-1950s, BMWs were powered by the pre-war six-cylinder engine. But BMW needed more power, and asked Fritz Fiedler to design a V8 powerplant. He produced an impressive piece of engineering: a five-bearing, 90-degree V8 engine with a light-alloy cylinder block and heads, which have wedge-shaped combustion chambers. In the 507 it displaces 3,168 cc and develops 140 bhp. This was later increased to 150 bhp with a higher compression ratio and two twin-choke carburetors.

Wedge-shaped combustion chamber

Two valves per cylinder

Five main bearings

Alloy cylinder block

First class

The 507 is one of the most sought-after post-war BMW road cars: elegant, sporty, classy and very rare. It was made as a roadster, but could be fitted with a hard top for winter or wet weather driving, effectively turning it into a coupe.

The handsome 507 was styled by Count Albrecht Goertz.

BMW 507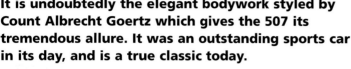

It is undoubtedly the elegant bodywork styled by Count Albrecht Goertz which gives the 507 its tremendous allure. It was an outstanding sports car in its day, and is a true classic today.

Aristocratic design

The faultless lines of the 507 were styled by Count Albrecht Goertz. He was approached by Max Hoffman, BMW's American sales representative, and submitted proposals for a sporty two-seater which were accepted, despite some resistance from BMW's board.

Rare V8 power

The technically advanced V8 engine was the mainstay of BMW's program in the late 1950s, providing all the torque and power its big luxury cars required.

Stylized kidney grill

The trademark upright split 'kidney' front grill—an unmistakable and universal BMW feature—at first appears to be absent from the 507. But Albrecht Goertz merely flattened the profile of the split grill so that it runs horizontally across the front of the car and, undoubtedly, suits this body design to perfection.

Close-ratio transmission

To suit its more sporting role, the four-speed manual transmission is fitted with a new cluster of close-set ratios for more spirited acceleration. The standard final drive ratio is 3.70:1, which is lower than other BMWs of the period, but an optional 3.42:1 or 3.90:1 differential was also available to suit a customer's driving style—sporty or touring.

Powerful brakes

The brakes are hydraulically-actuated servo-assisted. When launched, the 507 had four-wheel 11.2-inch drum brakes, but Alfin 10.5-inch front discs were installed on later cars. These were very advanced for the time and provide excellent stopping power.

Plenty of aluminum

To keep weight down, aluminum is used as much as possible. The bodywork and doors are handcrafted in alloy, as are the cylinder block and heads.

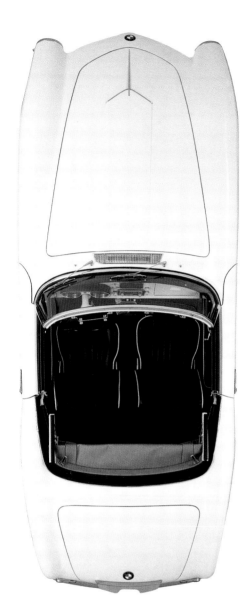

Specifications
1957 BMW 507

ENGINE
Type: V8

Construction: Light-alloy cylinder block and heads

Valve gear: Two overhead valves per cylinder operated by a single camshaft

Bore and stroke: 3.28 in. x 2.95 in.

Displacement: 3,168 cc

Compression ratio: 7.8:1

Induction system: Two twin-choke carburetors

Maximum power: 150 bhp at 5,000 rpm

Maximum torque: 174 lb-ft at 4,000 rpm

Top speed: 124 mph

0-60 mph: 8.8 sec.

TRANSMISSION
Four-speed manual

BODY/CHASSIS
Separate steel chassis with two-door aluminum convertible body

SPECIAL FEATURES

'Bullet' front marker lights show its American styling influence.

The highly distinctive side louvers have become a BMW hallmark; the current M Roadster has the same arrangement.

RUNNING GEAR
Steering: Pinion-and-sector

Front suspension: Upper and lower wishbones with torsion bars, and telescopic shock absorbers

Rear suspension: Live axle with torsion bars and Panhard rod, and telescopic shock absorbers

Brakes: Drums (front and rear); later front discs

Wheels: Steel, 16-in. dia.

Tires: 6.00H x 16 in. racing type

DIMENSIONS
Length: 173 in.   **Width:** 65 in.

Height: 49.5 in.   **Wheelbase:** 97.6 in.

Track: 56.9 in. (front), 56.1 in. (rear)

Weight: 2,840 lbs.

BMW ISETTA

Before BMW built some of the world's most desirable cars, it provided affordable motoring when it produced the miniscule Italian Iso Isetta— the world's first bubble car. Four wheels were soon cut down to three.

"...not as bizarre you'd expect."

"It's not as bizarre as you'd expect. Although the light steering feels very dead, the Isetta corners accurately but with strong understeer. Surprisingly, it doesn't lean through corners and, equally surprisingly, it doesn't pitch violently over bumps. The clutch and four-speed transmission are easy to use, which is just as well because you need them to extract all 13 bhp from the engine. The figures suggest that it's incredibly slow, but it doesn't feel it."

The Isetta doesn't have a dashboard and its steering wheel is horizontally mounted.

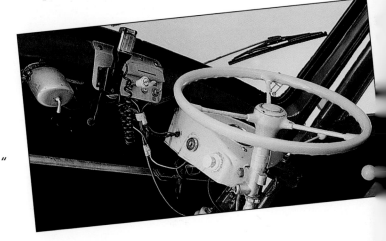

1953 Italian auto company Iso launches the tiny four-wheel Isetta in a Europe still struggling after World War II. It is powered by a 236-cc, air-cooled, 10-bhp, two-stroke engine.

1954 BMW builds a version of the Isetta in Germany, with a four-stroke engine.

BMW's 600 varied the theme, adding rear seats and a side door.

1957 After Isetta manufacturing spreads to France and Brazil, it goes to England in 250 and 300 form.

Front nudge bars were available as an option on the Isetta.

1959 Three-wheeled versions appear in order to qualify for less expensive road taxes.

1965 Rivals such as the Mini force production to end in Britain. BMW stopped in 1962.

UNDER THE SKIN

Original thinking

Although the Isetta is small, it is not a monocoque but has a separate steel chassis frame. The engine is mounted at the back in a unit with the transmission and usually (except for the three-wheeler) drives two rear wheels on a very short and rigid axle with no differential. Rear suspension is by quarter elliptic springs, and the front suspension uses coil spring/shock absorber units in a swinging arm. The brakes are hydraulic drums all around.

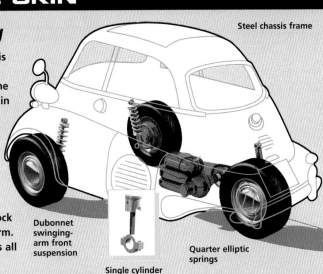

Steel chassis frame

Dubonnet swinging-arm front suspension

Single cylinder

Quarter elliptic springs

THE POWER PACK

Back to basics

By the time the Isetta had become a three-wheeler, a four-stroke single-cylinder BMW engine had replaced the original two-stroke single cylinder. Like its predecessor, it is a simple design, with a single cam and pushrod over-head valves together with air cooling. Cylinder dimensions are virtually 'square' and, to run on the least expensive fuel, the compression ratio is a low 6.8:1. That, together with the engine's small size of only 298 cc, means that power is limited to just 13 bhp. As with everything on the Isetta, the engine is designed to keep running costs to an absolute minimum.

Three versus four

Purists might well go for one of the very early cars, attracted by the fact that they have four wheels like a normal car, even if the rear wheels are only 20.5 inches apart, giving the smallest rear track of any car ever made. Unfortunately, the Isetta's small track makes the car unstable at speed. The early cars are also hampered by even tinier engines.

In the Isetta's case, three wheels are just as good as four.

BMW **ISETTA** ▬

The shape of the Isetta is extremely clever. Not only can two people fit inside easily, there is still room for a surprising amount of luggage. Also, the car is so short it can be parked nose-first curbside and in tiny spaces.

Single door

The key to the Isetta's design is that the whole front of the car swings out as a single door. The only drawback is the blindspots caused by the thickness of the front pillars.

Single-cylinder engine

The biggest engine used in the Isetta is BMW's 298-cc single-cylinder—an air-cooled overhead-valve design with an almost equal bore and stroke. Its output of 13 bhp sounds small, but at the time it was about the same output per liter as a conventional car.

Movable steering column

In the Isetta's rival, the Heinkel, the steering column is fixed, making entry and exit awkward. In the Isetta, a lower universal joint enables it to swing clear of the door and instrument panel, and it also acts as a convenient handle with which to pull the door closed.

Swinging arm suspension

Due to limited space, the front suspension uses Dubonnet-type swinging arms with integral coil spring/shock absorber units.

Single rear wheel

Although the early Isettas have four wheels, the design evolved into a three-wheeler, with a single chain-driven rear wheel on a swinging arm with a quarter elliptic leaf spring.

Specifications

1960 BMW Isetta 300

ENGINE
Type: BMW one-cylinder
Construction: Alloy block and head
Valve gear: Two valves operated by a single camshaft via pushrods and rockers
Bore and stroke: 2.83 in. x 2.87 in.
Displacement: 298 cc
Compression ratio: 6.8:1
Induction system: Single Bing carburetor
Maximum power: 13 bhp at 5,200 rpm
Maximum torque: Not quoted
Top speed: 55 mph
0-40 mph: 16.3 sec.

TRANSMISSION
Four-speed manual

BODY/CHASSIS
Separate tubular steel chassis with steel single-door body

SPECIAL FEATURES

A central fuel filler cap means the Isetta can be filled with ease from either side.

There was no shortage of imagination when it came to the design of details.

RUNNING GEAR
Steering: Worm-and-nut
Front suspension: Dubonnet swinging arms with enclosed coil spring/shock absorber units
Rear suspension: Single quarter elliptic leaf spring with telescopic shock absorber
Brakes: Drums (front and rear)
Wheels: Pressed steel disc, 10-in. dia.
Tires: 4.40-10

DIMENSIONS
Length: 90.0 in.   **Width:** 54.3 in.
Height: 52.8 in.   **Wheelbase:** 59.1 in.
Track: 47.2 in. (front)
Weight: 795 lbs.

Borgward ISABELLA

Dr. Karl Borgward's most famous car was named after his wife Isabella. This was his first unitary-construction car and it earned a strong reputation for being virtually indestructible.

"...simple and effective."

"Road testers driving the Isabella in the 1950s were instantly struck by its quality, power and solid road manners. That impression remains today. The pushrod engine seems more powerful than it actually is, feeling happy cruising at speeds approaching 90 mph. The column gearshift is both simple and effective to use, while the fast-geared steering has a nicely weighted action. The roadholding and handling are competent and the ride is comfortable."

The Isabella's wire steering wheel is a typical 1950s feature for a German car.

Milestones

1954 At the London International Motor Show, Borgward launches its Isabella in sedan form.

In sedan form, the Isabella was relatively inexpensive.

1955 The more powerful TS is launched at the Frankfurt Motor Show.

1956 An Isabella station wagon and convertible model are released.

The Isabella brought U.S. style and glamour to austere Europe.

1957 Alongside new De luxe models, Borgward launches the Deutsch-designed coupe and convertible models. Power goes up across the range.

1961 Soon after founder Carl Borgward retires, the company goes out of business. A Mexican company buys the tooling and makes Isabella derivatives until 1970.

UNDER THE SKIN

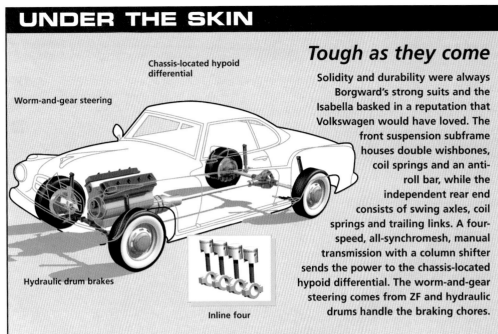

Chassis-located hypoid differential

Worm-and-gear steering

Hydraulic drum brakes

Inline four

Tough as they come

Solidity and durability were always Borgward's strong suits and the Isabella basked in a reputation that Volkswagen would have loved. The front suspension subframe houses double wishbones, coil springs and an anti-roll bar, while the independent rear end consists of swing axles, coil springs and trailing links. A four-speed, all-synchromesh, manual transmission with a column shifter sends the power to the chassis-located hypoid differential. The worm-and-gear steering comes from ZF and hydraulic drums handle the braking chores.

THE POWER PACK

Reliable modern power

The 1.5-liter, inline four was derived from the Hansa 1500, which was Germany's first new car after WWII. It had modern specifications, with overhead valves and, in the Isabella, an aluminum cylinder head. With 60 bhp in standard tune, it was also a relatively powerful engine for its time. In 1955 the Touring Sport (TS) version was released. It had a twin-choke carburetor and a higher compression ratio that helped it produce 75 bhp. Later TS models have a Solex dual-throat carburetor, pushing power up to 82 bhp. In racing tune, with fuel injection, these engines can pump out up to 115 bhp.

Cabriolet

The sedan and wagon have a definite following, but it is the coupe and convertible that attract collector interest. A good coupe will fetch more than twice the price of a sedan and the rare Deutsch-bodied Cabriolet is treasured among aficionados.

Coupes and cabriolets are the collectors' favorites.

Borgward ISABELLA

The Borgward Isabella remains one of the greatest unsung cars from Germany. Many of the qualities of the Isabella were adapted by BMW, so the Borgward has a right to be called the 1950s equivalent of today's BMW.

Elegant style

One German magazine said the Isabella coupe was perhaps the prettiest German car of the 1950s. Designed by Karl Deutsch of Cologne, it features an elegant body and shapely rear fenders.

Tough engine

The 1.5-liter, pushrod, four-cylinder engine is a model of quality and reliability. In postwar Germany, this quality was widely appreciated. The engine is also very capable, and in its day, had a lot of success in competition.

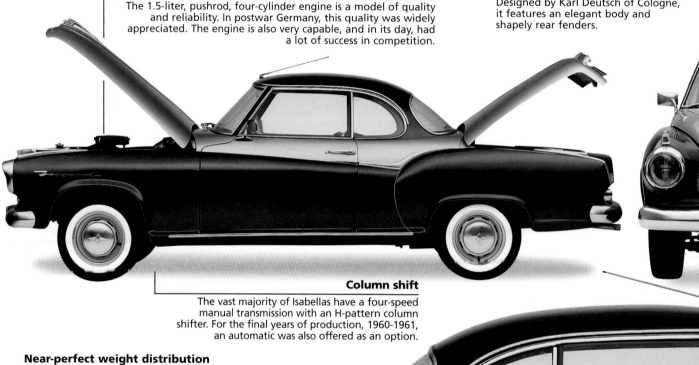

Column shift

The vast majority of Isabellas have a four-speed manual transmission with an H-pattern column shifter. For the final years of production, 1960-1961, an automatic was also offered as an option.

Near-perfect weight distribution

Part of the Isabella's handling prowess can be attributed to its perfect 50/50 weight distribution. Testers remarked on how adjustable the car was. Understeer and oversteer were virtually selectable.

Distinctive grill

Like all postwar Borgwards, the Isabella has a diamond-pattern badge in the middle of the grill. Horizontal bars emanate from both sides of the diamond.

Generous equipment

Befitting its image as a high-quality car, the Isabella is equipped with many luxury features. In TS form, these include deeply upholstered reclining seats, armrests, door pockets, clock, cigar lighter, multiple gauges and heater.

Specifications

1958 Borgward Isabella TS

ENGINE

Type: Inline 4-cylinder

Construction: Cast-iron cylinder block and aluminum cylinder head

Valve gear: Two valves per cylinder operated by single camshaft with pushrods and rockers

Bore and stroke: 2.95 in. x 3.27 in.

Displacement: 1,493 cc

Compression ratio: 8.2:1

Induction system: Single Solex dual-throat carburetor

Maximum power: 82 bhp at 5,200 rpm

Maximum torque: 84 lb-ft at 3,000 rpm

Top speed: 93 mph

0-60 mph: 16.0 sec.

TRANSMISSION

Four-speed manual (or automatic from 1960)

BODY/CHASSIS

Steel unitary construction chassis with two-door sedan, wagon, coupe or convertible

SPECIAL FEATURES

A padded armrest is one of the features that gives the Isabella its charm.

TS models have side markerlights on the front fenders.

RUNNING GEAR

Steering: Worm-and-roller

Front suspension: Unequal-length double wishbones with coil springs and shock absorbers

Rear suspension: Swing axles with coil springs and shock absorbers

Brakes: Drums (front and rear)

Wheels: Steel, 13-in. dia.

Tires: 5.90 x 13

DIMENSIONS

Length: 173.0 in.   **Width:** 67.7 in.

Height: 53.2 in.   **Wheelbase:** 102.4 in.

Track: 52.8 in. (front), 53.5 in. (rear)

Weight: 2,320 lbs.

Buick ROADMASTER

The combination of just about the most comfortable ride in any large sedan and the total convenience of the pioneering two-speed Dynaflow transmission made the 1949 Roadmaster a huge success.

"...comfortable and relaxing."

"Its incredibly soft suspension may not give the Roadmaster the best hand-ling, but it does mean that it is blissfully comfortable and relaxing. This is enhanced by the quiet, refined, and strong straight-eight engine. The pioneering and impressively smooth Dynaflow transmission comes into its own as you accelerate to around 30 mph, when it performs really well. You just select 'Drive' and forget the rest—the Buick can easily soak up hundreds of miles in a day."

The view of the gauges through the large steering wheel is excellent.

Milestones

1945 Buick production gets underway again after WWII. Its cars changed from the 1942 models. Among the range is a Roadmaster.

By 1953, the Roadmaster had an OHV V8 engine.

1949 There is a fundamental restyle for the Roadmaster, with the top line of the front fender carried all the way through the doors to the top of the rear fender. The modern look complements the pioneering two-speed automatic transmission, with Dynaflow-drive.

1958 is the last year for the Buick Roadmaster.

1953 The straight-eight engine is replaced by a new, overhead-valve, pushrod 322-cubic inch V8 producing 188 bhp.

1958 The name Roadmaster is discontinued. It is resurrected in 1991.

UNDER THE SKIN

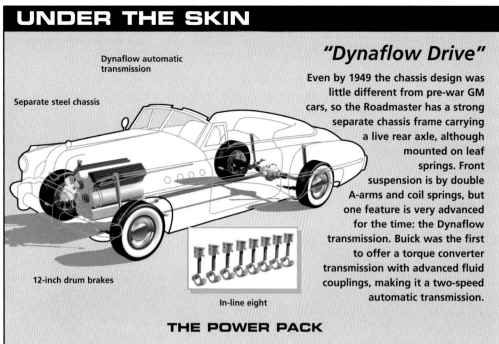

Dynaflow automatic transmission

Separate steel chassis

12-inch drum brakes

In-line eight

"Dynaflow Drive"

Even by 1949 the chassis design was little different from pre-war GM cars, so the Roadmaster has a strong separate chassis frame carrying a live rear axle, although mounted on leaf springs. Front suspension is by double A-arms and coil springs, but one feature is very advanced for the time: the Dynaflow transmission. Buick was the first to offer a torque converter transmission with advanced fluid couplings, making it a two-speed automatic transmission.

THE POWER PACK

Pre-war power

Buick's fine straight-eight engine, with its cast-iron block and cylinder head has its origins in the pre-war period. With the use of long crankshafts mounted on five bearings, by 1936 the capacity had increased to 320 cubic inches. A single block-mounted camshaft operates in-line overhead valves with pushrods and rockers. It is very unstressed and has a small 6.9:1 compression ratio. The engine is tuned for torque rather than outright power with its long stroke. The maximum power output of 150 bhp and 260 lb-ft of torque are produced, at 3,600 rpm and 2,400 rpm respectively.

Open-top joy

The two-door convertible is the most sought-after Roadmaster. At the time, it was more affordable than the two-door coupe. This helped account for its popularity, with over 8,200 sold in the model year—almost twice as many as the Riviera coupe.

The open-top Roadmaster is the ideal model for cruising.

Buick ROADMASTER

For 1949, the Roadmaster's new flatter side styling and the first appearance of portholes in the front fenders were an instant hit. Buick sales increased by more than 100,000.

Straight-eight engine

The design of Buick's straight-eight engine dates back to 1931. Straight-eights were built for prestige and, although very smooth, had drawbacks, such as length and the very long crankshaft, which limited engine speeds.

Foot starter

To start the Roadmaster, the ignition is switched on and then, with the transmission in 'Park' or 'Neutral,' the throttle is pressed right to the floor, activating the starter button.

Dynaflow transmission

Buick was not the first to offer an automatic transmission but was the first to have a torque converter. It called its new transmission dynaflow. It is a much more sophisticated version of a fluid coupling, which magnifies the effect of the torque produced by the engine, so Drive is the only selection really needed.

Rear wheel covers

The 1949 Buicks, including the Roadmaster, were the last to have enclosed rear wheels. A removable panel allows the wheel to be changed.

Split windshield

The 1949 Roadmaster was one of the last Buicks to have a split windshield. Soon technology enabled curved, one-piece windshields to be produced.

Recirculating-ball steering

The Roadmaster is a big and very heavy car, so the recirculating-ball steering needed more than five turns to go from lock to lock. This was improved with the power steering introduced in 1952. By 1954, there were 4.5 turns lock to lock, but the steering was still vague.

Drum brakes

Large, cast-iron drums give the Roadmaster good stopping power and can halt the car from 60 mph in 240 feet. Brake fade soon sets in if the car is driven hard.

A-arm front suspension

Coil-sprung double A-arm suspension and an anti-roll bar are used at the front to give the best possible ride.

Specification

1949 Buick Roadmaster

ENGINE
Type: In line eight-cylinder
Construction: Cast-iron block and head
Valve gear: Two valves per cylinder operated by a block-mounted camshaft.
Bore and stroke: 3.44 in. x 4.25 in.
Displacement: 320.2 c.i.
Compression ratio: 6.9:1
Induction system: One two-barrel Stromberg carburetor/ or carter carburetor
Maximum power: 150 bhp at 3,600 rpm
Maximum torque: 260 lb-ft at 2,400 rpm
Top speed: 100 mph
0-60 mph: 17.1 sec.

TRANSMISSION
Two-speed Dynaflow automatic with a torque converter

BODY/CHASSIS
Separate steel chassis with two-door convertible body

SPECIAL FEATURES

The Roadmaster has four portholes compared to the three of other Buicks.

The Dynaflow transmission was the first torque-converter automatic on a production car.

RUNNING GEAR
Steering: Recirculating-ball
Front suspension: Double A-arms with coil springs, telescopic shock absorbers and anti-roll bar
Rear suspension: Live axle with leaf springs, torque arm and telescopic shock absorbers
Brakes: Drums, 12-in. dia. (front and rear)
Wheels: Steel disc, 15-in. dia.
Tires: 8.20 x 15

DIMENSIONS
Length: 214.1 in.   **Width:** 80.0 in.
Height: 63.2 in.   **Wheelbase:** 126.0 in.
Track: 59.1 in. (front), 62.2 in. (rear)
Weight: 4,370 lbs.

Cadillac ELDORADO

The most expensive Cadillac of the 1950s, the Eldorado Brougham is a huge four-door hardtop derived from a show car. Each one was hand built and came with just about every conceivable option. However, its steep price resulted in it being dropped in 1960.

"...you can feel its quality."

"The most luxurious of all 1950s Cadillacs, the Eldorado Brougham is glitzy but not overtly so. You can almost feel the quality in the massive hand-stitched bench seat and door panels. The best part about this car is that it's whisper quiet at speed and the air suspension makes you feel like you're floating on a cloud. The automatic transmission is amazingly precise for a 1950s car. The steering is exceedingly light, while the brake pedal has almost no feel."

Buyers could choose from 44 trim and color combinations, including lamb's-skin seats.

Milestones

1956 In December, the Eldorado Brougham is announced for 1957. A total of 400 are built in its first year.

The Eldorado Seville was the next most expensive Cadillac after the Brougham.

1958 While regular Cadillacs receive an exterior facelift, the Brougham remains externally unchanged, although the interior door panels are now leather instead of metal.

1959-1960 Broughams were larger and sharper looking.

1959 All Cadillacs are new this year, and standard models have Detroit's tallest fins. The Brougham returns with more power and a new, four-door, hardtop body built by Pininfarina in Italy.

1960 As a result of high production costs and slow sales, the Brougham is dropped. Its styling previews 1961 Cadillacs.

UNDER THE SKIN

State of the art

When the Brougham arrived in 1957 it rode an exclusive 126-inch wheelbase; other Cadillacs were larger. It adopted a new X-braced separate chassis, and shunned conventional coil springs in favor of air suspension. Separate piston-operated airbags were used at each corner and operated with a central air pump. Braking was less high tech, with power-assisted drums in the front and rear.

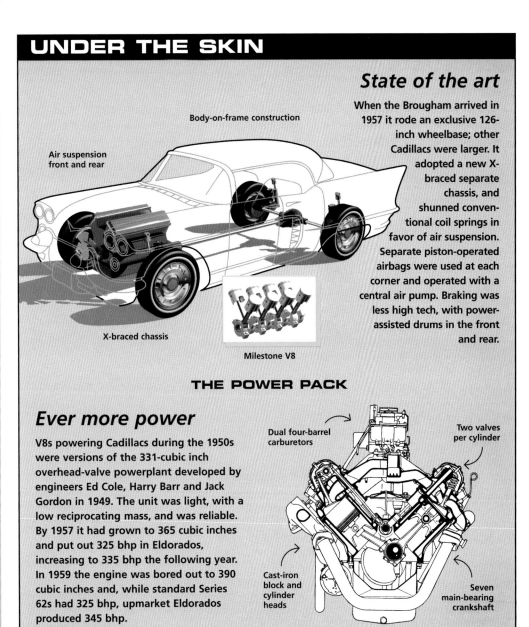

Air suspension front and rear

Body-on-frame construction

X-braced chassis

Milestone V8

THE POWER PACK

Ever more power

V8s powering Cadillacs during the 1950s were versions of the 331-cubic inch overhead-valve powerplant developed by engineers Ed Cole, Harry Barr and Jack Gordon in 1949. The unit was light, with a low reciprocating mass, and was reliable. By 1957 it had grown to 365 cubic inches and put out 325 bhp in Eldorados, increasing to 335 bhp the following year. In 1959 the engine was bored out to 390 cubic inches and, while standard Series 62s had 325 bhp, upmarket Eldorados produced 345 bhp.

Dual four-barrel carburetors

Two valves per cylinder

Cast-iron block and cylinder heads

Seven main-bearing crankshaft

U.S.-built

Broughams can be divided into two distinct series, the 1957-1958 cars, hand-built in Detroit, and the later 1959-1960 models. These Pininfarina-built cars are larger and have much sleeker styling that other Cadillacs. Collectors tend to prefer the earlier models.

Earlier Broughams have proved to be very popular with collectors.

Cadillac ELDORADO

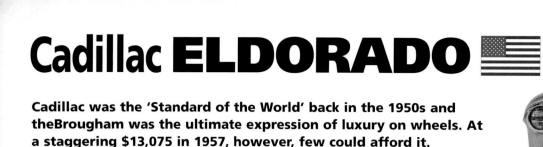

Cadillac was the 'Standard of the World' back in the 1950s and theBrougham was the ultimate expression of luxury on wheels. At a staggering $13,075 in 1957, however, few could afford it.

Powerful V8

By 1957 the 1949 vintage Cadillac V8 had been stroked to 365 cubic inches and produced a muscular 325 bhp on Eldorados (300 bhp on other models). All Cadillacs got an extra 10 bhp for 1958.

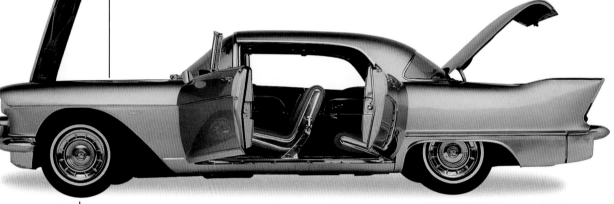

Air suspension

A state-of-the-art feature, air suspension, was introduced on the Brougham. It basically consisted of a rubber diaphragm and piston at each wheel controlled by a central compressor. The system was not very reliable and many owners chose to replace it with coil springs.

Suicide doors

Another feature unique to the 1957-1958 Eldorado Brougham are the suicide doors. Those at the front open in the normal manner, but the back doors are hinged at the rear. This allows easy access for passengers and also means that the Brougham was a pillarless four-door sedan that allowed the elimination of the rear quarter windows.

Modest fins

Cadillac pioneered fins among domestic manufacturers as far back as 1948. In 1955 Eldorados gained tall blade-like items, and these were adopted for the Brougham when it was launched in 1958. Interestingly, although regular Cadillacs had fins of gigantic proportions for 1959, Broughams had fairly small fins with dagger-shaped taillight lenses.

Sumptuous interior

Eldorado Broughams were laden with luxury options inside, including power steering, brakes and windows, plus air-conditioning, electric memory seats and cruise control. Buyers also had the choice of 44 interior and exterior trim and color combinations.

Huge chrome grill

Broughams have a unique eggcrate mesh-pattern grill which is neater than those on other Cadillacs. Broughams were also the first to get quad headlights.

Smooth styling

Panoramic windshields were first seen on the limited production Eldorado convertible in 1953. By 1958 all Cadillacs had them. They offered good visibility, but were costly to replace and necessitated a front dog-leg A-pillar which could make entry into the car rather difficult.

Specifications

1957 Cadillac Eldorado Brougham

ENGINE

Type: V8

Construction: Cast-iron block and heads

Valve gear: Two valves per cylinder operated by a single camshaft via pushrods and rockers

Bore and stroke: 4.00 in. x 3.63 in.

Displacement: 365 c.i.

Compression ratio: 10.0:1

Induction system: Two four-barrel carburetors

Maximum power: 325 bhp at 4,800 rpm

Maximum torque: 435 lb-ft at 3,400 rpm

Top speed: 110 mph

0-60 mph: 11.4 sec.

TRANSMISSION

Three-speed automatic

BODY/CHASSIS

Separate chassis with two-door steel convertible body

SPECIAL FEATURES

A full-length stainless-steel roof was standard on 1957-1958 Broughams—a feature lifted virtually intact from the Eldorado show car of 1954.

A gold anodized air cleaner is mounted atop the 365-cubic inch V8.

RUNNING GEAR

Steering: Recirculating ball

Front suspension: Wishbones with airbags and shock absorbers

Rear suspension: Live axle with airbags and shock absorbers

Brakes: Drums (front and rear)

Wheels: Steel, 15-in. dia.

Tires: 8.0 x 15.0 in.

DIMENSIONS

Length: 216.3 in.   **Width:** 78.5 in.

Height: 55.5 in.   **Wheelbase:** 126.0 in.

Track: 61.0 in. (front and rear)

Weight: 5,315 lbs.

Cadillac 62/DEVILLE

In response to Chrysler's tail-finned cruisers General Motors fielded all-new C-body cars in 1959—all with outrageous styling. The 1959 Cadillac was the most flamboyant of all and became etched in the public's imagination because of its classy styling and large tail fins.

"...the definitive Cadillac."

"For its size the 1959 Cadillac is quick in a straight line, with lots of low rpm torque to get it moving. It's easily capable of maintaining a smooth, silent 80 mph. Feather-light power steering makes for easy turning, but over-enthusiastic cornering reveals the Caddy's tendency to pitch and roll in an unsettling manner. But as we already know, this isn't designed to be a race car. Rather it's a sleek and sophisticated luxury cruiser. And to most people, it's the definitive Cadillac."

The emphasis is on luxury. This car has power everything, including cruise control.

Milestones

1955 Eldorados get a revised body with a new gold anodized grill and larger, more protruding fins than the Series 62s.

In 1953 the Series 62 was the entry-level Cadillac.

1957 The ultra-exclusive Eldorado Brougham, costing $13,074, is a new flagship built to challenge the Lincoln Continental. Among a huge list of luxuries this model previews the air suspension available on the 1959 cars. The fins are made larger too.

By 1964, fins on Cadillacs had become quite modest.

1959 Totally restyled on a massive 130-inch wheelbase, the 1959 has some of the wildest fins ever, plus a huge chrome grill. All Cadillacs are powered by a V8 stretched to 390 cubic inches. The 1960 models have cleaner styling.

UNDER THE SKIN

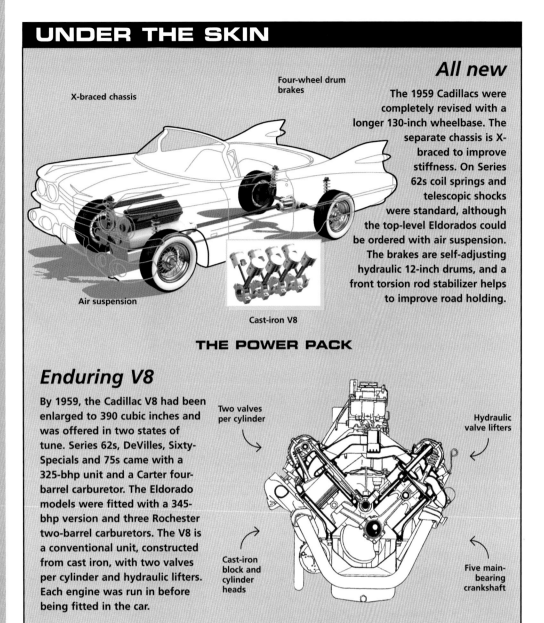

X-braced chassis

Four-wheel drum brakes

All new

The 1959 Cadillacs were completely revised with a longer 130-inch wheelbase. The separate chassis is X-braced to improve stiffness. On Series 62s coil springs and telescopic shocks were standard, although the top-level Eldorados could be ordered with air suspension. The brakes are self-adjusting hydraulic 12-inch drums, and a front torsion rod stabilizer helps to improve road holding.

Air suspension

Cast-iron V8

THE POWER PACK

Enduring V8

By 1959, the Cadillac V8 had been enlarged to 390 cubic inches and was offered in two states of tune. Series 62s, DeVilles, Sixty-Specials and 75s came with a 325-bhp unit and a Carter four-barrel carburetor. The Eldorado models were fitted with a 345-bhp version and three Rochester two-barrel carburetors. The V8 is a conventional unit, constructed from cast iron, with two valves per cylinder and hydraulic lifters. Each engine was run in before being fitted in the car.

Two valves per cylinder

Hydraulic valve lifters

Cast-iron block and cylinder heads

Five main-bearing crankshaft

Biarritz special

Next up the scale from the series 62 is the DeVille, offered in hardtop coupe and sedan form. The four window sedan De Ville may not have quite the allure of a drop top but it is distinctive nonetheless and presently is cheaper to buy than a convertible.

in 1959 Sedan DeVilles came in either four- or six-window forms.

Cadillac 62/DEVILLE

The 1959 Cadillacs were at their most glamorous in convertible form, either as Series 62 models or the flagship Eldorado Biarritz. As one of the world's premier luxury cars of the late 1950s, they were almost unchallenged.

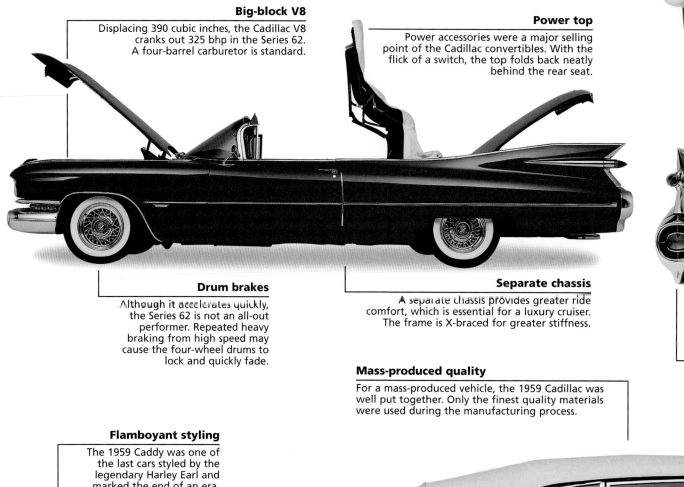

Big-block V8
Displacing 390 cubic inches, the Cadillac V8 cranks out 325 bhp in the Series 62. A four-barrel carburetor is standard.

Power top
Power accessories were a major selling point of the Cadillac convertibles. With the flick of a switch, the top folds back neatly behind the rear seat.

Drum brakes
Although it accelerates quickly, the Series 62 is not an all-out performer. Repeated heavy braking from high speed may cause the four-wheel drums to lock and quickly fade.

Separate chassis
A separate chassis provides greater ride comfort, which is essential for a luxury cruiser. The frame is X-braced for greater stiffness.

Mass-produced quality
For a mass-produced vehicle, the 1959 Cadillac was well put together. Only the finest quality materials were used during the manufacturing process.

Flamboyant styling
The 1959 Caddy was one of the last cars styled by the legendary Harley Earl and marked the end of an era.

utomatic headlights

adillac's 'Twilight Sentinel'
eadlights switch on automatically at
usk and also switch from high to
ow beams for oncoming traffic.

Chromed bumper

In the 1950s, designers looked to
the space program for inspiration.
The 1959 Cadillac has a heavy,
full-width chromed rear bumper
with back-up lights built into the
center of its fins.

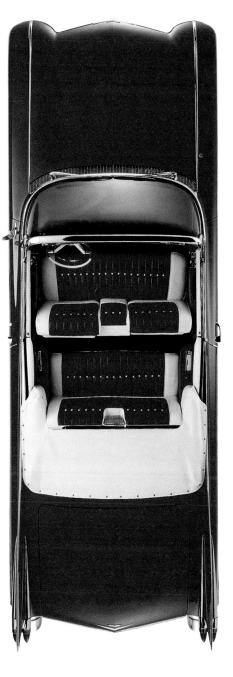

Specifications

1959 Cadillac Series 62

ENGINE

Type: V8

Construction: Cast-iron block and heads

Valve gear: Two valves per cylinder operated by a single camshaft via pushrods and rockers

Bore and stroke: 4.00 in. x 3.88 in.

Displacement: 390 c.i.

Compression ratio: 10.5:1

Induction system: Carter four-barrel carburetor

Maximum power: 325 bhp at 4,800 rpm

Maximum torque: 435 lb-ft at 3,400 rpm

Top speed:, 110 mph

0-60 mph: 11.4 sec.

TRANSMISSION

GM TurboHydramatic automatic

BODY/CHASSIS

Steel body on steel X-frame chassis

SPECIAL FEATURES

By 1959, quad headlights were in fashion. For the ultimate in excess, all 1959 Cadillacs have dual parking lights in chrome housings which form the lower part of the bumper.

The most recognizable feature are the fins—the tallest ever on a production car. Huge chrome bumpers further accentuate its advanced styling.

RUNNING GEAR

Steering: Recirculating ball

Front suspension: Wishbones with coil springs and telescopic shock absorbers

Rear suspension: Live axle with coil springs and telescopic shock absorbers

Brakes: Drums, 12-in. dia. (front and rear)

Wheels: Steel discs, 15-in. dia.

Tires: 8.20-15

DIMENSIONS

Length: 224.8 in.   **Width:** 79.9 in.

Height: 55.9 in.   **Wheelbase:** 130.0 in.

Track: 61.0 in. (front), 60.2 in. (rear)

Weight: 4,885 lbs.

Chevrolet CORVETTE '53-'55

Chevrolet was the first major car company in the world to dare to make a regular production car out of fiberglass. It was a crude affair at first but the sleek body and throaty engine captured the hearts of the American public, kick-starting the Corvette legend.

"...impressive in its day."

"You forget the modified sedan car origins of the Blue Flame Special six-cylinder engine when the throttle is floored and it roars to life. Despite the handicap of the two-speed Powerglide automatic, its 11 second 0-60 mph time is impressive for the day. Dynamically, the Corvette was closer to its traditional British sports car rivals than anything else made in the U.S. at the time, with stiff springs and a taut ride."

The interiors on early Corvettes were a bit confined and had a simple dashboard Layout.

Milestones

1952 The first full-size plaster model of the Corvette is presented to the GM president Harlow Curtice by Harley Earl. Curtice likes it and the Corvette is all set for production.

By 1957 the Corvette's V8 had gained optional fuel injection.

1953 The public sees the Corvette for the first time at the GM Motorama Show. Production begins later in the year and all cars are painted Polo White. Changes are made for the 1954 model year with more colors and increased power.

A major facelift came for the Corvette in 1961.

1954 For the 1955 model year Chevrolet's proposed facelift is shelved and the car's future is in doubt until the new V8 engine is used.

1955 It's the end of the line for the six-cylinder Corvette. The small block V8 is now the preferred power unit.

UNDER THE SKIN

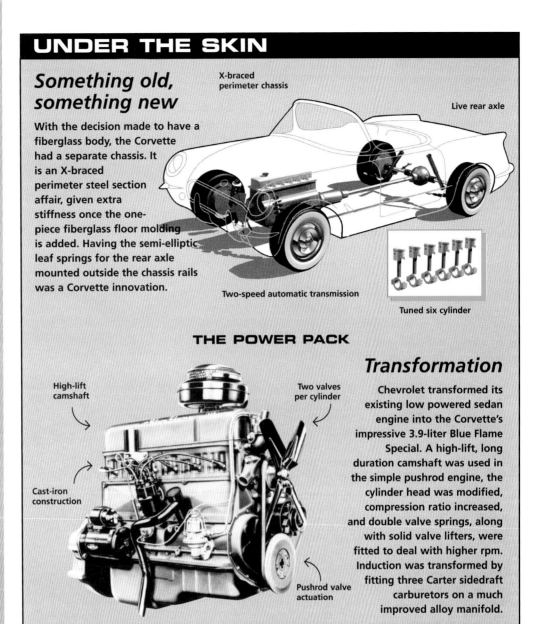

Something old, something new

With the decision made to have a fiberglass body, the Corvette had a separate chassis. It is an X-braced perimeter steel section affair, given extra stiffness once the one-piece fiberglass floor molding is added. Having the semi-elliptic leaf springs for the rear axle mounted outside the chassis rails was a Corvette innovation.

X-braced perimeter chassis

Live rear axle

Two-speed automatic transmission

Tuned six cylinder

THE POWER PACK

High-lift camshaft

Two valves per cylinder

Cast-iron construction

Pushrod valve actuation

Transformation

Chevrolet transformed its existing low powered sedan engine into the Corvette's impressive 3.9-liter Blue Flame Special. A high-lift, long duration camshaft was used in the simple pushrod engine, the cylinder head was modified, compression ratio increased, and double valve springs, along with solid valve lifters, were fitted to deal with higher rpm. Induction was transformed by fitting three Carter sidedraft carburetors on a much improved alloy manifold.

Rare original

Although the six-cylinder Chevrolet Corvettes aren't the best performing examples of the breed, they're now very valuable. Collectors value the 1953 and 1954 cars for their relative rarity, historical importance and purity of shape.

The early six-cylinder Corvettes are highly collectable today.

Because of poor sales, GM almost gave up on the little sports car. In 1955 it got a husky V8 engine and the car was making the power it lacked. Luckily, sales picked up and the Corvette has been in Chevrolet's line up ever since.

Wishbone front suspension

The Corvette's double wishbone and coil spring front suspension was a modified version of the contemporary Chevrolet sedans, with different spring rates to suit the sports car.

Six-cylinder engine

The first Corvettes used a modified Chevrolet sedan engine. Tuning made it an effective sports car powerplant with 150 bhp.

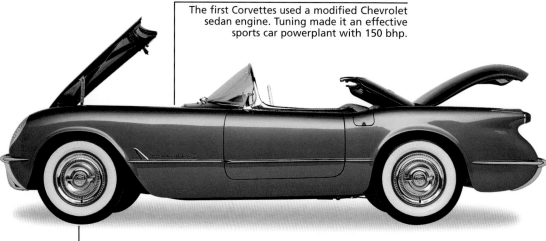

Whitewall tires

Whitewall tires were very fashionable in the 1950s. One advantage was that they broke up the high sided look of the tall sidewalls.

Fiberglass body

Although there were a number of fiberglass-bodied specialty and kit cars around in the U.S. in the early 1950s General Motors was the first to make a regular production car out of the material. In production the fiberglass panels used were about half as thick as the prototype's.

Two-speed transmission

Incredibly, the only available GM transmission which would take the power and torque of the modified engine was the two-speed Powerglide automatic. A three-speed manual became available for the 1955 model year cars.

Wrap-around windshield

The wrap-around style of windshield was popular in the early 1950s. Apart from looking great, it improved three-quarter vision compared with a conventional flat front glass with thick pillars.

Live rear axle

Because it was a limited-production car, the first Corvettes had to use many off-the-shelf Chevrolet components and the engineering had to be as simple as possible.

Specifications

1954 Chevrolet Corvette

ENGINE
Type: Inline six cylinder
Construction: Cast iron block and head
Valve gear: Two valves per cylinder operated by single block-mounted camshaft via pushrods and solid valve lifters
Bore/stroke: 3.56 in. x 3.94 in.
Displacement: 235 c.i.
Compression ratio: 8.0:1
Induction system: Three Carter YH sidedraft carburetors
Maximum power: 150 bhp at 4,200 rpm
Maximum torque: 233 lb-ft at 2,400 rpm
Top speed: 107 mph
0-60 mph: 11.0 sec

TRANSMISSION
Two-speed Powerglide automatic

BODY/CHASSIS
X-braced steel chassis with fiberglass two-seater convertible body

SPECIAL FEATURES

The first Corvettes have very curvaceous rear ends with subdued fins and prominent taillights.

Stone guards over the front headlights were purely a styling feature and unnecessary on ordinary roads.

RUNNING GEAR
Steering: Worm-and-sector
Front suspension: Double wishbones with coil springs, telescopic shocks and anti-roll bar
Rear suspension: Live axle with semi-elliptic leaf springs and telescopic shocks
Brakes: Drums (front and rear), 11-in. dia.
Wheels: Steel disc, 15-in. dia.
Tires: Crossply 5.5 x 15

DIMENSIONS
Length: 167 in.   **Width:** 72.2 in.
Height: 51.3 in.   **Wheelbase:** 102 in.
Track: 57 in. (front), 59 in. (rear)
Weight: 2,851 lbs.

Chevrolet **CORVETTE**

As one of the U.S.'s few sports cars, the Corvette has been desirable since the day it first rolled of the assembly line in 1953. Although fast in stock trim, some people just cannot resist the urge to make these cars even more powerful.

"...A 409-powered Corvette?"

"A 409-powered Corvette? It is a fact that no such production car was built, but then, this is not your run-of-the-mill sports car. There are few creature comforts inside, but once on the move, this ceases to matter. The classic Chevy V8 gives plenty of power right through the rev range, and six speeds enable you to get the most from it. Turn-in is sharp thanks to the steering, and a low center of gravity results in race car-type handling."

Cream leather seats are the only concession to luxury in the functional interior.

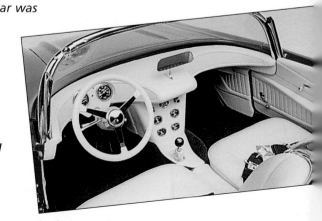

1958 The Corvette is heavily facelifted, with chrome accents on the coves and trunk, plus quad headlights, vents on the hood and revised wheel covers. In this recession year, production jumps from 6,339 to 9,168. The base 283 gets an extra 10 bhp while the fuelie version makes up to 290.

The Corvette entered production in 1953. They were all painted white and had red interiors.

1959 Minor changes, including the elimination of the trunk straps and hood vents conspire to give a cleaner appearance. Power ratings remain unchanged, but sales near the 10,000 mark.

The 1963 Sting Ray® marked a new direction for the Corvette.

1961 New rear styling, inspired by the '57 Sting Ray racer, mates well with the front-end design. The grill is changed to a mesh pattern and the headlight bezels are painted instead of chrome. The fuelie V8 is up to 315 bhp.

UNDER THE SKIN

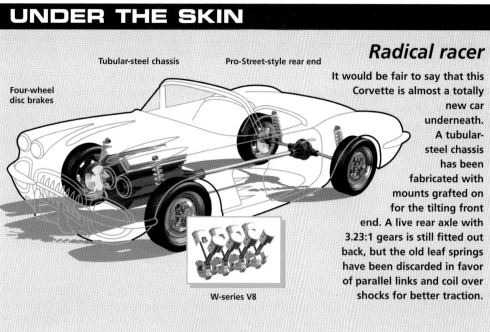

Four-wheel disc brakes

Tubular-steel chassis

Pro-Street-style rear end

W-series V8

Radical racer

It would be fair to say that this Corvette is almost a totally new car underneath. A tubular-steel chassis has been fabricated with mounts grafted on for the tilting front end. A live rear axle with 3.23:1 gears is still fitted out back, but the old leaf springs have been discarded in favor of parallel links and coil over shocks for better traction.

THE POWER PACK

Not as it seems

Solid-axle Corvettes came from the factory with 283 and 327 small-block V8s, but this one was built with a little more performance in mind. One of the most legendary engines of the early 1960s now sits between the fenders: a 409-cubic inch W-series engine. Outside, the engine looks almost stock, but it has Venolia 10.3:1 compression pistons, ported and polished heads with 2.19 intake valves, Competition Cams valve springs and a Lunati camshaft. It is fully balanced and blue printed like a real race engine.

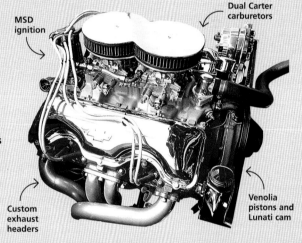

MSD ignition

Dual Carter carburetors

Custom exhaust headers

Venolia pistons and Lunati cam

Solid axle

Somewhat overshadowed by the Sting Ray, the 1958-1962 Corvettes still have strong collector interest and are among the most popular Corvettes with the custom fraternity. They are fairly rare and considerably expensive, but the end result is often worth it.

Pre-1963 Corvettes are nicknamed 'solid axles' because of their live rear axle.

Chevrolet CORVETTE

Few cars can capture the spirit of the late 1950s as well as the Corvette. This tasteful though radically modified example does a lot more than capture spirits—it captures show trophies, too.

Fiberglass body

Since its introduction in 1953, the Corvette has always had fiberglass bodywork. This was decided late in the development stage, as it would prove more cost effective than steel and Kirksite—which was originally intended.

Performance engine

The Beach Boys sang its praise, justifiably, considering the 409 was one of the most potent hi-po V8s of the early 1960s. Although expensive to build and not easy to modify, experienced engine builders are able to coax tremendous power from it.

Lowered suspension

By dropping the front and rear ends, the center of gravity is lowered, which, combined with the gas shocks and Goodyear GSC tires results in one of the sharpest-handling Corvettes around.

Spartan interior

Everything about this car screams performance and function. The interior may be draped in cream colored leather, but there is no convertible roof, air conditioning or stereo. However, a full set of Stewart-Warner gauges keeps the driver fully informed.

Cleaned-up body

The 1958 Vette has more glitz than its predecessors, but this was only in keeping with buyer tastes of the time. This one looks positively demure, with its monochromatic Rally Orange paint and absence of chrome accents on the door coves.

Tubular chassis

A completely custom-fabricated chassis lies beneath the bodywork, though thanks to considerable ingenuity, the stock front suspension has been mated to it.

Small windshield

It may look cut down, but the windshield is actually the stock full-length piece, just lowered four inches into the cowl.

Stock hood

Even though the whole front end can be tilted forward, the hood can still open independently for routine maintenance and tuning so essential for hot rods.

Specifications

1959 Chevrolet Corvette

ENGINE
Type: V8
Construction: Cast-iron block and heads
Valve gear: Two valves per cylinder operated by pushrods and rockers
Bore and stroke: 4.31 x 3.50 in.
Displacement: 416 c.i.
Compression ratio: 10.3:1
Induction system: Dual Carter AFB four-barrel carburetors
Maximum power: 454 bhp at 5,500 rpm
Maximum torque: 460 lb-ft at 5,500 rpm
Top speed: 164 mph
0-60 mph: 4.6 sec.

TRANSMISSION
Richmond six-speed manual

BODY/CHASSIS
Tubular-steel chassis with fiberglass convertible body

SPECIAL FEATURES

The whole front end tilts forward for access to the engine.

Auxiliary gauges are neatly housed in the center console, which is color-keyed with the rest of the interior.

RUNNING GEAR
Steering: Worm-and-ball
Front suspension: Unequal-length A-arms with coil springs, telescopic shock absorbers and sway bar
Rear suspension: Live axle with upper and lower parallel links, coil springs and telescopic shock absorbers
Brakes: Discs, (front and rear)
Wheels: Slotted Magnesium 15.0-in. dia.
Tires: Goodyear Eagle GS-C

DIMENSIONS
Length: 177.2 in. **Width:** 70.5 in.
Height: 48.2 in. **Wheelbase:** 102.0 in.
Track: 56.2 in. (front), 55.6 in. (rear)
Weight: 2,620 lbs.

Chevrolet **CORVETTE '56-'62**

By the end of the 1950s, the Corvette had grown into one of the fastest sports cars in the world and one of the biggest performance bargains too. With so many power and handling options, the Vette™ could be just what you wanted it to—from civilized sportster to awesome mile-eater.

"...a unique experience."

"For the lucky few that will ever own or even drive a vintage Corvette, it's a unique experience. What's it like? Well, if you exploited the option list, your Corvette turned into a fearsome sports car, which by 1962, could have 360 bhp. Brakes were never its strong suit and even the optional linings are no solution. Despite the live axle, the handling is excellent for the time and the power steering is surprisingly precise. It has to be, because you need to be quick to catch the sudden power-oversteer."

There are few car interiors that can rival the dramatic styling of an early Corvette, which used contemporary fighter planes as its inspiration.

1956 Corvettes are introduced with a streamlined body style; powered by the 265-cubic inch small-block V8.

1958 Revised styling adds twin headlights, among other body modifications. The Vette is about 2 inches wider, 10 inches longer and 200 lbs. heavier. Cockpit is improved and the base engine power rises to 230 bhp.

Twin headlights were added for the 1958 restyle.

1961 Styling changes again, but like the 1958, the 1961 change is more major, with a new design for the rear of the car that gives a welcomed boost to the trunk space.

1962 Styling is toned down again and a larger engine installed, the bored and stroked 327-cubic inch V8 with power ranging from 250 bhp to 360 bhp.

1963 A new generation of Corvette, the Sting Ray®, appears totally restyled and with independent rear suspension.

The 1961 Corvette has a restyled rear, a hint of what was to come with the 1963 Sting Ray.

UNDER THE SKIN

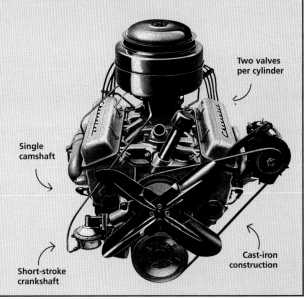

Simple ladder-frame chassis

Leaf-sprung live rear axle

Fiberglass bodywork

Double-wishbone front suspension

Traditional American V8

Cover-up

The Corvette's spectacular looks mask a very simple ladder-frame chassis with its two main rails joined and strengthened by a massive cruciform brace. The live rear axle is located and sprung by semi-elliptic leaf springs. At the front is a double-wishbone system with anti-roll bar. Although the big V8 is mounted up front with the transmission, it is set well back to give a very reasonable distribution of weight.

THE POWER PACK

Rumbling V8s

Corvettes of this generation are all V8-powered. All of these V8s are simple cast-iron, single camshaft, pushrod designs with two valves per cylinder. All have a short stroke and increasingly larger bore. Displacement rose from 265-cubic inches in 1956, through 283 and then, in the last year of this type, to 327. Outputs ranged from 210 bhp for a carbureted 265, right up to 360 bhp at 6,000 rpm, with the high, 11.25:1 compression ratio of the rare Rochester 'Ramjet' fuel-injected version, available as an option from 1957.

Two valves per cylinder

Single camshaft

Short-stroke crankshaft

Cast-iron construction

Best Vette

The best of the second generation of Corvettes was the 1957 model-year—after that they became bigger and more sleek. A 1957 equipped with Rochester Ramjet fuel injection produced 283 bhp and could reach 135 mph with 0-60 mph in 6.8 seconds.

The 1957 is the best vintage of second-generation Vette.

Chevrolet CORVETTE '56-'62

Style, power and performance. In the 1950s and early-1960s, the Corvette had it all. Despite its fiberglass body it was no lightweight but no one cared—it had power to burn.

Color schemes

In 1961, the Corvette was available in a choice of seven colors: Tuxedo Black, Ermine White, Roman Red, Sateen Silver, Jewel Blue, Fawn Beige and Honduras Maroon. For an extra $16, you could have the side cove highlighted in silver or white, an option deleted the next year.

Concealed hood

Unlike some of its European convertible rivals, the Corvette has a top which folds down completely to be hidden out of sight under a lockable cover.

Front vents

When the Corvette was widened for the 1958 model year, some of that extra width was taken up by vents behind the front bumper, there purely for styling.

Jaguar wheelbase

Chevrolet evaluated the Jaguar XK120 while developing the Corvette, but the only sign of any influence is that both cars have exactly the same wheelbase.

Limited slip differential

To stop the Corvette from spinning away its power on relatively narrow tires, the option of a Positraction limited slip differential was offered from 1957 on.

Power windows

From 1956 onward, Vettes were available with electrically-operated windows. In 1961, that option would have cost you just under $60.

'Duck tail' rear

The major styling change introduced for the 1961 model is this 'duck tail' rear, created by stylist Bill Mitchell and carried over into the '62 models.

Fiberglass body

Vettes have always been fiberglass and Chevrolet became better at producing it as the years passed. Early bodies were made from 46 different panels but that process had been streamlined by 1961.

Live rear axle

By 1961, the Corvette was only two years away from independent rear suspension. Until then it soldiered on with an old-fashioned live axle.

Specifications
1961 Chevrolet Corvette

ENGINE
Type: V8
Construction: Cast-iron block and heads
Valve gear: Two valves per cylinder operated by single block-mounted camshaft, pushrods and rockers
Bore and stroke: 3.87 in. x 2.99 in.
Displacement: 283 c.i.
Compression ratio: 11:1
Induction system: Rochester Ramjet mechanical fuel injection
Maximum power: 315 bhp at 6,200 rpm
Maximum torque: 295 lb-ft at 4,000 rpm
Top speed: 135 mph
0-60 mph: 6.1 sec.

TRANSMISSION
Four-speed manual

BODY/CHASSIS
X-braced ladder frame with fiberglass two-seat convertible body

SPECIAL FEATURES

All 1958-1962 Corvettes have a side cove, but the detail design and amount of chrome was changed every year.

From 1957 a Rochester Ramjet fuel injection option offered owners even more power to play with.

RUNNING GEAR
Steering: Worm-and-ball
Front suspension: Double wishbones with coil springs, telescopic shocks and anti-roll bar
Rear suspension: Live axle with semi-elliptic leaf springs and telescopic shocks
Brakes: Drums, 11 in. dia. (front and rear)
Wheels: Steel discs 6 in. x 17 in.
Tires: Crossply 6.70 in. x 16 in.

DIMENSIONS
Length: 177.5 in.   **Width:** 72.8 in.
Height: 52.4 in.   **Wheelbase:** 102 in.
Track: 57 in. (front), 59 in. (rear)
Weight: 2,905 lbs.

Chevrolet NOMAD

One of the most stylish wagons of all time, the 1955-1957 Chevrolet Nomads are a favorite with both collectors and customizers. The owner of this car has taken a traditional approach when customizing his 1956 Nomad.

"...supercharged performance."

"With its bucket seats and thick-rimmed steering wheel, this 1956 Nomad has a sporty edge. Push down on the throttle and feel its supercharged performance that can only come from a 1970 Corvette® small-block V8 with a B&M blower. It rockets the car to 60 mph in less than six seconds. No expense has been spared underneath either, and the 1986 Corvette suspension enables this car to corner much better than it did stock.

The dashboard is original, but the Connolly leather bucket seats have been added and give the car a more upmarket feel.

Milestones

1955 Chevrolet announces its new models, totally restyled and with magnificent new V8 engines. Top of the range is the distinctive Nomad, combining hardtop styling with station wagon practicality.

Designed by Carl Renner, the Nomad first appeared in 1955.

1956 Performance s improved with up to 265 bhp available from the small-block V8. Nomads, like the rest of the line, adopt busier styling.

The Nomad was subtly restyled for the 1956 model year.

1957 The two-door Nomad is again listed and receives another, and arguably more attractive, facelift. A amjet mechanical fuel injection ystem is available with the 283 '8 giving up to 283 bhp. Due to ts high cost, its two-door styling nd several seal problems, sales re moderate. Chevrolet decides o drop the model for its 1958 model line-up.

UNDER THE SKIN

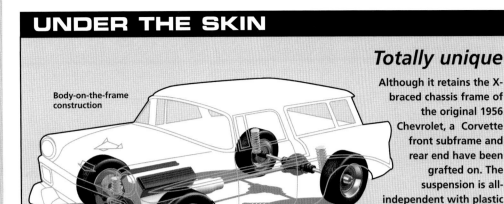

Body-on-the-frame construction

Lowered Corvette suspension

Four-wheel disc brakes

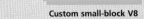

Custom small-block V8

Totally unique

Although it retains the X-braced chassis frame of the original 1956 Chevrolet, a Corvette front subframe and rear end have been grafted on. The suspension is all-independent with plastic transverse leaf springs front and rear, and four-wheel disc brakes to help improve stopping power.

THE POWER PACK

Old school mill

Many hot rodders use a small-block Chevy® to power their cars. The owner of this Nomad has installed a 1970-vintage Corvette LT-1®, (similar to the one shown here) and had it overbored to 358-cubic inches. The reciprocating assembly has been balanced, while the rest of the engine features ported heads, stainless-steel valves, roller-rocker arms, a forged steel crankshaft and a B&M supercharger.

Two valves per cylinder

Single camshaft

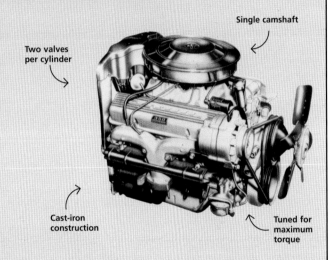

Cast-iron construction

Tuned for maximum torque

The Cormad

Although it looks like a mild custom, this Nomad has been drastically modified. Underneath is a 1986 Corvette front and rear suspension, complete with brakes and shocks. With a reworked LT-1 engine, this car will surprise many drivers on the road.

With their classic lines, Shoebox-Chevy Nomads are collector's favorites.

Chevrolet NOMAD

This Shoebox-Chevy Nomad combines style with performance. Using a Corvette powerplant and running gear, this 1956 Nomad can surprise many newer performance cars.

Modern paint

The body has been resprayed in two-tone Corvette dark red metallic and tan pearl.

Modified transmission

A 1976 Turbo 400 automatic transmission backs up the sinister LT1 engine. To extract maximum power from the engine, it has a high-stall torque converter.

Custom wheels

No street machine would be complete without aftermarket wheels. This Nomad is fitted with a set of custom chromed 16-inch wheels.

Clean lines

Even in 1956, the Nomad was a fairly clean-looking car. The two-tone paintwork and chrome spears accentuate the classic lines of this Chevrolet.

Corvette front end

The front suspension employs a 1986 Corvette subframe. Not only does it lower the car, giving it a ground-hugging stance, but it greatly improves the car's handling.

Small-block power

For massive performance, this ubiquitous 1970 LT-1 small-block V8 has been bored over .060-inch in and features a forged-steel crank, ported and polished cylinder heads, roller rocker arms plus a B&M supercharger and a Holley carburetor.

Specifications

1956 Chevrolet Nomad

ENGINE
Type: V8

Construction: Cast-iron block and heads

Valve gear: Two valves per cylinder operated by pushrods and rockers

Bore and stroke: 4.06 in. x 3.48 in.

Displacement: 358 c.i.

Compression ratio: 10.5:1

Induction system: B&M supercharger and Holley four-barrel carburetor

Maximum power: 400 bhp at 4,800 rpm

Maximum torque: 320 lb-ft at 3,000 rpm

Top speed: 131 mph

0-60 mph: 5.5 sec.

TRANSMISSION
1976 Turbo HydraMatic 400 with a high-stall torque converter

BODY/CHASSIS
Separate two-door station wagon steel body on X-braced steel frame and Corvette front subframe.

SPECIAL FEATURES

The fuel cap is neatly hidden behind the tail light.

With the rear seat folded down, luggage space is cavernous.

RUNNING GEAR
Steering: Recirculating ball

Front suspension: Double wishbones with plastic transverse leaf spring and shocks

Rear suspension: Trailing arms with plastic transverse leaf spring and shocks

Brakes: Discs (front and rear)

Wheels: Custom Boyds, 15-in. dia.

Tires: Goodyear P22560VR15

DIMENSIONS
Length: 196.7 in. **Width:** 77.2 in.

Height: 53 in.   **Wheelbase:** 115 in.

Track: 59.5 in. (front), 55.8 in. (rear)

Weight: 3,352 lbs.

Chevrolet **BEL AIR**

Think of America in the 1950s and an image of a 1957 Chevy® will appear, parked outside a period diner. This, the most popular of the so-called classic 'Shoebox-Chevys,' is also a favorite basis for a hot rod.

"...apple pie dynamite."

"This is what American hot-rodding is all about: a classic '57 Chevy® with some serious get-up-and-go. Think of it as apple pie with a stick of dynamite baked right in. Tap the throttle and the whole car rocks with the engine's inertia. Off the line, this car could beat almost any modern production car. Once the huge Mickey Thompson racing rear tires have stopped spinning, the violent acceleration shoves you back into your seat as you hang, white-knuckled, onto the tiny steering wheel."

Flame theme is apparent inside the car, with the graphic appearing on the steering wheel, interior trim and upholstery.

1955 Chevrolet releases its new modern line of cars, the 150, 210 and Bel Air series. It is the first sedan to use the new 265-cubic inch V8 small-block engine. Harley Earl's design team matches the engine to well-balanced and modern styling. Its box-styling and clean looks give it the name 'shoebox Chevy.'

The 1957 Bel Air convertible was the top of the line.

1956 The car receives a $40 million restyle for the new model year. Power is boosted on both six- and eight-cylinder models. The top spec V8 with Power-Pak produces 225 bhp.

The 150-series models are identifiable by the 1955-styled side trim.

1957 Another restyle produces the classic 1950s American sedan. The 1957 model uses a larger 283-cubic inch version of the small-block engine with fuel injection for 283 bhp.

1990s By this time, the 1955-57 'shoebox-Chevys' have become true classics in standard and hot-rod forms.

UNDER THE SKIN

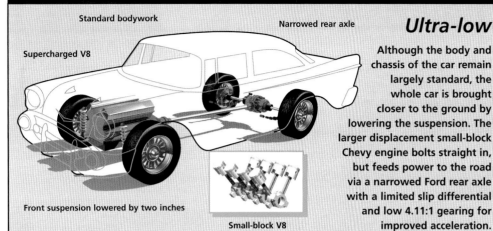

Standard bodywork

Narrowed rear axle

Supercharged V8

Front suspension lowered by two inches

Small-block V8

Ultra-low

Although the body and chassis of the car remain largely standard, the whole car is brought closer to the ground by lowering the suspension. The larger displacement small-block Chevy engine bolts straight in, but feeds power to the road via a narrowed Ford rear axle with a limited slip differential and low 4.11:1 gearing for improved acceleration.

THE POWER PACK

Powerful small block

It is possible to get a huge amount of power from the 350-cubic inch small-block V8 engine without forced induction. The car overleaf, however, uses a B&M supercharger to help it produce truly monstrous power and torque outputs. Other modifications include custom-fabricated tubular exhaust headers and electronic exhaust cut-outs. The rest of the exhaust system uses 2.5-inch diameter tubing and Mac mufflers to create a very free-flowing system.

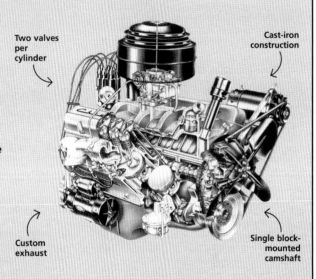

Two valves per cylinder

Cast-iron construction

Custom exhaust

Single block-mounted camshaft

Boyd's best

Master hot-rod builder Boyd Coddington created the Boydair as a showcase for his hot-rod building company. It has a custom-made chassis clothed in modified 1957 Chevy panels. It's centered around the cowl and windshield of a 1959 Chevrolet Impala®. The engine and running gear are from a 1997 Corvette®.

Ultra-low 'Boydair' uses modern Corvette mechanicals.

Chevrolet BEL AIR

Huge tires, an immaculate custom paint job, a wild interior, low aggressive stance and a powerful blown V8 engine installed in a classic American car—all the ingredients of a great hot rod.

Chromework
Although this car has been built as a high-performance vehicle, little has been done to reduce its weight. Even the heavy chrome bumpers are retained.

Blown engine
A B&M supercharger gives a huge boost to the power and torque outputs of this car's 350-cubic inch small-block Chevy V8 engine.

Custom interior
It looks just as good inside. The flame motif is carried through to the interior and even appears on the headlining and steering wheel.

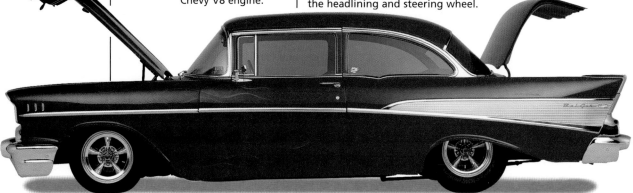

Alloy wheels
The popular American Racing Torq-Thrust five-spoke wheels are used. They are similar in style to racing wheels often used in the 1960s.

Lowered suspension
To lower the lines of the car and give it that road-hugging stance, the suspension has been lowered. Two-inch drop spindles and chopped coil springs lower the front, while custom semi-elliptic leaf springs, relocated on the chassis, ease down the rear end.

Huge rear tires
The Mickey Thompson tires added to the rear of the car are designed to give maximum traction off the line.

Smoothed hood and trunk
Both the hood and rear deck have been smoothed off and stripped of badges to give the car a much cleaner look.

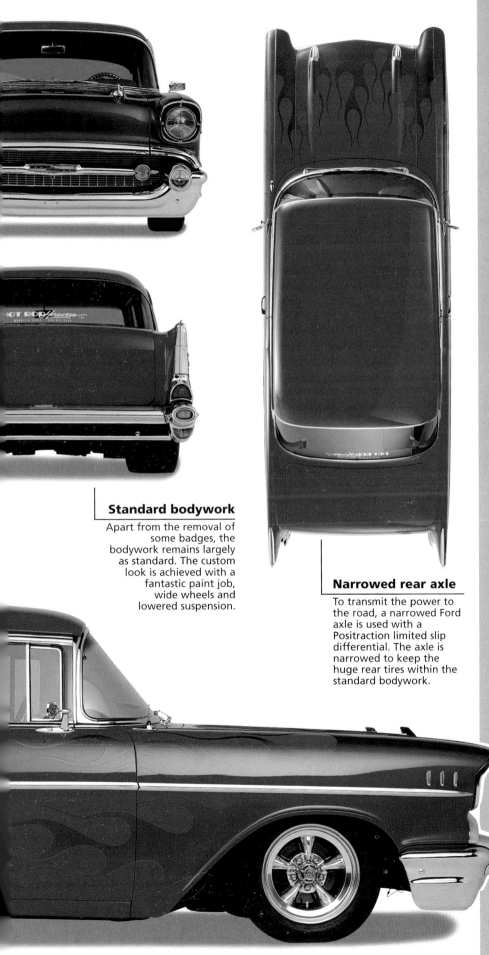

Standard bodywork

Apart from the removal of some badges, the bodywork remains largely as standard. The custom look is achieved with a fantastic paint job, wide wheels and lowered suspension.

Narrowed rear axle

To transmit the power to the road, a narrowed Ford axle is used with a Positraction limited slip differential. The axle is narrowed to keep the huge rear tires within the standard bodywork.

Specifications

1957 Modified Chevrolet Bel Air

ENGINE

Type: V8

Construction: Cast-iron block and heads

Valve gear: Single block-mounted camshaft operating two valves per cylinder via pushrods

Bore and stroke: 4 in. x 3.5 in.

Displacement: 350 c.i.

Compression ratio: 8.5:1

Induction system: B&M 4-71 mechanical supercharger with Holley four-barrel carb

Maximum power: 420 bhp at 5,400 rpm

Maximum torque: 435 lb-ft at 2,500 rpm

Top speed: 147 mph

0-60 mph: 3.9 sec.

TRANSMISSION

350 Turbo automatic

BODY/CHASSIS

Standard 1957 Bel Air steel body with smoothed hood and rear deck on steel perimeter chassis

SPECIAL FEATURES

Above: To achieve its enormous power output, the hot 350-cubic inch V8 uses a B&M supercharger.

Left: This car features outstanding chromework. The hidden gas filler cap is a typical feature for a car of the '50s.

RUNNING GEAR

Steering: Power-assisted recirculating ball

Front suspension: Fabricated tubular wishbones, 2-in. drop spindles, chopped coil springs, telescopic shock absorbers

Rear suspension: Custom semi-elliptic leaf springs, lowering blocks, traction bars and air shock absorbers

Brakes: Discs (front and rear)

Wheels: American Racing Torq-Thrust D, 7.5 in. x 15 in. (front), 11 in. x 15 in. (rear)

Tires: BF Goodrich 205/60-15 (front), Mickey Thompson Sportsman I N50/15

DIMENSIONS

Length: 200 in.   **Width:** 73.9 in.

Height: 46.9 in.   **Wheelbase:** 115 in.

Track: 58 in.(front), 58.8in. (rear)

Weight: 3,197 lbs.

Chevrolet **IMPALA**

In 1958, Chevrolet tried to reach a more upscale market by offering its base full-size model, the Bel Air® with more plush features calling it the Impala. With soft lines and lots of chrome, it lends itself well to customizing.

"...period-enhanced hot rod."

"Jazzy tuck n' roll upholstery take you back to the golden era of automobiles. Your first impression might be that this is a slow, all-garb, no-go sled, but once the engine reaches its peak rpm, you realize there is much more to this period-enhanced hot rod. The V8 is choppy at idle, but once you tap the gas the Impala rockets away accompanied by a harmonious bellow from the exhaust pipes. With an adjustable suspension you can practically scrape the bumper on the pavement at low speeds, too."

A chrome-faced dash and a white-on-red interior give this Impala a real 1950s flavor.

Milestones

1957 Late in the year, the all-new restyled Chevrolets go on sale for the 1958 model year. Model names were revised and include Del Ray™, Biscayne™ and Bel Air. A new range-topping hardtop coupe and convertible, known as the Impala, arrive as a sporty Bel Air sub-series.

The Impala convertible was top of the 1958 Chevrolet range.

1959 Another restyle introduces a new chassis accompanied by longer, lower bodywork with 'cat's-eye' taillights and 'bat-wing' fins. The Impala returns but is now a full model range that includes sedans, coupes and convertibles.

The Del Ray was the entry-level 1958 Chevrolet.

1960 Styling is toned down, but Impala production climbs to over 40,000 units, making it one of Chevrolet's best-selling cars.

UNDER THE SKIN

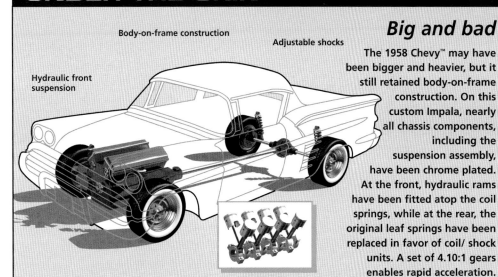

Body-on-frame construction

Adjustable shocks

Hydraulic front suspension

Powerful V8

Big and bad

The 1958 Chevy™ may have been bigger and heavier, but it still retained body-on-frame construction. On this custom Impala, nearly all chassis components, including the suspension assembly, have been chrome plated. At the front, hydraulic rams have been fitted atop the coil springs, while at the rear, the original leaf springs have been replaced in favor of coil/ shock units. A set of 4.10:1 gears enables rapid acceleration.

THE POWER PACK

A stoke of power

First-year Impalas came standard with a 236-cubic inch inline six, but this one has something a little bit hotter. A late model Firebird donated its 350 small-block which has been endowed with a .030-inch overbore and fitted with a 400-cubic inch crankshaft upping its displacement to 383 cubic inches. Ported and polished Corvette heads are fitted and a three-angle valve job ensures the perfect valve seal. Flat-top pistons, an Iskendarian camshaft and a vintage Tri-Power intake with three Rochester carburetors help this stroker engine make 430 bhp at 6,700 rpm and its heady 420 lb-ft of torque comes on at 3,400 rpm.

High style

Entering production during the eclipse of the 1950s, the 1958 Impala had unusual styling compared to all other Impalas. Only the 1958s were endowed with small tail fins, and very 1950s styling. The 1959 models were toned down to pave the way for the more upright and boxier cars of the 1960s.

During the 1960s, first-year Impalas were very popular for customizing.

Chevrolet IMPALA

A striking paint job combined with generous portions of chrome give this 1958 Chevrolet a very nostalgic look. The performance, too, comes from some time-honored, hot-rodding tricks.

Worked V8

With a 400 stroker kit and a .030-inch overbore, this tri-carbed small-block makes almost three time the power output of the straight six it replaces. Its list of modifications reads like that of a race car-spec engine: fully balanced reciprocating assembly, double roller timing chain, fat camshaft, high compression forged pistons, stainless-steel valves and a high-pressure fuel pump. Did we mention it makes more than 400 bhp?

Chromed underpinnings

This car is all about attention to detail. Underneath, nearly everything is chrome plated, including the wishbones, anti-roll bar, motor mounts, springs and rear axle assembly.

Custom exhaust

In order for the engine to fully exploit its power, a low-restriction exhaust system is essential. Custom headers and 2½-inch pipes with Glasspack mufflers not only help increase power but give a low, deep bellow, too.

Hydraulic front suspension

On this Impala, the front shocks have been replaced by a hydraulic system. This enables the front of the car to be raised or lowered with interior mounted controls. A dump valve and a heavy-duty battery are located in the trunk.

Triple taillights

Distinguishing Impalas from lesser Chevys in 1958 was its triple taillight lenses per side, which soon became a hallmark of the series. On this car, the stock items have been replaced by bullet-style lenses from a 1959 Cadillac.

Specifications

1958 Chevrolet Impala

ENGINE
Type: V8

Construction: Cast-iron block and heads

Valve gear: Two valves per cylinder operated by a single, centrally-mounted mounted camshaft

Bore and stroke: 4.03 in. x 3.75 in.

Displacement: 383 c.i.

Compression ratio: 10.5:1

Induction system: Three Rochester two-barrel carburetors

Maximum power: 430 bhp at 6,700 rpm

Maximum torque: 420 lb-ft at 3,400 rpm

Top speed: 102 mph

0-60 mph: 6.5 sec.

TRANSMISSION
TH400 three-speed automatic

BODY/CHASSIS
Separate steel chassis with two-door hardtop coupe body

SPECIAL FEATURES

Chrome horizontal bars give the grill a clean appearance.

An aftermarket tach and auxiliary gauges hint at the car's performance.

RUNNING GEAR
Steering: Recirculating ball

Front suspension: Unequal-length wishbones with coil springs, hydraulic rams and anti-roll bar

Rear suspension: Live axle with coil springs and telescopic adjustable shock absorbers

Brakes: Discs (front), drums (rear)

Wheels: Saturn smoothie, 6 x 14 in.

Tires: Coker Classic (front), Commando (rear)

DIMENSIONS
Length: 197.6 in.   **Width:** 83.0 in.

Height: 55.0 in.   **Wheelbase:** 117.5 in.

Track: 62.5 in. (front), 61.5 in. (rear)

Weight: 3,447 lbs.

Chevrolet EL CAMINO

It isn't a car and it isn't a pick-up. The idea was to combine the luxury, comfort, and style of the 1959 Chevrolets with the convenience and practicality of a large and handy load bed.

"...more car than truck."

"When driving the El Camino without the optional heavy-duty springs and with a load on board, you'll realize it's more car than truck as it bottoms over even small bumps. With a ride that is both soft and comfortable, the driver must take care through the turns. The steering takes a lot of effort, requiring six turns lock-to-lock. When fitted with one of the optional big-block V8 engines the El Camino's performance is outstanding, although traction is poor."

The interiors of 1959 El Caminos were typical of most cars from the late 1950s.

Milestones

1958 Launched as a 1959 model in response to Ford's fast-selling Ranchero, the El Camino is based on the full-size Chevy wagon. Top-of-the-line models are extremely fast and can be fitted with an optional Corvette close-ratio four-speed transmission.

The similarity of the El Camino and the Chevrolet Impala is clear to see.

1959 Despite a minor restyle, sales fall by over a quarter in the 1960 model year to a figure that is unacceptable to Chevrolet.

Over the years, a popular modification is dropping an El Camino body on a 4x4 chassis.

1960 There is no place for the El Camino in the 1961 model year line; poor sales have doomed it to extinction.

1964 Chevrolet decides that the El Camino concept is worth reviving and produces a new model based on the sporty mid-size Chevelle.

UNDER THE SKIN

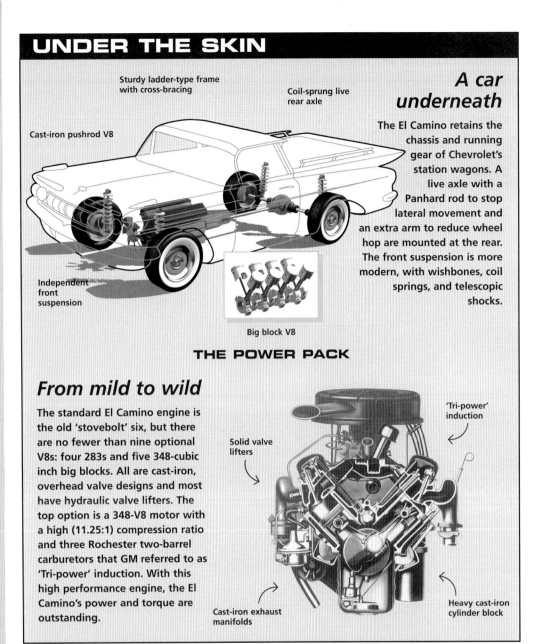

Sturdy ladder-type frame with cross-bracing

Coil-sprung live rear axle

Cast-iron pushrod V8

Independent front suspension

Big block V8

A car underneath

The El Camino retains the chassis and running gear of Chevrolet's station wagons. A live axle with a Panhard rod to stop lateral movement and an extra arm to reduce wheel hop are mounted at the rear. The front suspension is more modern, with wishbones, coil springs, and telescopic shocks.

THE POWER PACK

From mild to wild

The standard El Camino engine is the old 'stovebolt' six, but there are no fewer than nine optional V8s: four 283s and five 348-cubic inch big blocks. All are cast-iron, overhead valve designs and most have hydraulic valve lifters. The top option is a 348-V8 motor with a high (11.25:1) compression ratio and three Rochester two-barrel carburetors that GM referred to as 'Tri-power' induction. With this high performance engine, the El Camino's power and torque are outstanding.

'Tri-power' induction

Solid valve lifters

Heavy cast-iron cylinder block

Cast-iron exhaust manifolds

Cats-eye

Being the first of the line and having been built in the most glamorous era of American cars, the 1959 El Camino is the collector's dream. Big fins, 'cats-eye' taillamps and headlamp 'eyebrows' make it the most stylish of all luxury pick-up trucks.

The 1959 El Camino had all the stylish embellishments of the era.

Chevrolet EL CAMINO

Stung by the success of the Ford Ranchero luxury sedan/pick-up, Chevrolet hit back with the El Camino. In its most powerful form, the El Camino was the fastest utility vehicle in the world.

Engine options

The standard engine is a six-cylinder, but nine V8s were available. The 283-cubic inch was offered in four states of tune, from 185 bhp to 290 bhp. The five 348-cubic inch big block V8s produce between 250 bhp and 315 bhp.

Limited slip differential

With the big block engines, traction off the line is poor. A Positraction limited slip differential was a sensible option at just $48.

Horizontal fins

One of the most distinctive features of all 1959 Chevrolets is the tailfin.

Luggage area in cab

You don't have to carry all your luggage in the cargo area; there is a small space behind the bench seat.

Double-skinned bed

Although much of the El Camino is for show, Chevrolet made sure it was practical, too. The cargo area has a double-skinned load bed with a strong, ribbed-steel floor.

Live axle

Following typical Detroit fashion in the 1950s, the El Camino has a solid rear axle. Like Chevy wagons, the rear suspension has a Panhard rod and control arms to help to keep the axle in place. Rear coil springs help to smooth out the ride.

Twin headlights

Introduced on passenger cars in 1958, twin headlights remained a feature on the 1959 El Camino.

Air-conditioning

Despite the utilitarian interior, air-conditioning was available for $468.

Wraparound windshield

Panoramic windshields were in fashion during the 1950s and offer excellent visibility.

Corvette transmission

Although a three-speed manual column shift was standard, the El Camino could be ordered with either an automatic or a floor-mounted Corvette four-speed transmission.

Specifications
1959 Chevrolet El Camino

ENGINE

Type: V8

Construction: Cast-iron block and heads

Valve gear: Two valves per cylinder operated by single central camshaft via pushrods, rockers and solid lifters

Bore and stroke: 4.13 in. x 3.27 in.

Displacement: 348 c.i.

Compression ratio: 11.25:1

Fuel system: Triple Rochester two-barrel carburetors

Maximum power: 315 bhp at 5,600 rpm

Maximum torque: 357 lb-ft at 3,600 rpm

Top speed: 131 mph

0-60 mph: 8.7 sec.

TRANSMISSION

Optional three-or four-speed manual or two-speed automatic

BODY/CHASSIS

Steel box section cruciform chassis with two-door pick-up body

SPECIAL FEATURES

The back of the roof projected outward and had the same 'flyaway' style feature as seen on 1959 Chevrolet hardtop sedans.

'Cats eye' tail-lights were a unique feature on Chevys of the period and were neatly split for the El Camino's tailgate.

RUNNING GEAR

Steering: Recirculating ball

Front suspension: Double wishbones with coil springs and telescopic shocks

Rear suspension: Live axle with trailing arms, Panhard rod and central torque reaction arm, coil springs and telescopic shocks

Brakes: Drums, 11-in. dia.

Wheels: Pressed steel, 14-in. dia.

Tires: Crossply 8.00 x 14

DIMENSIONS

Length: 210.9 in.

Width: 79.9 in.

Height: 58.7 in.

Wheelbase: 119.7 in.

Track: 60.2 in. (front), 59.5 in. (rear)

Weight: 3,881 lbs.

Chrysler C-300

The Chrysler 300 is widely recognized as one of America's first muscle cars. However, the 300 wasn't about brute power; it also was a refined, full-size sportster with an abundance of luxury features.

"...immensely powerful."

"The immensely powerful 331-cubic inch Hemi engine produces superb performance by 1950s standards. It pushes the 4,005-lbs. Chrysler to 60 mph in less than 9 seconds, and cruising at over 120 mph is easily possible. Despite its considerable size, the big C-300 remains rock-steady at speed, and although it leans through corners, it manages to hold the line better than any of its contemporaries. It truly deserves its legendary status."

Power windows and a 150-mph speedometer are standard in the C-300.

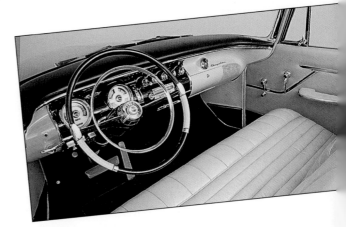

Milestones

1951 Chrysler
introduces its first mass-produced, widely available overhead-valve V8—the 331-cubic inch firepower Hemi. Although a late entry in the OHV V8 race, Chrysler's engine gains a fine reputation for its rugged, powerful and technically well-engineered design.

1958 was the last year for the original Hemi in Chrysler cars, here a DeSoto Adventurer.

1955 Chrysler
installs a tuned 300-bhp Hemi into a two-door Windsor coupe and adds heavy-duty suspension and an Imperial grill. The result is the potent C-300.

The last of the tailfinned 300s was the 1961 300G.

1956 More power
(340 bhp) and integrated fins mark the second-season 300B, which also starts the letter legacy, culminating in the square-rigged 300L of 1965.

UNDER THE SKIN

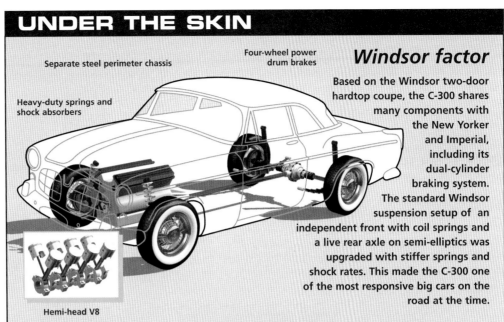

Separate steel perimeter chassis

Four-wheel power drum brakes

Heavy-duty springs and shock absorbers

Hemi-head V8

Windsor factor

Based on the Windsor two-door hardtop coupe, the C-300 shares many components with the New Yorker and Imperial, including its dual-cylinder braking system. The standard Windsor suspension setup of an independent front with coil springs and a live rear axle on semi-elliptics was upgraded with stiffer springs and shock rates. This made the C-300 one of the most responsive big cars on the road at the time.

THE POWER PACK

Hemi Legacy

Chrysler gained a lead on its competition when it launched its new overhead-valve V8 in 1951. This 331-cubic inch cast-iron engine featured hemispherical combustion chambers, which enabled it to produce more power than rival V8s at a lower compression ratio. In initial form, it was rated at 180 bhp, but more power was easily possible. For 1955, engineers fitted a tuned version into a two-door Windsor hardtop and christened it the 300. This engine featured bigger valves, a higher-lift camshaft, and a slightly higher compression. The result was nearly 1 bhp per cubic inch and staggering performance.

Bargain Blaze

Competing in the great American horsepower race, the C-300 packed a fearsome punch. It was faster than nearly every other car on sale in the U.S. in 1955, and although it cost a towering $4,110, this early muscle car was a bargain.

Back-up lights and external mirrors were not available on the C-300.

Chrysler **C-300**

America's first mass-produced car to break the 300-bhp ceiling, the C-300 was also incredibly stylish and dominated NASCAR, winning 37 races in the hands of drivers like Buck Baker and Tim Flock.

Stiffened suspension

While the front coil springs of the New Yorker are rated at 480 lbs./in., those on the C-300 are rated at 800 lbs./in. Likewise, the New Yorker's rear leaf springs are rated at 100 lbs./in., whereas the C-300's are 160 lbs./in.

Solid lifters

Chrysler engineers replaced the hydraulic lifters with solid lifters for the 300. Revving up to 5,200 rpm, the heat generated by the engine could 'pump up' hydraulic lifters as they expand and hold the valves open.

Automatics only

All C-300s came with two-speed PowerFlite automatic transmissions. However, experts agree that there was one car (number 1206) that was built with a three-speed manual transmission.

Unique wheels

Chrysler C-300 buyers had a choice of two wheel styles. The standard ones are steel with Imperial wheel covers and unique 300 center caps; or, for an extra $617, buyers could opt for a set of chrome, 48-spoke wheels by Motor Wheel.

Specifications

1955 Chrysler C-300

ENGINE
Type: V8

Construction: Cast-iron block and heads

Valve gear: Two valves per cylinder operated by a single camshaft with pushrods and rockers

Bore and stroke: 3.81 in. x 3.63 in.

Displacement: 331.1 c.i.

Compression ratio: 8.5:1

Induction system: Two Carter four-barrel carburetors

Maximum power: 300 bhp at 5,200 rpm

Maximum torque: 345 lb-ft at 3,200 rpm

Top speed: 130 mph

0-60 mph: 8.9 sec.

TRANSMISSION
PowerFlite two-speed automatic

BODY/CHASSIS
Separate chassis with steel two-door body

SPECIAL FEATURES

The protruding stalk shifter was only found on 1955 300s.

Fins on the C-300 were little more than extra chrome pieces grafted on.

RUNNING GEAR
Steering: Recirculating-ball

Front suspension: A-arms with coil springs and telescopic shock absorbers

Rear suspension: Live axle with semi-elliptic multileaf springs and telescopic shock absorbers

Brakes: Drums (front and rear)

Wheels: Wire, 15 x 5 in.

Tires: Goodyear Super Cushion Nylon Special tubeless white sidewalls 6-ply, 8.00 x 15

DIMENSIONS
Length: 218.8 in.   **Width:** 79.1 in.

Height: 60.1 in.   **Wheelbase:** 126.0 in.

Track: 60.2 in. (front) 59.6 in. (rear)

Weight: 4,005 lbs.

Axle ratios

The standard rear axle ratio for the C-300 is a 3.54:1 ring-and-pinion, but steeper cogs were available.

Citroën **TRACTION AVANT**

It's hard to imagine just how revolutionary Citroën's Traction Avant was in the mid-1930s. It came decades before any other popular front-wheel drive car and was still in production more than 20 years later. Its legendary handling made it a popular choice.

"...unrivaled grip for its time."

"The Traction was a revelation to drive in the 1930s. The combination of its solid structure, which did not twist or shake, and an advanced suspension combined to give an unrivaled combination of ride, handling, and grip for its time. Even today, the Traction can be hurried through bends at high speeds. The trick is not to lose momentum as the Traction takes its time to build up speed. Drawbacks are few: the gearshift cannot be rushed, the turning circle is wide and the steering is heavy at low speeds."

Don't slow down. The Traction has great handling, but the asthmatic engine means it gathers speed rather than actually accelerating.

1932 André Citroën decided to revolutionize his full range of cars with the most modern family car in the world, giving his engineering team just two years to design and produce it.

...odies included various ...briolets.

1934 Traction Avant appears on schedule but its development bankrupts Citroën. The company is taken over by its chief creditor, Michelin.

1938 Supplementing the standard 1,911-cc models, the Economy 1,628-cc and Performance 1,911-cc models are introduced and built until 1940.

1945 Production restarts in June and the Traction Avant, in Light Fifteen and the larger-bodied Big Fifteen styles, are produced until 1957, using the 56-bhp engine.

...e Traction changed little in ...s 25 years of production.

UNDER THE SKIN

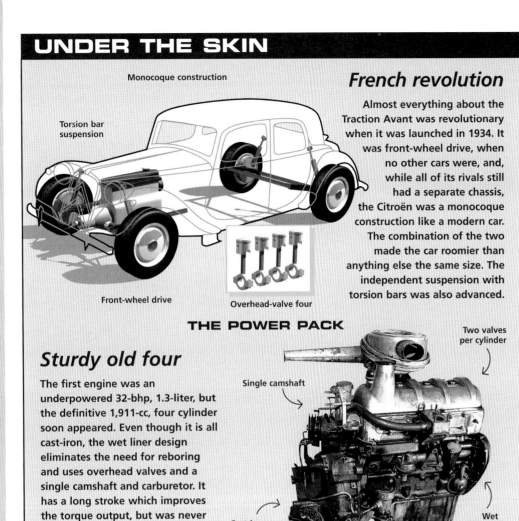

Monocoque construction

Torsion bar suspension

Front-wheel drive

Overhead-valve four

French revolution

Almost everything about the Traction Avant was revolutionary when it was launched in 1934. It was front-wheel drive, when no other cars were, and, while all of its rivals still had a separate chassis, the Citroën was a monocoque construction like a modern car. The combination of the two made the car roomier than anything else the same size. The independent suspension with torsion bars was also advanced.

THE POWER PACK

Sturdy old four

The first engine was an underpowered 32-bhp, 1.3-liter, but the definitive 1,911-cc, four cylinder soon appeared. Even though it is all cast-iron, the wet liner design eliminates the need for reboring and uses overhead valves and a single camshaft and carburetor. It has a long stroke which improves the torque output, but was never tuned for outright power.

Single camshaft

Two valves per cylinder

Cast-iron construction

Wet cylinder liners

Citroën's big six

The Traction Avant's chassis could handle much more power than the standard car, so in 1938 Citroën introduced the 77-bhp, 2,866-cc straight-six engine. It has a higher maximum speed of around 80 mph and stayed in production as late as 1957. The rare 15CV 6H (only 3,079 built) had Citroën's pioneering hydropneumatic self-levelling suspension at the rear.

Ultimate Traction Avant was 2,866-cc, six-cylinder version.

Citroën **TRACTION AVANT**

By forcing his engineers to design and develop the revolutionary front-wheel drive Traction Avant, André Citroën bankrupted the company. However, the result was a car that was way ahead of its time.

Citroën emblem
The double chevron emblem represented meshing gears, an iro[n] considering the weakness of the three-speed transmission.

Wet liner engine
The engine has wet liners—cylinder sleeves inserted into the block and surrounded by the water jacket. These could be replaced where a conventional engine would need to be rebuilt.

Monocoque design
The main structure of the Traction was a steel monocoque. Citroën once demonstrated its great strength by pushing one off a cliff.

Front-wheel dri[ve]
It was the first front-wheel drive car to solve the problem of getting universal joints to work reliab[ly] on front driveshafts, and the first to go into mass productio[n]

Transmission ahead of engine
Since the Traction Avant is a front-wheel drive, the transmission is mounted ahead of the engine. It helped weight distribution, but made for a very long gear linkage which needed precise adjustment to work well.

Michelin radial tires

Michelin took over the company when Citroën went bankrupt— naturally the Traction used Michelin tires. After the war, they were replaced with the new and hard-wearing X radials.

'Floating Power' engine mounts

Citroën wanted the car to be comfortable and refined. Using 'Floating Power' mounts helped to isolate the movement and vibration of the engine and transmission.

Specifications
1952 'Big Fifteen' Citroën 11CV Traction Avant

ENGINE
Type: In-line four cylinder
Construction: Cast-iron block and head with wet liner cylinder sleeves.
Valve gear: Two valves per cylinder operated by single block-mounted camshaft, pushrods and rockers
Bore and stroke: 3.07 in. x 3.93 in.
Displacement: 1,911 cc
Compression ratio: 6.5:1
Induction system: Single Solex 32 PBI downdraft carburetor
Maximum power: 56 bhp at 4,250 rpm
Maximum torque: 90 lb-ft at 2,200 rpm
Top speed: 71 mph
0-50 mph: 16.4 sec.

TRANSMISSION
Three-speed manual

BODY/CHASSIS
Steel monocoque with, at one stage, choice of sedan, coupe or open-roadster body

SPECIAL FEATURES

The wind-shield can be wound open with a handle in the cabin to improve ventilation.

The shifter sprouts from the dashboard in an unconventional fashion for Citroën. It can be difficult to use if it is out of adjustment.

RUNNING GEAR
Steering: Rack-and-pinion
Front suspension: Upper wishbones, lower radius arms, torsion bars and shocks
Rear suspension: Beam axle, trailing arms, radius arms, torsion bars and hydraulic shocks
Brakes: Hydraulically operated drums, 12 in. dia. (front), 9.8 in. dia. (rear)
Wheels: Pressed steel disc
Tires: 6.5 in. x 15 in.

DIMENSIONS
Length: 186.5 in. **Width:** 70 in.
Height: 61 in. **Wheelbase:** 21.5 in.
Track: 58.5 in. (front), 57.8 in. (rear)
Weight: 2,349 lbs.

Daimler **MAJESTIC MAJOR**

British royalty always favored Daimlers, so the Majestic name was not at all misplaced. What makes this Daimler special—or 'Major' in the company's words—is its smooth V8 engine. In style, the Majestic is regal, but it is a truly fast car, comfortably capable of 120 mph.

"...wood, wool and leather."

"One tongue-in-cheek journalist called the Majestic Major a '120-mph funeral express' because of its dour demeanor. Certainly you feel transported back to the early days of driving, the decor being a rich, 'gentleman's club' mix of wood, wool and leather. The engine has that smooth sound of the best U.S. V8s, and the three-speed automatic transmission provides seamless gear shifts."

The flat, wood veneer dashboard with multiple gauges and toggle switches dates from the conservative end of the 1950s.

Milestones

1958 Daimler updates its traditional sedan style to become the Majestic, with a wide body and a 3.8-liter straight-six engine.

1959 Just before the company's takeover by Jaguar, Daimler shows its new V8-powered Majestic Major.

Daimler's SP250 sports car packed a smaller version of the V8.

1960 Production begins this year.

1961 A long-wheelbase DR450 limousine version of the model appears on the price lists.

Daimler's other V8-powered sedan was the 250.

1964 Power steering becomes standard.

1968 Production of the Major and DR450 comes to an end.

UNDER THE SKIN

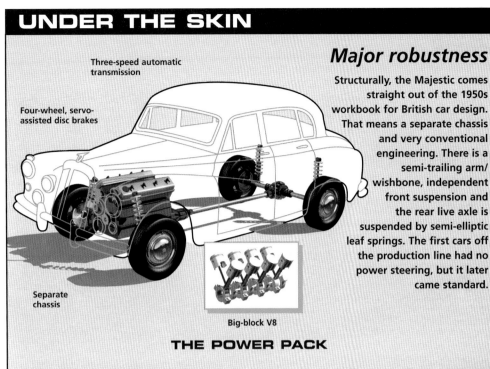

Three-speed automatic transmission

Four-wheel, servo-assisted disc brakes

Separate chassis

Big-block V8

Major robustness

Structurally, the Majestic comes straight out of the 1950s workbook for British car design. That means a separate chassis and very conventional engineering. There is a semi-trailing arm/wishbone, independent front suspension and the rear live axle is suspended by semi-elliptic leaf springs. The first cars off the production line had no power steering, but it later came standard.

THE POWER PACK

Majestic motor

Designed by Daimler's legendary engineer Edward Turner, the 4.6-liter V8 was a very large engine for a British car maker in those days. Notably, it had alloy cylinder heads and hemispherical combustion chambers. With a power output of 220 bhp and adequate torque output of 283 lb-ft, it could provide trouble-free driving. Indeed Jaguar trial-fitted this V8 in its own very large Mark X sedan and recorded a 0-100 mph time of 30.9 seconds—impressive stuff. But Jaguar favored its XK engine range, so the Daimler V8 withered away.

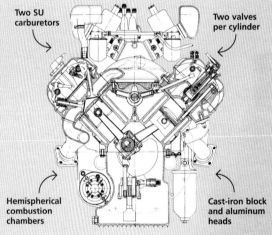

Two SU carburetors

Two valves per cylinder

Hemispherical combustion chambers

Cast-iron block and aluminum heads

Major benefits

The V8-powered Major has slightly more power than the standard six-cylinder Majestic, and its value in the classic market reflects this. Apart from the Rolls-Royce Silver Cloud, it is the only British sedan with 1950s style and 1960s sports performance.

Few cars combine 1950s style with 1960s performance as well as the Majestic.

Daimler MAJESTIC MAJOR

With its unique blend of dignified lines, relaxed performance and competitive pricing, the Majestic Major was a British favorite for those who liked its adequate power. But this made it a popular and safe driver's car.

Unique V8 power
Though Daimler did produce a popular 2.5-liter V8 for its smaller models, the 4.6-liter V8 engine in the Majestic Major was never fitted to any other model. It has light alloy cylinder heads and hemispherical combustion chambers.

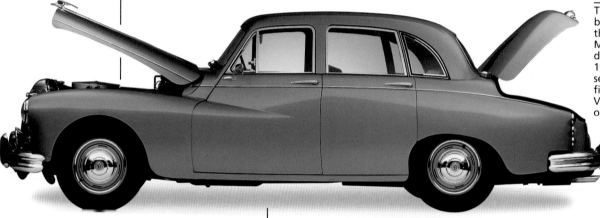

Unique V grills
The bodywork is basically the same as that on the six-cylinder Majestic, itself a development of the 1955 One-O-Four sedan. A major identification mark was the V-grills on either side of the radiator.

Two wheelbase lengths
A 114-inch wheelbase may seem long enough, but the eight-passenger DR450 limousine version is nearly 19 feet long and weighs more than two tons.

Leather interior
The Major has a beautifully crafted interior that resembles a living room rather than an automobile interior. The seats are hand-stitched leather and the dashboard is styled with wood veneer.

Four-wheel disc brakes
Dunlop supplied Daimler with its disc brakes which were fitted to all four wheels. They were just barely adequate to haul down the two tons of metal.

Optional power steering
After early buyers had struggled with the non-assisted steering, power assistance became an option—and a popular one. It was fitted as standard only in 1964.

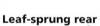

Leaf-sprung rear axle
The chassis is very conventional. It has coil-sprung front suspension and a live rear axle on semi-elliptic leaf springs.

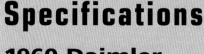

Specifications

1960 Daimler Major

ENGINE
Type: V8
Construction: Cast-iron block and aluminum heads
Valve gear: Two valves per cylinder operated via pushrods and rockers
Bore and stroke: 3.75 in. x 3.15 in.
Displacement: 4,561 cc
Compression ratio: 8.0:1
Induction system: Two SU carburetors
Maximum power: 220 bhp at 5,500 rpm
Maximum torque: 283 lb-ft at 3,200 rpm
Top speed: 120 mph
0-60 mph: 10.3 sec.

TRANSMISSION
Borg-Warner three-speed automatic

BODY/CHASSIS
Separate chassis with steel four-door sedan body

SPECIAL FEATURES

Daimler's distinctive emblem sits atop a fluted grill.

The opulence of the interior includes fold-away wood-veneer tables.

RUNNING GEAR
Steering: Recirculating ball
Front suspension: Semi-trailing arms with lower wishbones, coil springs and telescopic shock absorbers
Rear suspension: Live axle with semi-elliptic springs and telescopic shock absorbers
Brakes: Discs (front and rear)
Wheels: Steel, 16-in. dia.
Tires: 6.70 x 16

DIMENSIONS
Length: 202.0 in.   **Width:** 73.25 in.
Height: 62.75 in.   **Wheelbase:** 114.0 in.
Track: 57.0 in. (front and rear)
Weight: 4,228 lbs.

DeSoto **PACESETTER**

Arriving midway through 1956 was a new top-of-the line DeSoto—the Adventurer. Packing a bigger 341-cubic inch version of the Hemi engine, it was distinguished by gold anodized trim. A convertible version, which was the Indianapolis 500 pace car that year, was aptly named the Pacesetter.

"...majestic interior design."

"The majestic interior design in the Pacesetter really strikes a chord. Sitting on sofa-like seats, you grasp a huge, narrow-rimmed steering wheel with push button shift controls to the left of the wheel. The wonderful-sounding Hemi V8 sings enthusiastically, combining seamlessly with the PowerFlite transmission. Despite its bulk, the DeSoto was quick for its day and will keep pulling past 100 mph long after its competition has reached its terminal top speed."

Anodized gold on the dash and door panels was an Adventurer/Pacesetter exclusive.

Milestones

1956 DeSoto launches a limited-production hardtop, the Adventurer. A convertible version, the Pacesetter, is also built in very small numbers.

1957 As part of an all-new Chrysler range, a new DeSoto lineup debuts, with the Adventurer coupe and convertible (replacing the Pacesetter) at the top of the range. The Hemi is bored out to 345 cubic inches and has 345 bhp.

1951 saw the arrival of the Hemi V8 in DeSotos.

1958 With a larger bore, the engine size grows to 361 cubic inches. There are minor changes to the grill and trim.

For 1958, the Pacesetter and Adventurer gained a 361-cubic inch engine.

1959 The size of the V8 increases again, to 383 cubic inches.

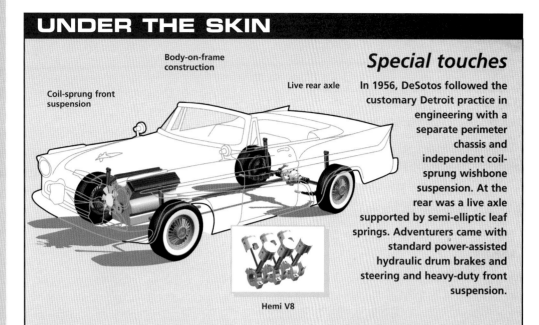

Body-on-frame construction

Coil-sprung front suspension

Live rear axle

Hemi V8

Special touches

In 1956, DeSotos followed the customary Detroit practice in engineering with a separate perimeter chassis and independent coil-sprung wishbone suspension. At the rear was a live axle supported by semi-elliptic leaf springs. Adventurers came with standard power-assisted hydraulic drum brakes and steering and heavy-duty front suspension.

Highland Park power

Regular Firedomes and Fireflites came with 330-cubic inch versions of Chrysler's superb hemi-head V8, rated at 230 and 255 bhp, respectively. In 1956, the Adventurer name first appeared and was the perfect limited-edition showcase for a larger, more powerful 341-cubic inch Hemi. With 320 bhp coupled to a PowerFlite automatic transmission, the new DeSoto flagship was a star performer with 0-60 mph acceleration in the 10- to 12-second range. This engine formed part of the so-called 'Highland Park' performance stable of that year, which included the legendary Chrysler 300B and Dodge D-500.

THE POWER PACK

Trendsetter

Although the 1956 Adventurer is an undisputed collectible, offering fine performance and style, its lesser known derivative, the Pacesetter, is worth a look. For 1956, its only year, just 100 were built compared to 996 hardtops.

Pacesetters are extremely rare these days.

DeSoto PACESETTER

DeSotos were always clean, stylish and classic. The Adventurer and Pacesetter, with their 320-bhp Hemi V8s and luxury trim, were flagships, and still look fresh and stylish today.

DeSoto Fireflite Eight

Chrysler's Hemi V8 was an engineering milestone of the 1950s. In the DeSoto Pacesetter it was known as the Fireflite Eight. It had smoother porting and manifold passages and better spark plug and valve location than rival V8s, which helped produce more power.

Coil-sprung suspension

Like rivals of the time, the Pacesetter has independent front suspension with upper and lower wishbones and telescopic shocks. Adventurers and Pacesetters have standard heavy-duty suspension, which slightly improves roadholding.

126-inch wheelbase

The Pacesetter is a full-size car riding a 126-inch wheelbase. In 1957, when Virgil Exner's 'Forward look' cars arrived, the entry-level Firesweep got a shorter 122-inch wheelbase; other DeSotos had a 126-inch wheelbase.

Single color scheme

In its debut year, the Adventurer and the Pacesetter were available only in two-tone white and gold. Special gold badging, interior paneling, grill and wheel covers completed the package. The result was one of the most striking Detroit cars in 1956.

Tailfins

1956 was a pivotal year for Chrysler products, which began sprouting true fins. Those on the Pacesetter were tasteful and mated well with the rest of the body. As the decade wore on, Desotos gained increasingly taller and more outlandish fins.

Convenience options

Pacesetters came with standard power steering, chrome exhaust tips and whitewall tires, which were optional on the Firedome and Fireflite. Air Temp air conditioning, power antenna and Solex safety glass were also available to Pacesetter buyers in 1956.

1956 DeSoto Pacesetter

ENGINE

Type: V8

Construction: Cast-iron block and heads

Valve gear: Two valves per cylinder operated by a single camshaft via pushrods and rockers

Bore and stroke: 3.78 in. x 3.80 in.

Displacement: 341 c.i.

Compression ratio: 9.5:1

Induction system: Two Carter four-barrel carburetors

Maximum power: 320 bhp at 5,200 rpm

Maximum torque: 365 lb-ft at 2,800 rpm

Top speed: 115 mph

0-60 mph: 10.2 sec.

TRANSMISSION

PowerFlite two-speed automatic

BODY/CHASSIS

Separate steel chassis with two-door convertible body

SPECIAL FEATURES

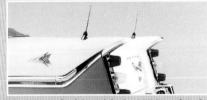

Fins were fashionable in 1956 and twin antennas were a popular option.

A dealer installed record player was just one of the DeSoto's unusual options.

RUNNING GEAR

Steering: Recirculating ball

Front suspension: Double wishbones with coil springs and telescopic shock absorbers

Rear suspension: Live axle with semi-elliptic leaf springs and telescopic shock absorbers

Brakes: Drums (front and rear)

Wheels: Pressed steel, 15-in. dia.

Tires: 7.60 x 15

DIMENSIONS

Length: 220.9 in.   **Width:** 76.5 in.

Height: 58.12 in.   **Wheelbase:** 126.0 in.

Track: 60.4 in. (front), 59.6 in. (rear)

Weight: 3,870 lbs.

Edsel CITATION

Recognized as one of the biggest flops of all time, the Edsel, in all honesty, was not really a bad car. The 1958 Citation convertible, in particular, was fast and well equipped, and had fairly restrained looks for its time.

"...cruises happily."

"Sitting on the big, padded bench seat, the Citation feels similar to most 1958 Detroit cars. Give her a little gas, however, and the picture begins to change. It has noticeably more urge off the line than many of its contemporaries, and on the highway, it cruises happily at speeds around 70 mph. Throw the Edsel into a sharp corner and it leans alarmingly, but then again, so does any other car built during the 1950s."

Citation was the top-of-the-line Edsel in 1958 and was loaded to the gills.

Milestones

1954 With Ford returning to prosperity after near collapse, chairman Ernest R. Breech lays plans to match GM with a five-make hierarchy.

Rarest of all the 1958 Edsels is the 9-seater Bermuda wagon—just 779 were built.

1958 After various delays, Ford launches its new medium-priced car—the Edsel—into a depressed market. Four series are offered (Ranger, Pacer, Corsair and Citation).

Citations and Corsairs shared their chassis with Mercurys.

1959 As a result of sluggish sales, the Edsel lineup is pared back to just Corsair, Ranger and station wagons, on a single 118-in. wheelbase. Less than 45,000 cars are built for the 1959 model year.

1960 Edsel production ends.

UNDER THE SKIN

Separate steel chassis with X-bracing

Four-wheel drum brakes

Live rear axle

Big-block V8

Mercury chassis

Citations used the 124-inch wheelbase Mercury chassis. It was a substantial affair with long side members kicking up at the rear to go over the live axle. On the convertible, a center cruciform X-bracing helped to increase overall stiffness. Suspension was straight-forward, with double wishbones and coils at the front and a live axle on semi-elliptic leaf springs at the rear. Like the vast majority of U.S. cars in the late 1950s, the Citation had four-wheel drum brakes.

Continental power

For the larger Edsels, Ford used basically the same engine as in the Lincoln Continental, but with a smaller (4.20 inch) bore, resulting in a displacement of 410 cubic inches instead of 430. Construction was typical for its time with a cast-iron block and cylinder heads, single cam, pushrods, rockers and hydraulic lifters. One different feature was having flat cylinder heads, with the wedge-shaped combustion chambers set in the block. With 345 bhp and 475 lb-ft of torque, the engine made the Edsel quite a performance-oriented car for its time.

THE POWER PACK

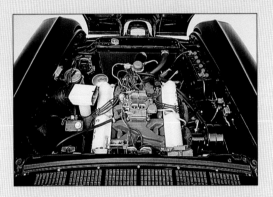

With only 930 built, the 1958 Citation was rare.

Collectible

Considered a disaster when new, the Edsel—especially convertible models—has gained strong collector interest in recent years. The big 401-powered Citation, of which only 25 are believed to exist today, is sought after, and often sells for over $30,000.

Edsel CITATION

There are many reasons the Edsel failed in the marketplace, but perhaps the greatest was poor quality control. This factor alone sent buyers scurrying almost immediately to other makes.

V8 engine

The Citation V8 was tuned for torque, as the output of 475 lb-ft at only 2,900 rpm indicates. Even the smaller 361 engine used in the Ranger and Pacer put out an impressive 303 bhp and 400 lb-ft of torque. That engine had its combustion chambers in the head, unlike the bigger 401 unit.

Convertible top

There was a choice of four colors available for the vinyl-covered convertible top on the Citation: black (seen here), white, turquoise and copper. The top folded down flush with the rear deck and was power-operated like most convertibles of the era. It had a flexible plastic rear window.

Mercury chassis

There were three different wheelbase lengths for 1958 Edsels: 116 inches for wagons; 118 inches for Pacer and Ranger coupes, sedans and convertibles; and 124 inches for Corsairs and Citations. The latter two actually rode on a Mercury chassis and were built on the same assembly line as the slightly plusher Mercurys.

Recirculating-ball steering

The recirculating-ball steering could be ordered with or without power assistance (an $85 option). If you went without, the steering ratio was altered accordingly to make the wheel easier to turn. There were 5.25 turns lock to lock, compared with 4.25 when power was added.

ower seats

Edsel Citation convertible was a luxury
ehicle and there was the $76 option of four-
ay power adjustable front seats which were
rmed by a 30/70 divided front bench seat.

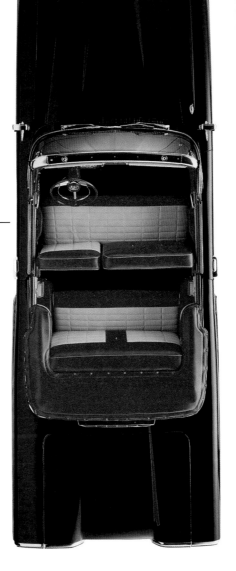

Specifications

1958 Edsel Citation

ENGINE
Type: V8
Construction: Cast-iron block and heads
Valve gear: Two valves per cylinder operated by single V-mounted camshaft
Bore and stroke: 4.20 in. x 3.70 in.
Displacement: 410 c.i.
Compression ratio: 10.5:1
Induction system: Single four-barrel carburetor
Maximum power: 345 bhp at 4,600 rpm
Maximum torque: 475 lb-ft at 2,900 rpm
Top speed: 105 mph
0-60 mph: 9.7 sec

TRANSMISSION
Three-speed automatic

BODY/CHASSIS
Separate curbed-perimeter chassis frame with center X-brace and convertible body

SPECIAL FEATURES

A station seeking radio with an electric antenna was an expensive ($143.90) option.

One interesting gimmick on 1958 Edsels was the Cyclops Eye rotating-drum speedometer.

RUNNING GEAR
Steering: Recirculating-ball
Front suspension: Double wishbones with coil springs, telescopic dampers and anti-roll bar
Rear suspension: Live axle with semi-elliptic leaf springs and telescopic shock absorbers
Brakes: Drums, 11.0-in. dia. front, 11.0-in. dia. rear
Wheels: Pressed steel disc, 14 in. dia.
Tires: 8.50 -14

DIMENSIONS
Length: 218.8 in.   **Width:** 79.8 in.
Height: 57.0 in.   **Wheelbase:** 124.0 in.
Track: 59.4 in front, 59.0 in rear
Weight: 4,311 lbs.

Ferrari 250GT CALIFORNIA

Like all Ferraris, the California Spyder was built to be raced. Powered by a smooth yet robust Colombo, 3-liter V12, this Pininfarina-designed, Scaglietti-built dream machine gives staggering acceleration and 150-mph performance. It has long since become one of the all-time great automotive icons.

"...the ultimate top-down ride."

"Look at its soft flowing lines; hear its sewing machine-smooth engine rev beyond 7,000 rpm; smell its rich leather seats. Take it all in because you are about to go for the ultimate top-down ride of your life. Don't let its half million dollar price tag scare you. This is a tough, competition-bred machine. It has a high revving Colombo V12 with plenty of power and handling to match. It shifts super smoothly, and the whole car feels solid and secure."

Its racing pedigree extends to the simple yet functional dash and Nardi steering wheel.

1957 U.S. Ferrari importer Luigi Chinetti is sure that a convertible version of the 250 GT Berlinetta will be a good seller in the U.S. A car converted by the Scaglietti coachbuilders. Its 3.0-liter V12 develops 250 bhp.

Most civilized of all the 250 family was the 1962-1964 Lusso.

1959 An alloy-bodied California with a lowered windshield wins the GT class at Sebring. Another finishes fifth overall at Le Mans.

Californias had the tuned V12 from the 250 Tour de France.

1960 Production f the long-wheelbase version ends after 40 cars have been built, and the new short-wheelbase version appears. All except three are steel-bodied.

1963 Production finally comes to an end.

UNDER THE SKIN

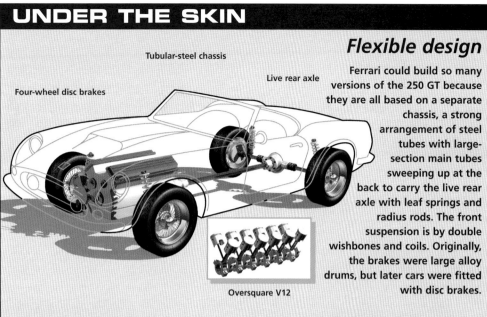

Tubular-steel chassis

Live rear axle

Four-wheel disc brakes

Oversquare V12

Flexible design

Ferrari could build so many versions of the 250 GT because they are all based on a separate chassis, a strong arrangement of steel tubes with large-section main tubes sweeping up at the back to carry the live rear axle with leaf springs and radius rods. The front suspension is by double wishbones and coils. Originally, the brakes were large alloy drums, but later cars were fitted with disc brakes.

Colombo power

One of Ferrari's most famous engines, the Colombo-designed V12 is made from alloy and has dry liners inserted in the block. Each cylinder head holds just one chain-driven, overhead camshaft that operates two angled valves in a hemispherical combustion chamber. Curved rocker arms with roller tips are used to reduce friction. Fuel is pumped in through three twin-choke Webers. Curiously, on early cars the valve springs were of the hairpin type rather than more common coils. This was as high tech in the late 1950s as pneumatic valves in Le Mans cars are today.

THE POWER PACK

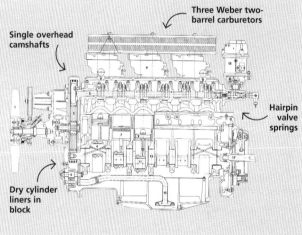

Three Weber two-barrel carburetors

Single overhead camshafts

Hairpin valve springs

Dry cylinder liners in block

Better-looking

The short-wheelbase models are a lot more desirable because their proportions are better suited to high speed driving. They have an extra 40 bhp from a revised V12, the suspension and damping are improved and the brakes are more impressive Dunlop discs.

California Spyders are among the most prized Ferraris of the entire 250 series.

Ferrari 250GT CALIFORNIA

When the first California Spyder appeared in 1957, it looked a little out of proportion, but the short-wheelbase model, which appeared in 1960, was much more attractive. Its Pininfarina lines were perfect, with the top up or down.

V12 engine

For the later short-wheelbase versions of the California, Ferrari installed an improved version of the 3.0-liter, V12 engine—the 168F, with 280 bhp. Changes included moving the spark plugs to the outside of the V, better-shaped combustion chambers and conventional coil valve springs instead of the hairpin type.

Wire wheels

Disc-type wheels were never used on Ferraris of this era—the California is fitted with very expensive Borrani wire-spoke wheels. These are strong and light, as well as extremely elegant.

Steel body

Although some of the early California long-wheelbase models were sold with an alloy hood and trunk, the later production run of short-wheelbase cars were almost all fitted with all-steel bodywork.

Hood scoop

Both the long-wheelbase and short-wheelbase versions have distinctive hood scoops, but on the shorter cars, they are recessed farther into the hood, which is one way of telling the two versions apart. This model is a short wheelbase variant.

Standard spotlights

The two small Marchal spotlights that were mounted above the bumper in the grill were standard. The headlight design varies; the majority have curved Plexiglas covers over the round head-lights, but approximately 25 cars were built without the covers.

Disc brakes

Huge, alloy-finned drums were used on the long-wheelbase models, but despite their size these are not very effective. It was only a matter of time before Ferrari switched to disc brakes.

Specifications

1960 Ferrari 250 GT California

ENGINE

Type: V12

Construction: Alloy block and heads

Valve gear: Two valves per cylinder operated by a single, chain-driven overhead camshaft and rockers

Bore and stroke: 2.87 in. x 2.31 in.

Displacement: 2,953 cc

Compression ratio: 9.2:1

Induction system: Three Weber 42 DCL twin-choke downdraft carburetors

Maximum power: 280 bhp at 7,000 rpm

Maximum torque: 203 lb-ft at 5,500 rpm

Top speed: 150 mph

0-60 mph: 7.0 sec.

TRANSMISSION

Four-speed manual

BODY/CHASSIS

Separate tubular-steel chassis with steel two-seat, two-door convertible body

SPECIAL FEATURES

Wide Borrani wire wheels with knockoff spinners are seen on the majority of Ferrari 250s. Fender vents are functional.

Unlike most supercars, the California Spyder has ample trunk space.

RUNNING GEAR

Steering: Worm-and-sector

Front suspension: Double wishbones with coil springs, telescopic shock absorbers and anti-roll bar

Rear suspension: Live axle with semi-elliptic leaf springs, radius arms and telescopic shock absorbers

Brakes: Dunlop discs (front and rear)

Wheels: Borrani knockoff wire, 6 x 15 in.

Tires: 185 x 15

DIMENSIONS

Length: 165.4 in.   **Width:** 67.7 in.

Height: 53.9 in.   **Wheelbase:** 94.5 in.

Track: 54.0 in. (front), 54.1 in. (rear)

Weight: 2,315 lbs.

Fiat **600 MULTIPLA**

It is generally accepted that the 1983 Dodge Caravan was the original minivan, but almost 30 years earlier Fiat had introduced the granddaddy of them all. In a masterstroke of packaging, the 600 Multipla could squeeze six passengers into a body that measured under 12 feet.

"...it is so unique."

"The best way to describe the Multipla is idiosyncratic. It's like no other vehicle. The driving position is similar to a VW Bus—you sit upright with the wheel horizontal in front of you. The Multipla is no hare in action, and when fully loaded progress is slow. While the roadholding is good, the handling can be tail happy if the little van is driven too fast. For all that, driving a Multipla can be great fun because it is so unique."

Its cab-forward design makes driving the Multipla feel like driving a tiny bus.

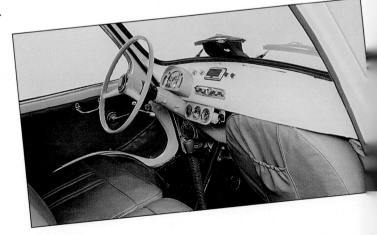

1956 A little behind schedule, the Fiat Multipla makes its debut at the Brussels Motor Show. It is based on the 600 sedan and can seat six people. A taxi and 4/5-seater version are also available.

The Multipla is based on the tiny Fiat 600 sedan.

1960 A larger 767-cc engine is installed along with improved and more efficient brakes.

Fiat is reviving the Multipla name with a new small MPV.

1966 As a victim of new safety rules concerning rear-hinged doors, the Multipla reaches a premature demise. The 600 sedan had changed to conventional doors two years earlier. About 160,000 Multiplas have been built during its 10-year production run.

Forward control

The Fiat 600 replaced the old 'Topolino' Fiat 500 in 1955, but a station wagon version was almost impossible to engineer around the rear-mounted engine. The solution was to move everything forward. The Multipla's platform is virtually identical to the 600 sedan: it has the same tiny wheelbase, but is 10 inches longer and has slightly wider front and rear treads. Naturally, there are some differences, notably to the steering gear.

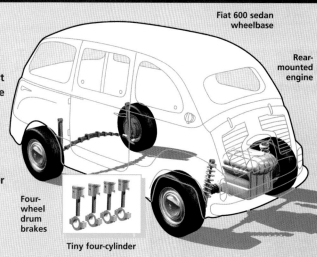

Fiat 600 sedan wheelbase

Rear-mounted engine

Four-wheel drum brakes

Tiny four-cylinder

THE POWER PACK

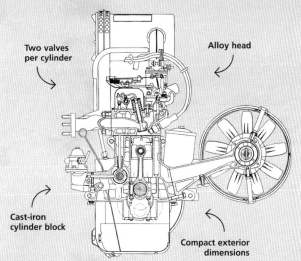

Two valves per cylinder

Alloy head

Cast-iron cylinder block

Compact exterior dimensions

Pint-pot motor

The Multipla uses the same 633-cc rear-mounted engine as the Fiat 600 sedan. This means a water-cooled four-cylinder unit that is compact and returns good gas mileage. The cast-iron cylinder block has an integral upper crankcase and an aluminum cylinder head. The whole engine/transmission unit weighs a mere 238 lbs. With a 7.0:1 compression ratio and a single Weber carburetor, it produces 22 bhp. In 1960, the engine was enlarged to 767 cc and power went up to 32 bhp.

Cult minivan

It would not be untrue to say that the Multipla has a cult following. It's a historic machine in one way—as the very first of the minivans—but it also has a design cuteness and a practicality that puts rivals in the shade. It's rare today, too, making it more valuable than the straight 600 sedan.

Historical importance and its cuteness give the Multipla a cult following.

Fiat 600 MULTIPLA

In Italy, the Multipla became an icon, a jack-of-all-trades that could act as a people carrier, small truck, taxi, camper or regular sedan. Its styling and layout may look odd but it worked well—and at a bargain price.

Rear-mounted engine

The small four-cylinder powerplant sits at the rear of the car and is easily accessible for servicing. It is unusual in that it incorporates the transmission within it as a single unit, saving weight and complexity.

'Suicide' front doors

Like many European small car designs of this era, the front doors hinge at the rear to provide better access for the driver and front passenger. The obvious safety implications of this setup led to the nickname 'suicide' doors.

600-based styling

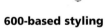

The Multipla's family lineage is obvious because the lower half of the rear body is identical to the Fiat 600 sedan. The rear engine lid is also the same. However, the body is some 8 inches taller overall and 2 inches wider.

Forward control

To maximize interior space, the driver is seated at the very front of the car. This posed problems for the steering, which had to have a right-angle joint between the driver's legs.

600 chassis

It may look like a mini truck but the Multipla is based on the platform of a Fiat 600 sedan. The wheelbase and rear engine/suspension are identical, although the steering, track and front suspension are altered.

Fiat 1100 front suspension

To cope with the extra weight over the front axle, the transverse leaf spring suspension of the 600 was substituted by the coil springs and anti-roll bar from the larger 1100 sedan.

Specifications

1957 Fiat 600 Multipla

ENGINE
Type: In-line four-cylinder
Construction: Cast-iron block and aluminum cylinder head
Valve gear: Two valves per cylinder operated by a single camshaft
Bore and stroke: 2.36 in. x 2.20 in.
Displacement: 633 cc
Compression ratio: 7.0:1
Induction system: Single Weber carburetor
Maximum power: 22 bhp at 4,600 rpm
Maximum torque: 29 lb-ft at 2,800 rpm
Top speed: 62 mph
0-60 mph: 54.0 sec.

TRANSMISSION
Four-speed manual

BODY/CHASSIS
Unitary monocoque construction with steel four-door minivan body

SPECIAL FEATURES

The compact four-cylinder engine is mounted at the rear.

This diminutive Multi-Purpose Vehicle (MPV) has three rows of seats.

RUNNING GEAR
Steering: Worm-and-roller
Front suspension: Wishbones with coil springs, telescopic shocks and anti-roll bar
Rear suspension: Semi-trailing arms with coil springs and telescopic shocks
Brakes: Drums (front and rear)
Wheels: Steel, 12-in. dia.
Tires: 5.20 x 12 in.

DIMENSIONS
Length: 140.8 in.   **Width:** 57.0 in.
Height: 62.3 in.   **Wheelbase:** 78.75 in
Track: 48.3 in. (front), 45.5 in. (rear)
Weight: 1,624 lbs.

Fiat **1500**

MG and Triumph did not have their own way with the American market in the 1950s and 1960s. Fiat produced the 90 mph-plus 1500 Spider, with handling to match any British sports car.

"...easy to drive."

"Fiat got so much right with the 1500. It looks great and is extremely easy to drive, with a light clutch, slick shift and light, accurate steering. Ride comfort is exemplary by small, 1960s sports car standards, and handling and balance are also strong suits. Throw the 1500 sharply into a tight turn and it will demonstrate progressive behavior with mild understeer. The only fault is a relative shortage of power."

Simple and elegant, the Spider boasts full instrumentation and a painted metal dash.

Milestones

1959 A combination of Pininfarina styling and Fiat engineering produces the new 1200/1500 Spider. The latter has a detuned OSCA engine, and is renamed the 1500S in 1961.

Fastest of the range is the 1500S, which packs 90 bhp.

1960 Brakes are improved with the switch from drums all round to a front discs/rear drums setup.

1962 A larger-engined version of the OSCA-powered car appears, with a 1,568-cc twin-cam powerplant and 90-bhp output.

Replacing the 1500 was the long-running 124 Spider.

1963 Late in the year Fiat introduces its new 1500 Spider, powered by a new 72-bhp crossflow engine. Sleeker sheetmetal also arrives.

1965 A five-speed transmission arrives for the Spider's final year.

UNDER THE SKIN

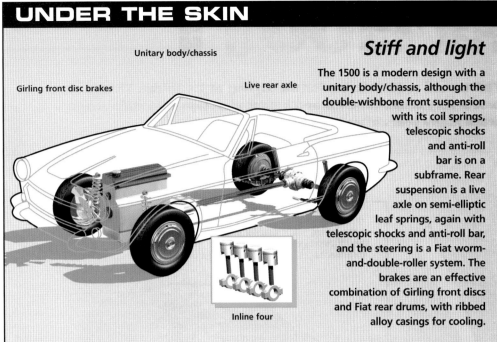

Unitary body/chassis

Girling front disc brakes

Live rear axle

Inline four

Stiff and light

The 1500 is a modern design with a unitary body/chassis, although the double-wishbone front suspension with its coil springs, telescopic shocks and anti-roll bar is on a subframe. Rear suspension is a live axle on semi-elliptic leaf springs, again with telescopic shocks and anti-roll bar, and the steering is a Fiat worm-and-double-roller system. The brakes are an effective combination of Girling front discs and Fiat rear drums, with ribbed alloy casings for cooling.

Complex yet simple

It may have lacked the twin-cam layout of its Alfa rivals, but the Fiat pushrod, overhead-valve 1500 was still a superb design. It has a cast-iron block with a crankshaft running on three large main bearings and an alloy crossflow cylinder head. This carries two valves per cylinder angled inside complex-shaped combustion chambers, in which three hemispheres are combined. The 1.34-inch intake valves are angled at almost 45 degrees, while the 1.22-inch exhausts are almost vertical, requiring two rocker shafts and different-length rockers.

THE POWER PACK

Five-speed

Probably the most desirable of this range is the 1500S, with its 72-bhp engine and front disc brakes. A later car with a five-speed transmission from 1965-on is the best bet, though as with all Fiats of this era, corrosion can be a tiresome problem.

The last of the 1500s are probably the best.

Fiat 1500

Fiat turned to Pininfarina for the styling of its Spider. The result was a very clean, timeless and balanced design that still looked fresh many years after it was introduced.

Four-cylinder engine

Because the valve gear was arranged to give a crossflow head with intake on one side and exhaust on the other, Fiat's simpler pushrod design could rival the efficiency of a twin-cam head despite theoretical disadvantages, such as the weight of the valve gear.

Radial tires

Although the Pirelli Cinturato 145-14 tires seem very small by today's standards, they suited the character of the car and were a compromise between handling and roadholding.

Convertible top

Having decided to make a serious attempt at selling its cars in the U.S. market, Fiat knew it would have to come up with a good convertible-top design as a selling point. The designers made sure it was easy to raise and lower, requiring just one arm while sitting in the driver's seat.

Wishbone front suspension

Upper and lower wishbones were used at the front. The coil spring/shock unit was mounted above the top wishbones, a more space-efficient arrangement that also helped to improve the handling.

Single carburetor

The four-cylinder engine is fed through a single twin-barrel Weber 28/36 DCD carburetor. It works well to give economical running at low rpms, with enough power for high-speed motoring.

Live rear axle

Rear-suspension design follows the live-rear axle layout of the 1500 sedan. However, instead of having four 1.97-inch wide leaves in the rear semi-elliptic springs, the Spider has six.

Specifications

Fiat 1500 Spider

ENGINE

Type: Inline four cylinder

Construction: Cast-iron block and alloy head

Valve gear: Two angled valves per cylinder operated by a single block-mounted cam with pushrods and rockers

Bore and stroke: 3.07 in. x 3.18 in.

Displacement: 1,481 cc

Compression ratio: 8.8:1

Induction system: Single Weber 28/36 DCD carburetor

Maximum power: 72 bhp at 5,200 rpm

Maximum torque: 87 lb-ft at 3,200 rpm

Top speed: 91 mph

0-60 mph: 14.7 sec.

TRANSMISSION

Four-speed manual

BODY/CHASSIS

Unitary monocoque construction with steel two-door convertible body

SPECIAL FEATURES

Like many sports cars of the early 1960s, the 1500 has a dash-mounted rear-view mirror.

1500 engines used alloy heads and a pushrod valvetrain.

RUNNING GEAR

Steering: Worm-and-roller

Front suspension: Double wishbones with coil springs, telescopic shock absorbers and anti-roll bar

Rear suspension: Live axle with semi-elliptic leaf springs and telescopic shock absorbers

Brakes: Discs, 9.38-in. dia. (front), alloy-cased drums, 10.6-in. dia. (rear)

Wheels: Pressed steel discs, 14-in. dia.

Tires: 145-14

DIMENSIONS

Length: 160.8 in.   **Width:** 59.8 in.

Height: 51.0 in.   **Wheelbase:** 92.1 in.

Track: 48.1 in. (front), 48.4 in. (rear)

Weight: 2,115 lbs.

Ford CRESTLINE SUNLINER

Although 1949-1951 Fords are often considered the classic post-war street machine, the later, more refined 1952-1954 Fords are also great for customizing. This period-looking 1952 Sunliner convertible complete with flames and a roof chop is a fine example.

"...glide by in style."

"Fuzzy dice and tuck 'n' roll upholstery were almost essential for a cruisin' custom back in the late 1950s. With a carbureted 302 small-block under the flamed hood, this classy custom can drive happily in modern traffic yet still offers plenty of old-fashioned torque. Power steering and brakes and a column-shifted automatic transmission make this Sunliner really easy to drive, giving you time to take in the stares of others as you glide by them in style."

Functional as well as tasteful, the white and black interior is almost timeless.

Milestones

1952 Squared-up styling
and a longer 115-inch wheelbase marks the new Ford line. Offered in Mainline, Customline and Crestline series, the latter includes a Sunliner convertible, Victoria hardtop and Country Squire wagon. The new cars prove to be a hit despite the ongoing Korean War; 671,733 Fords are built.

The basic design lasted through 1956—here is a Victoria glasstop.

1953 Ford celebrates
its golden anniversary and all models get special steering wheel medallions. A special 'Production Blitz' is intended to help steal sales from rival Chevrolet.

Fords were all-new in 1957 and were fitted with engines up to 312-cubic inches.

1954 A new Y-block, overhead-valve V8
replaces the venerable flathead. A new ball-joint front suspension also arrives.

UNDER THE SKIN

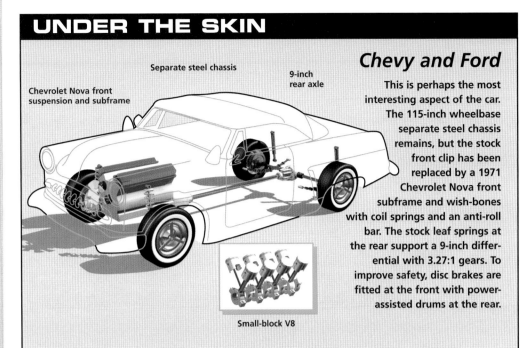

Separate steel chassis

9-inch rear axle

Chevrolet Nova front suspension and subframe

Small-block V8

Chevy and Ford

This is perhaps the most interesting aspect of the car. The 115-inch wheelbase separate steel chassis remains, but the stock front clip has been replaced by a 1971 Chevrolet Nova front subframe and wish-bones with coil springs and an anti-roll bar. The stock leaf springs at the rear support a 9-inch differential with 3.27:1 gears. To improve safety, disc brakes are fitted at the front with power-assisted drums at the rear.

The mighty 302

Originally, this Sunliner had a Y-block 239 V8 under the hood packing 110 bhp. In the interest of better reliability, it has been replaced by a 302-cubic inch engine sourced from a 1972 Ford F-100 pickup. Introduced in 1968, the 302 is one of the most versatile Ford V8s. It has a reputation for being a torquey, tractable engine that easily responds to simple modifications. Retaining the stock, cast-iron intake and two-barrel Autolite carburetor, this engine puts out 150 bhp and 240 lb-ft of torque. This may not seem much on paper, but it is more than enough to make this custom a real mover.

THE POWER PACK

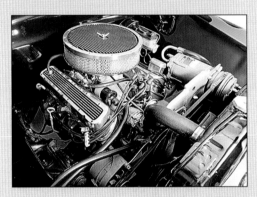

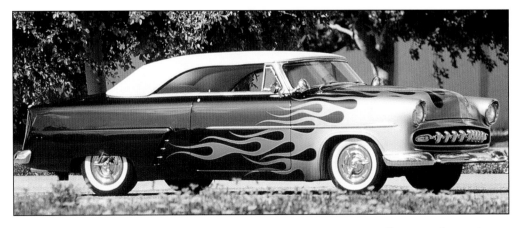

Still cool

It may be the earlier post-war Fords that are raved about by customizers, but the 1952-1954 models can be converted into rides that are just as cool. Some of the modifications on this car include a chopped carson top, flames and removed door handles.

Clever touches make this Sunliner really stand out.

123

Ford CRESTLINE SUNLINER

Flamed paint jobs are often depicted in contrasting hot/cold colors, but this Ford is ice-cool to the core, both inside and out. It puts a new face on the typical 1950s-style custom car.

Small-block V8

Replacing the less-than-satisfactory Y-block is a 1972 302-cubic inch V8. The small-block Windsor is often considered a latter-day flathead and a tuner's friend. In this application, it produces 150 bhp and 240 lb-ft of torque.

C4 transmission

As it was conceived for cruising rather than all-out performance, this ride has a C4 three-speed automatic behind the engine. Despite its age, this unit boasts smoothness that some modern transmissions are hard pressed to match.

Radial tires

The tires on this car combine the safety of modern radials with the appearance of classic, wide, white bias-plys.

Tuck 'n' roll interior

Most customized cars of the late 1950s had tuck 'n' roll upholstery. Both the front and rear seats of this Sunliner are upholstered in this way, and the addition of fuzzy dice completes the period picture. An A/C system adds a touch of comfort for those hot summer nights.

Chopped windshield

The windshield has been dropped by three inches. The top is actually a Carson removable type rather than the normal folding power item.

Toothy grill

One car that is notorious for its chromed tooth grill is the 1955 DeSoto. In keeping with its 1950s custom style, this Sunliner has a DeSoto grill mounted in place of the stock item.

Handmade taillights

The 1952 Fords marked the beginning of trademark circular taillights, but this one has custom, handformed lights.

Cool flames

The use of radiant 1990s colors like Jewel Green and black painted in the traditional 1950s-style flame pattern gives this Ford a classic, yet contemporary appearance.

Specifications

1952 Ford Crestline Sunliner

ENGINE

Type: V8

Construction: Cast-iron block and heads

Valve gear: Two valves per cylinder operated by a single camshaft with pushrods and rockers

Bore and stroke: 4.0 in. x 3.0 in.

Displacement: 302 c.i.

Compression ratio: 8.5:1

Induction system: Autolite two-barrel carburetor

Maximum power: 150 bhp at 4,200 rpm

Maximum torque: 240 lb-ft at 3,100 rpm

Top speed: 112 mph

0-60 mph: 10.5 sec.

TRANSMISSION

C4 three-speed automatic

BODY/CHASSIS

Separate steel chassis with two-door convertible body

SPECIAL FEATURES

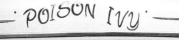

With its sharp green and black paint job, 'Poison Ivy' is an appropriate name.

Twin chrome spotlights were popular stock and custom accessories in the 1950s.

RUNNING GEAR

Steering: Recirculating ball

Front suspension: Unequal-length wishbones with coil springs, telescopic shock absorbers and anti-roll bar

Rear suspension: Live axle with leaf springs and telescopic shock absorbers

Brakes: Discs (front), drums (rear)

Wheels: Pressed steel, 14-in. dia.

Tires: Radial, 205/70 R14

DIMENSIONS

Length: 197.8 in. **Width:** 73.2 in.

Height: 56.8 in. **Wheelbase:** 115.0 in.

Track: 61.3 in. (front), 59.5 in. (rear)

Weight: 3,415 lbs.

Ford FAIRLANE

Ford's 1957 line-up was widely regarded as one of Detroit's most stylish. The Fairlane 500 sat at the top of the regular Ford tree, helping the company to achieve one of its best sales years.

"...effortless pulling power."

"This car was produced before the great horsepower race in which Detroit later indulged. Still, for a 1957 car, this Fairlane goes pretty well thanks to its Thunderbird engine. The V8 is tuned for low-down torque rather than absolute power, which means lazy cruising and effortless pulling power. But when you want to move a little faster, the big 312-cubic inch V8 pulls its weight. It's no slowcoach, and can easily deal with modern traffic conditions."

Getting behind the wheel of this Fairlane is like stepping back in time.

Milestones

957 Ford presents

s new line up including the
18-inch wheelbase Fairlane and
e range-topping Fairlane 500.
mid-1957 a new Skyliner
ersion is added with a
etractable hardtop roof.

*ne of the most desirable
ody styles is the Fairlane
onvertible.*

958 A facelift

cludes the addition of a
hunderbird-style bumper and
ill, quad headlights and tail
hts and a choice of two new
-series V8 engines (332-cubic
ch and 352-cubic inch). There
also the option of the new
uise-O-Matic transmission.

*e 1956 Fairlane had more
unded rear styling but a similar
ont end.*

959 A major reskin

ives a more simple style, with
sculpted V-shape back panel
d low-level grill with star-like
naments. A choice of new
laxie models is also available.

UNDER THE SKIN

Dependable

Excitement was mostly cosmetic on 1950s cars. Under the skin, simplicity was the order of the day. It comes as no surprise to find a separate chassis, a leaf-spring suspension at the rear, an independent coil-spring front end and four-wheel drum brakes.

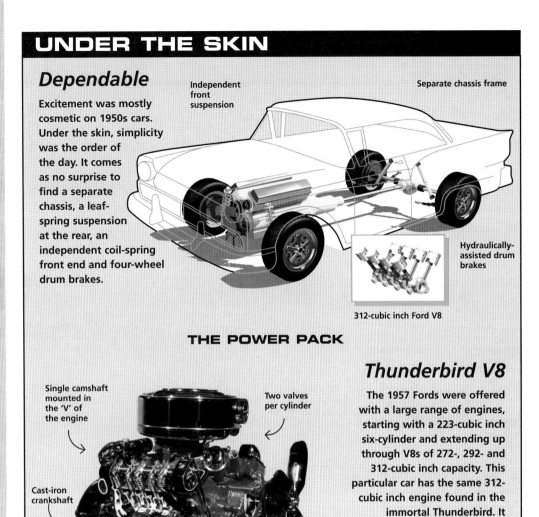

Independent front suspension

Separate chassis frame

Hydraulically-assisted drum brakes

312-cubic inch Ford V8

THE POWER PACK

Single camshaft mounted in the 'V' of the engine

Two valves per cylinder

Cast-iron crankshaft

Heavy iron block and heads

Thunderbird V8

The 1957 Fords were offered with a large range of engines, starting with a 223-cubic inch six-cylinder and extending up through V8s of 272-, 292- and 312-cubic inch capacity. This particular car has the same 312-cubic inch engine found in the immortal Thunderbird. It develops a healthy 245 bhp in stock form, but the mildly uprated exhaust system liberates a further 10 bhp—enough to power the car to 120 mph. This performance is not far from the sporty Thunderbird.

Range topper

The 1957 Ford range began with the entry-level, sub-$2,000 Custom and spanned up to the Fairlane 500 Club Victoria and Skyliner with a retractable hardtop at the top end. Ford offered the cars with a 144 bhp six cylinder to a 240 bhp supercharged V8.

The Fairlane hardtop coupe is one of the best-looking of the 1957 range.

Ford FAIRLANE

The 1957 Fairlane boasts tasteful styling for the period—a factor in its favor nowadays. Fords from this era are rarer than their popularity at the time might suggest.

Modern paint

The body of this restored and customized car has been resprayed in yellow and white acrylic paint.

Thunderbird engine

The base engine for the 1957 Fairlane was a modest six-cylinder. This car has received a useful increase in power by fitting a 255-bhp Thunderbird V8.

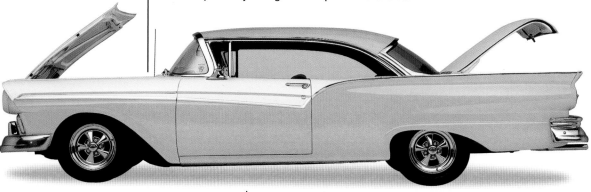

Automatic transmission

The Ford-O-Matic three-speed automatic transmission was optional on 1957 models and provides easy gear shifts.

Custom trim

The upholstery is black and charcoal velour, with yellow piping on the seats and rear package tray. Other additions include Auto Meter gauges, air-conditioning, and a powerful stereo.

Safety interior

Ford began its safety drive in 1956. This car is fitted with a dished steering wheel, padded dash, break-away rear-view mirror, and crash-proof door locks.

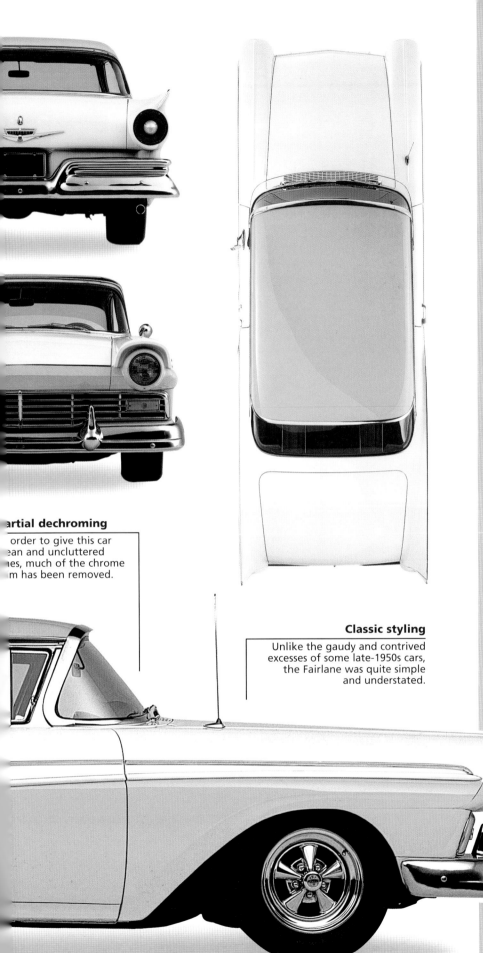

Specifications

1957 Ford Fairlane 500

ENGINE
Type: V8

Construction: Cast-iron cylinder block and cylinder heads

Valve gear: Two valves per cylinder operated by a single camshaft

Bore and stroke: 3.90 in. x 3.44 in.

Displacement: 312 c.i.

Compression ratio: 9.7:1

Induction system: Single Holley carburetor

Maximum power: 255 bhp at 4,600 rpm

Maximum torque: 354 lb-ft at 2,800 rpm

Top speed: 120 mph

0-60 mph: 10.2 sec.

TRANSMISSION
Ford-O-Matic three-speed automatic

BODY/CHASSIS
Separate chassis with steel two-door coupe bodywork

SPECIAL FEATURES

In 1957, the Fairlane had single rear lights; twin lights were fitted in 1958.

Chrome valve covers and air cleaner, and headers liven up the T-bird V8.

RUNNING GEAR
Steering: Recirculating ball

Front suspension: Independent with coil springs and telescopic shocks

Rear suspension: Rigid axle with leaf springs and telescopic shocks

Brakes: Four-wheel drums

Wheels: Cragar, 15-in. dia.

Tires: 235/60 x 15 in.

DIMENSIONS
Length: 207.5 in. **Width:** 77 in.

Height: 56.5 in. **Wheelbase:** 118 in.

Track: 59 in. (front), 56.4 in. (rear)

Weight: 3,400 lbs.

...artial dechroming
...order to give this car
...ean and uncluttered
...es, much of the chrome
...m has been removed.

Classic styling
Unlike the gaudy and contrived excesses of some late-1950s cars, the Fairlane was quite simple and understated.

Ford THUNDERBIRD

Although there's been a Thunderbird in the Ford lineup since 1955, the sporty two-seater convertible version only lasted until 1957. In those first three years, it had all the style—and almost the performance—to match the Chevrolet Corvette.

"...the real T-Bird."

"They're very rare now, so just seeing one of the original two-seat Thunderbirds is a treat. For true car enthusiasts, this is the only real T-Bird. Driving this 1956 model, one of the last off the line, instantly puts a smile on your face. Yes, it's a little loose and a little soft, but none of its faults matter: its looks and style make up for everything. With the V8 working hard, the T-Bird has the performance to match its style, easily exceeding 100 mph."

The Thunderbird's interior is typical of a 1950s American car— loud, brash and very stylized, a little like a jukebox of the period.

Milestones

1954 The T-Bird first appears at the Detroit Auto Show in February and goes on sale in October as a 1955 model. It's powered by a 292-cubic inch V8 with three-speed manual or three-speed automatic transmission.

After 1958 the Thunderbird became a four-seater.

1955 Changes for the 1956 model year are minor. Cooling flaps are added to the front fenders. To make more room in the trunk, the spare wheel is mounted vertically outside behind the body, making the whole car longer. A larger, 312-cubic inch V8 is also available with 215 or 225 bhp. Round 'porthole' windows are installed in the sides of the hardtop.

1956 Much more obvious changes are made for the 1957 model year with fins added at the rear. The car is also lengthened enough to allow the spare wheel back inside the trunk. The front grill and bumpers are also changed and smaller wheels added. Power increases to 270 bhp, but with a supercharger, the engine makes much more.

1957 The last 1957 model T-Birds are produced on December 13, replaced by a larger, four-seater car for 1958.

UNDER THE SKIN

Two-seater

The T-Bird has very simple construction, with a separate chassis and a live rear axle with leaf springs. Front suspension is independent wishbone and coil spring, with most parts coming from existing Ford sedans. The T-Bird had advanced features such as power brakes and steering.

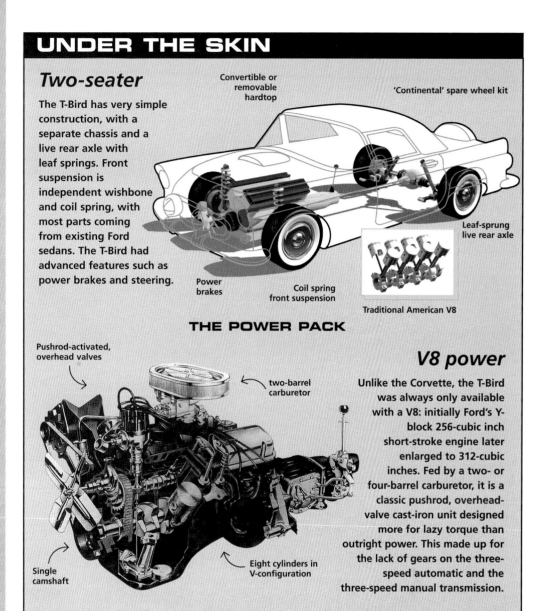

Convertible or removable hardtop

'Continental' spare wheel kit

Leaf-sprung live rear axle

Power brakes

Coil spring front suspension

Traditional American V8

THE POWER PACK

Pushrod-activated, overhead valves

two-barrel carburetor

Single camshaft

Eight cylinders in V-configuration

V8 power

Unlike the Corvette, the T-Bird was always only available with a V8: initially Ford's Y-block 256-cubic inch short-stroke engine later enlarged to 312-cubic inches. Fed by a two- or four-barrel carburetor, it is a classic pushrod, overhead-valve cast-iron unit designed more for lazy torque than outright power. This made up for the lack of gears on the three-speed automatic and the three-speed manual transmission.

Blown bird

The F-Bird, the Supercharged T-Bird, is the rarest, and now the most desirable, of all the early T-Birds. These are the supercharged 1957 models, with a Paxton-McCulloch supercharger added to a larger version (312 cubic inches) of the original V8 to give 300 bhp, or 340 bhp in race trim. Only 211 were sold.

Rare F-bird used 340-bhp, supercharged engine.

Ford THUNDERBIRD

The T-Bird was one of the smallest and most striking cars Ford built in the U.S. in many years. Ford called it a 'personal luxury' car rather than a sports car. It was never intended to be a serious rival to Jaguars or Ferraris.

Cooling flaps

The 1955 models had poor ventilation, so Ford added a flap in the front fenders which could be opened to let cold air into the footwells.

Wrap-around windshield

Like the Chevy Corvette, which came out two years before it, the T-Bird has a wrap-around-type front windshield, a design which avoided the blind spot caused by conventional front windshield pillars.

Choice of transmissions

There was a choice of three different transmissions: a three-speed Fordomatic automatic or the three-speed manual; and perhaps the best option—a manual transmission with high overdrive ratios.

V8 engine

From the beginning, the Thunderbird had a V8 engine. The prototype had only a 256-cubic inch engine with 160 bhp, but that was enlarged for production and became steadily more powerful year by year. By 1957, the most powerful engine—apart from the rare supercharged V8—was the 285-bhp, 312-cubic inch V8.

14/15-inch wheels

For its first two years, the Thunderbird ran on tall, 15-inch wheels. For the 1957 model year, they changed to 14-inch wheels which made the cars look sleeker.

Stretched rear

The original 1955 Thunderbird is very short, so the spare wheel had to be carried above the bumper. For 1957, Ford redesigned the back of the car to make the trunk longer so the spare wheel could be carried inside.

Open hardtop or convertible

As standard, the Thunderbird came with a bolt-on fiberglass hardtop. The car could also be ordered with a folding rayon convertible top instead of the hardtop, or in addition to it, for an extra $290.

Specifications
1957 Ford Thunderbird

ENGINE
Type: V8
Construction: Cast-iron block and heads
Valve gear: Two valves per cylinder operated via pushrods and rockers from a single block-mounted camshaft
Bore and stroke: 3.74 in. x 3.31 in.
Displacement: 292 c.i.
Compression ratio: 8.1:1
Induction system: two- or four-barrel carburetor
Maximum power: 212 bhp at 4,400 rpm
Maximum torque: 297 lb-ft at 2,700 rpm
Top speed: 122 mph
0-60 mph: 9.5 sec.

TRANSMISSION
Three-speed manual with optional overdrive or three-speed Fordomatic automatic

BODY/CHASSIS
Separate cruciform steel chassis with steel two-door body: choice of removable hardtop or convertible roof

SPECIAL FEATURES

Exhausts exiting through holes in the bumper are a typical 1950s American styling feature.

From 1956, the hardtop was available with 'porthole' windows to improve rear three-quarter vision.

RUNNING GEAR
Steering: Power-assisted recirculating ball
Front suspension: Double wishbones, coil springs and telescopic shocks
Rear suspension: Live axle with semi-elliptic leaf springs and telescopic shocks
Brakes: Drums front and rear with optional power assistance
Wheels: Steel 14 in. dia.
Tires: Crossply, 7.5 in. x 14 in.

DIMENSIONS
Length: 181.4 in.   **Width:** 70.3 in.
Height: 51.6 in.   **Wheelbase:** 102 in.
Track: 56 in. (front and rear)
Weight: 3,050 lbs.

Rear fenders
Setting the 1957 T-Bird apart from the 1955 and 1956 cars was the introduction of tail fins. This was the start of the fin era in the U.S., but those on the Thunderbirds are a little more restrained than those on some other models of the period.

Healey SILVERSTONE

Named after the most famous racing circuit in Britain, the Silverstone was a model designed to appeal to club and sprint racers, as well as sports car drivers. Extremely charismatic, today the Silverstone is the most highly sought-after Healey of all.

"...a well-mannered tourer."

"Swing open the tiny doors and step into the world of real sports cars. The view ahead over the curved dash is superb—made more remarkable by the drop-away windshield. There is plenty of torque from the engine, which pulls away effortlessly. It is not so happy at high revs, however, and in corners the Silverstone tends to understeer. Overall the feel is of a well-mannered tourer stripped down to deliver sports car performance."

Although it has a full set of gauges, the Healey is spartan in the extreme.

Milestones

1949 Racer Donald Healey

had proved his engineering skill with the Elliot, the fastest sedan in the world in 1946. Using the same chassis with a lightweight body, he launched the Silverstone.

The Riley RM donated its 2.4-liter in-line four for use in the Silverstone.

1950 The Series E model

supersedes the Series D. It has a better interior and expanded bodywork. The first Silverstones had no front bumper, but from this year British-market cars are so equipped. A Nash-powered Silverstone competes at Le Mans.

Healey's post-war sedans, like this Tickford, could top 100 mph.

1951 A slightly more powerful

106-bhp engine is fitted to the last of the Silverstones, which are withdrawn in May in favor of the new Nash-Healey.

UNDER THE SKIN

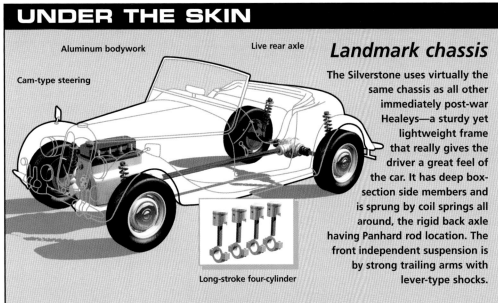

Aluminum bodywork

Cam-type steering

Live rear axle

Long-stroke four-cylinder

Landmark chassis

The Silverstone uses virtually the same chassis as all other immediately post-war Healeys—a sturdy yet lightweight frame that really gives the driver a great feel of the car. It has deep box-section side members and is sprung by coil springs all around, the rigid back axle having Panhard rod location. The front independent suspension is by strong trailing arms with lever-type shocks.

THE POWER PACK

Tuned Riley 'four'

One of the best engines in production following World War II was Riley's 2.4-liter overhead-valve four-cylinder unit. It was a very large capacity engine for a 'four' at 2,443 cc, thanks to a huge stroke of 120 mm, the longest stroke of any engine then in production. It features hemispherical combustion chambers and twin camshafts—one for inlet and one for exhaust—driving inclined overhead valves through short pushrods. Healey modified it slightly to produce 104 bhp (and later 106 bhp).

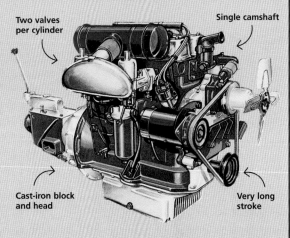

Two valves per cylinder

Single camshaft

Cast-iron block and head

Very long stroke

Prized Series E

Only 105 Silverstones were built in total and every one is highly prized. The production total is split roughly 50/50 into the Series D and Series E types, the latter having a slightly upgraded interior and a wider body. Silverstones were popular club racers due, in part, to their simple and rugged construction.

Many owners who went racing fitted aero windshields.

Healey **SILVERSTONE**

Many Silverstones were sold in the U.S. market where the car's speed and ability were well recognized. It was a car for drivers who had the right stuff—a stiff upper lip and racing blood in their veins.

Sliding windshield

One unusual feature is the retractable windshield. Unlike most vintage windshield arrangements, the Silverstone's windshield and frame disappear into the cowl to allow completely open motoring.

Cycle-type fenders

Separate cycle fenders with tiny parking lights mounted on them give the Silverstone an air of back-to-basics sports car true grit. They feature a tapering design that looks quite elegant.

Unique Healey steering

While most post-war specialist sports cars relied on proprietary components, the Healey is unusual in that it has its own unique steering gear. This is a Donald Healey design incorporating a swivelling plate and link rods, and is widely regarded as one of the most effective systems of its day.

Competition dimensions

Despite being based on the same 102-inch wheelbase as other 'touring' Healeys, the Silverstone was carefully scaled so that it fitted within the FIA's tight definition of body dimensions for the sports car category.

Light-alloy body

The streamlined bodywork was crafted by hand in lightweight aluminum. Unlike other Healey models, which used an ash frame, the Silverstone's panel work is stressed over a channel framework with tubular bracing.

Specifications

1950 Healey Silverstone

ENGINE

Type: In-line four-cylinder

Construction: Cast-iron block and head

Valve gear: Two valves per cylinder operated by twin camshafts via pushrods and rockers

Bore and stroke: 3.17 in. x 4.72 in.

Displacement: 2,443 cc

Compression ratio: 6.9:1

Induction system: Two SU carburetors

Maximum power: 104 bhp at 4,500 rpm

Maximum torque: 132 lb-ft at 3,000 rpm

Top speed: 110 mph

0-60 mph: 11.0 sec.

TRANSMISSION

Four-speed manual

BODY/CHASSIS

Separate chassis with aluminum two-door open body

SPECIAL FEATURES

Chrome-rimmed 'portholes' allow hot air to escape from the engine bay.

The rear-mounted spare tire protrudes slightly and acts as a sort of bumper.

RUNNING GEAR

Steering: Cam-type

Front suspension: Trailing link with coil springs, shock absorbers and anti-roll bar

Rear suspension: Live axle with torque tube, radius arms, coil springs and shock absorbers

Brakes: Drums (front and rear)

Wheels: Perforated steel, 15-in. dia

Tires: 5.50 x 15 (front), 5.75 x 15 (rear)

DIMENSIONS

Length: 168.0 in.   **Width:** 63.0 in.

Height: 43.0 in.   **Wheelbase:** 102.0 in.

Track: 54.0 in. (front), 53.0 in. (rear)

Weight: 2,072 lbs.

Jaguar **MK V**

Intended as a stopgap while Jaguar readied its modern XK twin-cam powered MKVII for production, the MKV used the old Standard 3.5-liter overhead-valve engine, yet it handled and performed impressively.

"...feels small and nimble."

"Don't be fooled by the looks, as the MKV is quite a performer. All-new front double-wishbone suspension helped give it balanced handling quite out of keeping with its appearance. The Standard pushrod six is smooth and refined, with enough bottom-end torque to make the car accelerate effortlessly, although the transmission is a little crude. Big and luxurious, it makes driver and passenger feel at ease, yet it feels small and nimble."

A huge steering wheel and a solid wood dash ooze quality.

Milestones

1949 With the XK120 being the star of the 1948 London Motor Show, Jaguar realizes it has to produce the car in far greater numbers than it originally thought—delaying the launch of the Jaguar MKVII sedan. The solution is to introduce an interim model, with the chassis design of the MKVII but using the established Standard six-cylinder engine.

Bentley's MKVI meant Jaguar called its next car the MKVII.

1950 Late in the year, the MKVII appears with the XK engine, as well as an all-new body. Surprisingly, the seemingly obsolete MKV stays in production.

The delayed MKVII used the same chassis as the MKV.

1951 With the MKVII extremely popular from the very beginning, there's no need for the MKV and it goes out of production, having been a successful interim model.

UNDER THE SKIN

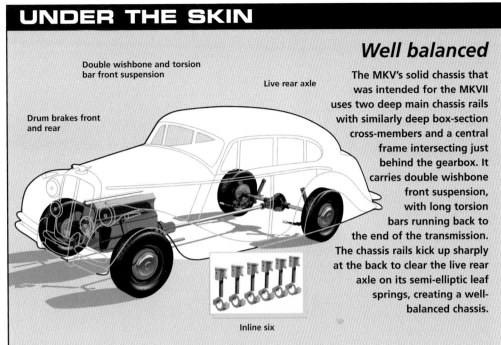

Double wishbone and torsion bar front suspension

Live rear axle

Drum brakes front and rear

Inline six

Well balanced

The MKV's solid chassis that was intended for the MKVII uses two deep main chassis rails with similarly deep box-section cross-members and a central frame intersecting just behind the gearbox. It carries double wishbone front suspension, with long torsion bars running back to the end of the transmission. The chassis rails kick up sharply at the back to clear the live rear axle on its semi-elliptic leaf springs, creating a well-balanced chassis.

THE POWER PACK

Advanced head design

Before Jaguar developed its famous twin-cam six, it brought engines in from the Standard company, so the MKV used a 3.5-liter straight six. It was a conventional design, with a cast-iron block and head, plus a single block-mounted camshaft operating two valves per cylinder with pushrods and rockers. The head was an advanced crossflow design, with twin carburetors on one side of the head and a two-branch exhaust manifold on the other. Being a long-stroke design, it produced lots of low-down torque, with 184 lb-ft available at only 2,000 rpm. Maximum power is just 125 bhp.

Drophead

The MKV was produced with two engine sizes (2.6 and 3.5 liters) and two body styles, a conventional four-door sedan and a drophead coupe. It's no surprise that it's the 3.5-liter drophead that is the most desirable, even though it's slightly slower than the sedan.

The MKV is viewed by enthusiasts as being a transitional car for Jaguar.

Jaguar MK V

One of Jaguar's strongest assets was the styling, which was overseen by William Lyons. Even on the MKV, which was intended purely as a stopgap, it was clearly visible.

Standard engine

Although Jaguar brought in its engines, it decided on the specification. The six-cylinder pushrod engine had an advanced free-flowing cylinder head design and could easily have produced more power.

Tool kit in trunklid

The MKV had a huge trunklid, which was hinged at the bottom and folded down almost flat. Inset into it under a cover is a tool kit running the full width and depth of the trunk.

Leather interior

As the MKV was a genuine luxury car, it was trimmed accordingly, with leather seats as well as the door side panels (complete with zipped side pockets). Complementing the leather is traditional walnut trim for the dash and the door cappings.

Torsion-bar front suspension

The front suspension system used in the MKV was so good it was used by Jaguar for years. The lower wishbone works a longitudinally mounted torsion bar, while the telescopic shock absorber is placed between the wishbones, angled inward at the top.

Turn signals

In 1949, the side opening and illuminated turn signals were still considered adequate. Modern turn signals at front and rear were added later.

Side opening hood

The MKV's bodywork was essentially pre-war in design, and it showed in features like the side opening hood (which would be replaced by a front-opening one on the MKVII) as well as the flat windshield.

Specifications

1950 Jaguar MkV

ENGINE

Type: Inline six cylinder

Construction: Cast-iron block and head

Valve gear: Two valves per cylinder operated by single block-mounted camshaft with pushrods and rockers

Bore and stroke: 3.28 in. x 4.40 in.

Displacement: 3,485 cc

Compression ratio: 6.8:1

Induction system: Two sidedraft carburetors

Maximum power: 125 bhp at 4,500 rpm

Maximum torque: 184 lb-ft at 2,300 rpm

Top speed: 92 mph

0-60 mph: 14.9 sec.

TRANSMISSION

Four-speed manual

BODY/CHASSIS

Separate steel chassis with steel four-door sedan body

SPECIAL FEATURES

The well-equipped tool kit is an integral part of the car and came standard.

Illuminated turn signals were standard on early postwar British cars.

RUNNING GEAR

Steering: Recirculating-ball

Front suspension: Double wishbones with longitudinal torsion bars, telescopic shock absorbers and anti-roll bar

Rear suspension: Live axle with semi-elliptic leaf springs and lever-arm hydraulic shock absorbers

Brakes: Drums, 12-in. dia.

Wheels: Pressed-steel discs, 16-in. dia.

Tires: 6.70 x 16

DIMENSIONS

Length: 187.0 in.   **Width:** 69.0 in.

Height: 62.5 in.   **Wheelbase:** 120.0 in.

Track: 56.0 in. (front and rear)

Weight: 3,696 lbs.

Jaguar **XK120**

In a world where other manufacturers were still recycling old pre-war designs Jaguar came up with a complete contrast; the XK120 was sleek, fast, modern, and also one of the cheapest sports cars on the market.

"...wonderful, smooth straight-six."

"It doesn't take long to see why the XK120 would have been astonishing in 1948. There's masses of power and torque from that wonderful, smooth straight-six and the performance is incredible. It's easy to drive too; that big steering wheel set close to your chest is necessary at slow speeds but the steering lightens up as speed rises. The crossply tires don't generate very much grip but are more progressive in their behavior than modern radials."

Although more sporty than Fixed Head or Drophead Coupes, the Roadster's interior was still luxurious by any standard.

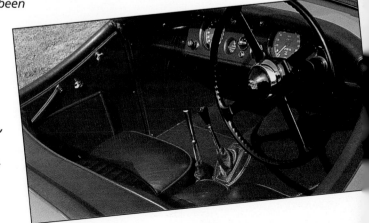

UNDER THE SKIN

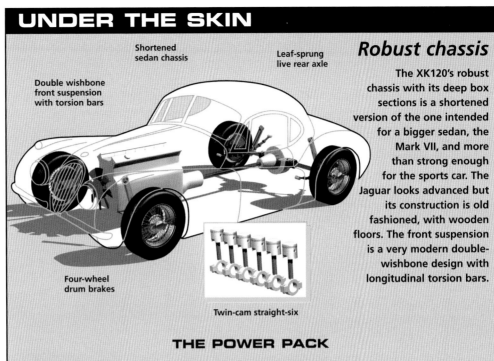

Shortened sedan chassis

Double wishbone front suspension with torsion bars

Leaf-sprung live rear axle

Four-wheel drum brakes

Twin-cam straight-six

Robust chassis

The XK120's robust chassis with its deep box sections is a shortened version of the one intended for a bigger sedan, the Mark VII, and more than strong enough for the sports car. The Jaguar looks advanced but its construction is old fashioned, with wooden floors. The front suspension is a very modern double-wishbone design with longitudinal torsion bars.

THE POWER PACK

Classic XK

Jaguar's most famous engine was designed during the war and lasted until 1985. It is a classic straight-six twin-cam with an alloy head, but its cast-iron block made it rather heavy, although very strong. First engines produced 160 bhp from 3.4 liters but that was soon improved to 180 bhp in M models and then to 210 bhp in the Le Mans-winning C-type Jaguars developed from the XK120. There were plans to introduce a four-cylinder model with a cut-down version of the XK engine.

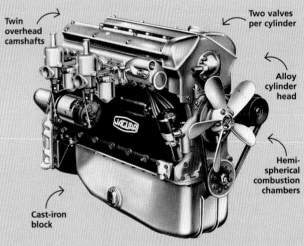

Twin overhead camshafts

Two valves per cylinder

Alloy cylinder head

Hemispherical combustion chambers

Cast-iron block

Early alloy

Rarest of all the XK120s are the first 240 cars, all Roadsters, which have bodies hand-formed in aluminum. When demand for the XK120 took off, the cars were made with steel bodywork and are about 110 lbs. heavier than the earlier cars.

Early, alloy-bodied XK120s are lightweight and very rare.

Jaguar **XK120**

Where the pre-war Jaguar SS100 had been the absolutely typical 1930s sports car, the XK120 looked to the future. It was in a class of its own because none of its rivals could come close in looks or performance.

Wishbone front suspension

Engine apart, the XK120's most advanced feature is its double-wishbone front suspension with torsion bars and telescopic shock absorbers instead of lever arm devices.

Twin-cam engine

The XK twin-cam six, which started life in the XK120, went on to power the C- and D-type racers, the XK140 and XK150, and the Jaguar sedans up to and beyond the XJ6.

Fitted rear luggage

To make the best possible use of the Jaguar's trunk space, fitted luggage was an option.

Alloy bodywork

Very early XK120s have all aluminum-alloy bodywork, joined to the chassis in 12 places. The alloy panels were soon replaced by steel.

Connolly leather seats

On the cars fitted with leather trim, high-quality Connolly leather is used for the seats and the trim around the doors.

Live rear axle

The XK120 uses a traditional live axle located and sprung on semi-elliptic leaf springs with lever arm shocks.

Rear wheel skirts

The removable wheel skirts are for style and aerodynamic efficiency, but they can only be fitted with steel disc wheels because the spinners on the wire wheels project too far.

No rear bumper

To begin with, only these small rear over-riders were fitted, but later XK models grew larger and larger bumpers.

Removable windshield

On the roadster, the windshield can be completely removed if you really want wind-in-the-hair motoring. The windshield pillars unbolt from the bodywork. On the coupe and convertible model, the windshield pillars are part of the bodywork.

Specifications
1951 Jaguar XK120 M

ENGINE
Type: In-line six
Construction: Cast-iron block, aluminum alloy cylinder head
Valve gear: Two valves per cylinder operated by twin overhead camshafts
Bore and stroke: 3.26 in. x 4.17 in.
Displacement: 3,442 cc
Compression ratio: 8.0:1
Induction system: Two SU H6 carburetors
Maximum power: 180 bhp at 5,300 rpm
Maximum torque: 203 lb-ft at 4,000 rpm
Top speed: 121 mph
0-60 mph: 11.3 sec.

TRANSMISSION
Four-speed manual

BODY/CHASSIS
Separate box section chassis with steel open-roadster body

SPECIAL FEATURES

XK120's curvaceous and wind-cheating lines were a revelation in 1948.

The rear wheels are covered by skirts which improve the aerodynamics.

RUNNING GEAR
Steering: Recirculating ball
Front suspension: Double wishbones with longitudinal torsion bars and telescopic shocks
Rear suspension: Live axle with semi-elliptic leaf springs and lever arm shocks
Brakes: Drums (front and rear)
Wheels: Steel disc or wire spoke, 16-in. dia.
Tires: Crossply 6 in. x 16 in.

DIMENSIONS
Length: 174 in.   **Width:** 62 in.
Height: 53 in.   **Wheelbase:** 102 in.
Track: 51 in. (front), 50 in. (rear)
Weight: 3,039 lbs.

Jaguar **C TYPE**

Conceived specifically to win the 24 Hours of Le Mans race, the C-type was based on the sensational XK120 sports car. An aerodynamic body combined with a lightweight steel frame made it an outstanding success in the 1950s.

"...superbly responsive."

"Perhaps the most impressive aspect about driving the C-type is that it is so easy. The XK engine pulls without question and is superbly responsive. All the controls are laid out perfectly: the pedals are just right for heel-and-toeing, the shifter is inches from the steering wheel, the dials are large and easy to read, and handling is finely balanced. Not too many cars from the 1950s have power, glory and prestige. But the Jaguar C-type has it all."

The bare interior greatly contributes to the race car's light weight.

Milestones

1950 Development work begins on Jaguar's Le Mans competitor, dubbed the XK120C (C stands for competition).

1951 Three C-types are entered in the Le Mans 24 Hours race and take the top three places. The Whitehead/Walker example triumphs in its first-ever race.

The highly successful D-types followed on from the C-types.

1952 Jaguar's restyled Le Mans fails as a result of overheating problems.

The very successful C-type incorporates many engineering features from the 1948 XK120.

1953 Mechanical changes, including Weber carburetors and disc brakes, ensures another Le Mans victory for Jaguar.

UNDER THE SKIN

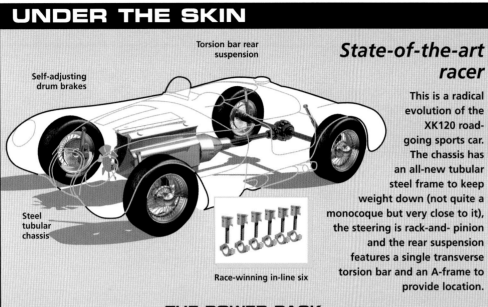

Torsion bar rear suspension

Self-adjusting drum brakes

Steel tubular chassis

Race-winning in-line six

State-of-the-art racer

This is a radical evolution of the XK120 road-going sports car. The chassis has an all-new tubular steel frame to keep weight down (not quite a monocoque but very close to it), the steering is rack-and-pinion and the rear suspension features a single transverse torsion bar and an A-frame to provide location.

THE POWER PACK

Celebrated XK engine

William Lyons' brilliant XK engine first appeared in 1948. It has twin overhead camshafts, an aluminum head, with hemispherical combustion chambers and inclined valves. The engine is built on a lightweight block, with a seven-bearing counterbalanced crank. In the racing C-type the engine features an improved cylinder head with larger exhaust valves and larger ports, plus longer valve springs and a more aggressive camshaft. The compression ratio was raised to 9.0:1, and the power output of 204 bhp was enough to ensure glory on the track.

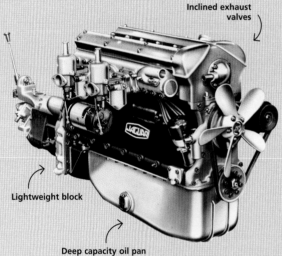

Inclined exhaust valves

Lightweight block

Deep capacity oil pan

Exclusive

Each example of the ultra-rare C-type is a coveted piece of automotive history and a story in its own right. The values of individual cars vary according to their racing pedigree, with genuine works factory-built race cars being more valuable than customer cars.

The C-type was the first of Jaguar's dominant Le Mans racers in the 1950s.

Jaguar C TYPE

The anatomy of Jaguar's superlative race winner is simple, but brilliant: lightweight construction, an unparalleled engine and a beautiful aerodynamic body.

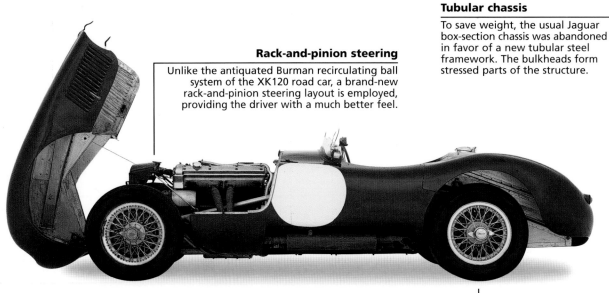

Tubular chassis

To save weight, the usual Jaguar box-section chassis was abandoned in favor of a new tubular steel framework. The bulkheads form stressed parts of the structure.

Rack-and-pinion steering

Unlike the antiquated Burman recirculating ball system of the XK120 road car, a brand-new rack-and-pinion steering layout is employed, providing the driver with a much better feel.

Racing wheels and tires

Wire wheels were a must for racing cars from the early 1950s, as they help with brake cooling. The C-type has knock-off wheels for quick removal.

Unique rear suspension

Jaguar replaced the leaf spring system of the XK120 rear end with a live rear axle with single transverse torsion bar.

Aerodynamic bodywork

Built from aluminum for lightness, the body has a smooth, low front end designed to minimize drag.

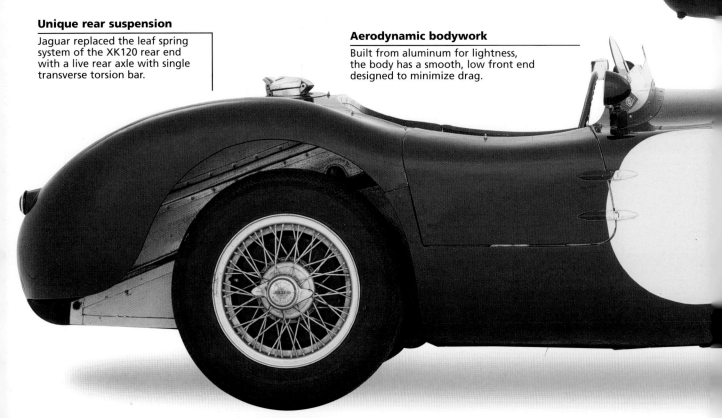

Specifications
1953 Jaguar C-type

ENGINE

Type: In-line six-cylinder

Construction: Cast-iron cylinder block and aluminum head

Valve gear: Two valves per cylinder operated by twin overhead camshafts

Bore and stroke: 3.26 in. x 4.17 in.

Displacement: 3,442 cc

Compression ratio: 9.0:1

Induction system: Three SU or Weber carburetors

Maximum power: 204 bhp at 5,500 rpm

Maximum torque: 220 lb-ft at 4,000 rpm

Top speed: 143 mph

0-60 mph: 6.8 sec.

TRANSMISSION

Four-speed manual

BODY/CHASSIS

Tubular steel chassis with two-door aluminum sports body

SPECIAL FEATURES

Faired-in headlights improve the car's aerodynamics, but were unusual in the early 1950s.

The cockpit is as bare as possible, but Le Mans rules stated that there had to be a passenger seat.

RUNNING GEAR

Steering: Rack-and-pinion

Front suspension: Wishbones with torsion bar and anti-roll bar

Rear suspension: Live axle with torsion bar, and telescopic shocks

Brakes: Discs (front and rear)

Wheels: Wires, 15-in. dia.

Tires: Dunlop racing

DIMENSIONS

Length: 157.4 in.   **Width:** 64.5 in.

Height: 42.5 in.   **Wheelbase:** 96.0 in.

Track: 51 in. (front), 51 in. (rear)

Weight: 2,240 lbs.

Tried-and-tested transmission

The four-speed transmission is nearly identical to that of the XK120. However, a one-piece input shaft, in addition to a lighter flywheel and a Borg & Beck 10-inch solid center-section clutch, is fitted to accomplish quick changes between ratios.

Jaguar **D TYPE**

Jaguar designed the D-type with one aim in mind—to create a car that could win the most important race in the world, the 24 Hours of Le Mans. It achieved three straight victories in the mid-1950s.

"...tractable in traffic."

"By any standards, the D-type is an astonishing car with straight-line power to frighten many current supercars. A lack of cockpit space is emphasized by the big central rib, and the steering wheel feels big and skinny. The gearshift is positive, but heavy. None of the other controls are unduly heavy. Surprisingly for a race car, the D-type is tractable in traffic. But find an open road and it rockets to 60 mph in just over 5 seconds and tops 162 mph."

A bulky transmission tunnel results in a snug fit inside the cockpit.

1953 Jaguar's XK120C Mk 2 is first seen in October, when it achieves nearly 180 mph on a closed Belgian highway.

The C-type started Jaguar's run of success at Le Mans.

1954 Now known as the D-type, three cars are entered in the 24 Hours of Le Mans. Two drop out, but the third car takes second place.

1955 Fitted with longer noses, two D-types take first and third at Le Mans.

Jaguar's next specialist racer was the lightweight E-type.

1956 An Ecurie Ecosse D-type wins at Le Mans, with a poor showing from the works cars.

1957 Jaguar no longer campaigns the D-type, but an Ecurie Ecosse car wins Le Mans again. New regulations result in the D-type's demise.

UNDER THE SKIN

Proven and new

The D-type's chassis owes as much to aircraft-industry thinking as to conventional race-car engineering. Whereas most racing sports cars in the mid-1950s still relied on a ladder-type frame, or at best a tubular spaceframe, the D-type uses a strong central monocoque with a separate subframe to support the engine and front suspension. Like its predecessor, the D-type has a live rear axle and four-wheel disc brakes.

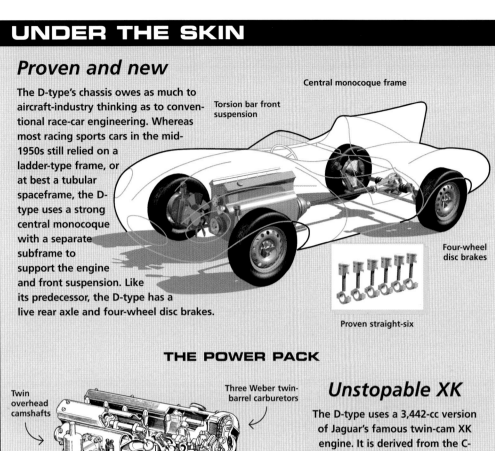

Central monocoque frame

Torsion bar front suspension

Four-wheel disc brakes

Proven straight-six

THE POWER PACK

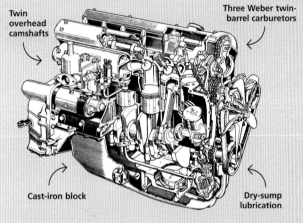

Twin overhead camshafts

Three Weber twin-barrel carburetors

Cast-iron block

Dry-sump lubrication

Unstopable XK

The D-type uses a 3,442-cc version of Jaguar's famous twin-cam XK engine. It is derived from the C-type's iron-block, alloy-head unit, but has a dry sump, bigger inlet valves, a new exhaust manifold and hotter camshafts. In its original form, with three twin-barrel Weber carburetors, it produces 250 bhp—more than 30 bhp more than the C-type unit. This unit was later increased to 3,781 cc and with fuel injection and an improved cylinder head, it produces up to 304 bhp.

Road racer

If the D-type is a little too stark for your tastes, the roadgoing version—the XKSS—is the one to choose. This later model is fitted with a proper windshield and a folding soft top. It has a road-car style interior without the central divider.

The last 16 cars were XKSS versions and were fully street legal.

Jaguar **D TYPE**

Jaguar's D-type broke new ground with its semi-monocoque construction and aerodynamic design. It was perfectly at home on the fast circuit of Le Mans, where it won for three consecutive years (1955-1957).

Dry-sump lubrication

Although the D-type's XK engine is essentially identical to that used in Jaguar's roadgoing sports cars, it has a dry sump rather than a conventional wet one. The oil is kept in a separate tank and circulated by a pump, which prevents oil surge during high-speed cornering.

Disc brakes front and rear

Jaguar pioneered the use of disc brakes in motor racing with the C-type. The Dunlop system was also used in the D-type, being employed both front and rear.

Two-seater bodywork

Racing regulations decreed that the D-type had to be a two-seater. In reality, it raced with just a driver; a fixed cover was put over the second seat to aid aerodynamics.

Rear stabilizing fin

Part of the aerodynamic package designed by ex-Bristol Aircraft aerodynamicist Malcolm Sayer is the fin that runs back from behind the driver's headrest. This provides important directional stability when racing on very fast circuits like Le Mans.

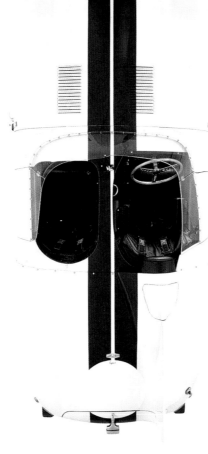

Monocoque center section

To give it the very stiff but light structure needed for a racing car, the D-type pioneered the use of an alloy monocoque to replace the spaceframe chassis used on the C-type. It is not a full monocoque, however, as the engine and front suspension are held in a separate subframe.

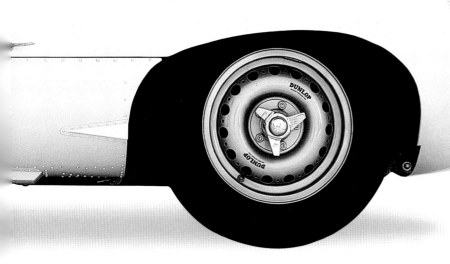

Specifications

1957 Jaguar D-type*

ENGINE

Type: In-line six

Construction: Cast-iron block and alloy head

Valve gear: Two valves per cylinder operated by two overhead camshafts

Bore and stroke: 3.27 in. x 4.17 in.

Displacement: 3,442 cc

Compression ratio: 9.0:1

Induction system: Three Weber sidedraft carburetors

Maximum power: 250 bhp at 6,000 rpm

Maximum torque: 242 lb-ft at 4,000 rpm

Top speed: 162 mph

0-60 mph: 5.4 sec.

TRANSMISSION

Four-speed manual

BODY/CHASSIS

Center monocoque with separate front subframe

SPECIAL FEATURES

The spare wheel is stored in a small trunk which hinges down for access.

A leather strap on each side keeps the clamshell hood secured.

RUNNING GEAR

Steering: Rack-and-pinion

Front suspension: Double wishbones with longitudinal torsion bars and telescopic shock absorbers

Rear suspension: Live axle with single transverse torsion bar, trailing links, single A-bracket and telescopic shock absorbers

Brakes: Dunlop discs (front and rear)

Wheels: Dunlop light alloy Center-lock, 5.5 x 16 in.

Tires: Dunlop racing, 6.50 x 16 in.

DIMENSIONS

Length: 154.0 in.   **Width:** 65.4 in.

Height: 44.0 in.   **Wheelbase:** 90.0 in.

Track: 50.0 in. (front), 48.0 in. (rear)

Weight: 2,460 lbs.

* Model illustrated is a Lynx replica

Jowett **Javelin**

Made in northern England, the Jowett developed a reputation for solidity and hill-climbing ability. Considering the austerity of post-war times, the 1947 Javelin was unusually ambitious, boasting a flat-four engine and a roomy six-seat interior.

"…surprisingly accomplished."

"Sitting in the Javelin for the first time, you'd think this car came from the 1960s rather than the 1940s. It has a curved windshield, plenty of instruments, a plastic-and-metal steering wheel and an airy feel. The flat-four engine may be more vocal than an equivalent in-line unit, but it offers plenty of torque, and the ride is amazingly good for such an old car. The steering is heavy at low speeds, but the handling is surprisingly accomplished."

The smart finish and luxurious feel of the Javelin's interior was way ahead of its time.

UNDER THE SKIN

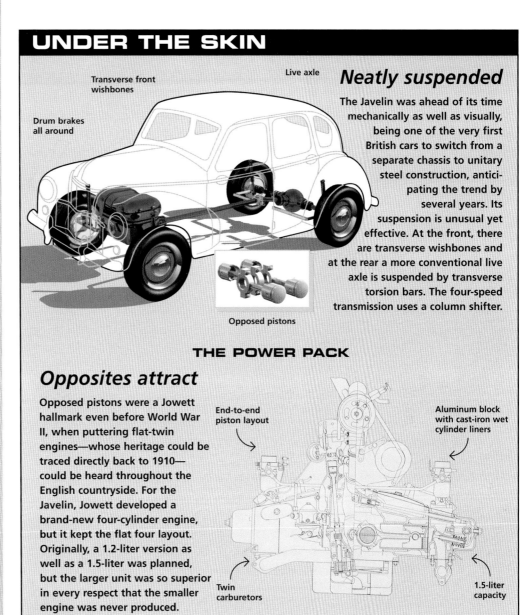

Transverse front wishbones

Live axle

Drum brakes all around

Opposed pistons

Neatly suspended

The Javelin was ahead of its time mechanically as well as visually, being one of the very first British cars to switch from a separate chassis to unitary steel construction, anticipating the trend by several years. Its suspension is unusual yet effective. At the front, there are transverse wishbones and at the rear a more conventional live axle is suspended by transverse torsion bars. The four-speed transmission uses a column shifter.

THE POWER PACK

Opposites attract

Opposed pistons were a Jowett hallmark even before World War II, when puttering flat-twin engines—whose heritage could be traced directly back to 1910—could be heard throughout the English countryside. For the Javelin, Jowett developed a brand-new four-cylinder engine, but it kept the flat four layout. Originally, a 1.2-liter version as well as a 1.5-liter was planned, but the larger unit was so superior in every respect that the smaller engine was never produced.

End-to-end piston layout

Aluminum block with cast-iron wet cylinder liners

Twin carburetors

1.5-liter capacity

Solid Series PE

Early Javelins suffered from a reputation for poor reliability, but that was cured by the series PE of 1952. This model boasted a Series III engine with more horsepower and it had hydraulic brakes that were standardized across the range in 1950. Late models also have leather upholstery.

Introduced late in the production run, the series PE was the ultimate Javelin.

Jowett JAVELIN

To a post-war nation being fed warmed-over remnants of dull 1930s automobiles, the sleek, advanced Javelin was a breath of fresh air. It might have been expensive, but it was probably the most desirable British sedan of its day.

Six-seat interior

For a car that measured only 14 feet long, the Javelin is extremely roomy inside—front and rear bench seats comfortably fit six adults. Legroom is particularly generous because the axles are positioned to the extreme ends of the car, and access is excellent with four perpendicular doors.

Generous equipment

The Javelin was well equipped for 1947. A built-in jacking system, ashtrays and interior mirror were standard. Deluxe models included leather trim, a spotlight, picnic trays and a walnut-faced radio.

Aerodynamic shape

Engineers discovered aerodynamics in the 1930s and Jowett was one of the first companies to embrace the new science in a popular car.

Large trunk

Under the sloping rear styling is a deceptively large trunk. The lid hinges upward for access to an extremely generous load bay. A built-in toolbox is also supplied.

ndependent front uspension

Vishbones and torsion ars made up the ndependent front uspension, which was ery effective by the tandards of the day.

Flat-four engine

In the immediate post-war period, Jowett's choice of a horizontally-opposed four-cylinder engine was brave and innovative. It was torquey, but early models were unreliable.

Specifications

1950 Jowett Javelin

ENGINE
Type: Horizontally-opposed four-cylinder
Construction: Aluminum cylinder block and cast-iron heads
Valve gear: Two valves per cylinder operated by a single camshaft
Bore and stroke: 2.85 in. x 3.54 in.
Displacement: 1,486 cc
Compression ratio: 7.25:1
Induction system: Two Zenith carburetors
Maximum power: 50 bhp at 4,100 rpm
Maximum torque: 76 lb-ft at 2,600 rpm
Top speed: 80 mph
0-60 mph: 25.4 sec.

TRANSMISSION
Four-speed manual

BODY/CHASSIS
Integral chassis with four-door steel sedan body

SPECIAL FEATURES

The deluxe model boasted a number of options such as picnic trays.

Flush-fitting, easy-release door handles were a major style innovation.

RUNNING GEAR
Steering: Rack-and-pinion
Front suspension: Live axle, transverse wishbones with torsion bars and shock absorbers
Rear suspension: Transverse torsion bars with shock absorbers
Brakes: Drums (front and rear)
Wheels: Steel, 16-in. dia.
Tires: 5.25 x 16

DIMENSIONS
Length: 168.0 in.   **Width:** 61.0 in.
Height: 60.5 in.
Wheelbase: 102.0 in.
Track: 51.0 in. (front), 49.0 in. (rear)
Weight: 2,254 lbs.

Land Rover SERIES 1

The Jeep paved the way as the standard all-purpose vehicle in WWII; Rover followed by building its own version. Modifying a Willys Jeep chassis, it installed Rover mechanicals. The result was a supreme and effective off-roader.

"...an unbeatable off roader."

"It's the Land Rover's no-nonsense character that appeals to its owners. It's devoid of any sort of frills and everything that is included has a specific and important function. As a result, the Series I Land Rover is an uncomfortable and stark beast. However, the truck's strengths quickly begin to show. The engine is very torquey at a low rpm, and the off-road ability is second to none. For mud-plugging and hill-climbing it is an unbeatable off roader."

Stark and functional, the cabin is not a place for those looking for creature comforts.

Milestones

1947 Land Rover makes its first prototype with a war-surplus Willys Jeep and Rover engine and transmission.

The work horse was elevated to royal status in 1959.

1948 The Land Rover is launched at the Amsterdam Motor Show. It has an 80-inch wheelbase and uses a 1.6-liter engine.

A modern equivalent of the Series 1 is the Defender.

1951 The headlights are moved from behind the grill and the engine grows to 2.0 liters.

1953 New 86- and 107-inch wheelbase lengths are offered.

1958 The Series 1 gives way to the much improved Series II.

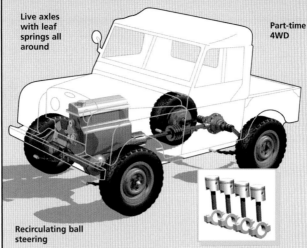

Live axles with leaf springs all around

Part-time 4WD

Recirculating ball steering

In-line four

Jeep-inspired

Rover's chief engineer, Maurice Wilks, happened to be using a Willys Jeep on his Welsh estate when Rover considered building its own agricultural machine. Two war-surplus Jeeps with 80-inch wheelbases were used as prototypes. There was permanent four-wheel drive with free-wheeling front hubs. This system changed in 1950 when the front wheels could be locked and unlocked for four- or two-wheel driving.

THE POWER PACK

Tough Rover engines

Partly to keep costs down and partly because they were tough and therefore ideal for the Land Rover, the Series 1 used a detuned regular production engine from its passenger car range. The first production cars had Rover 60 four-cylinder 1,595-cc engines, with their unusual intake-over-exhaust valve layout. For military use, some 33 trucks were fitted with Rolls-Royce 2.8-liter engines. In 1951, the capacity of the Rover engine was increased to 1,997 cc. This only marginally increased power but boosted torque to 101 lb-ft.

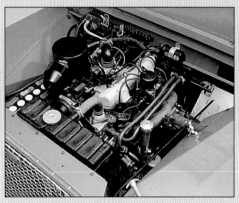

Early to rise

Workhorses are now collectable items, as the Jeep has proved. Here, the maxim is 'the earlier, the better'—collectors prefer the Series I Land Rovers. However, the Series II which debuted in 1958 is bigger, more use-able, less expensive and offered in a greater variety of models. Its basic design lasted until 1983 and its legacy lives on in the current Defender.

Series II Land Rovers came in both short and long wheelbase form.

Land Rover **SERIES 1** 🇬🇧

The Series I may have been basic, but it was supposed to be. The Land Rover had to be reliable, easy to service, and able to maintain its go-anywhere reputation. A worldwide legend was very quickly born.

Basic specification

Inexpensive, rugged and basic were Land Rover's basic principles and the specification was deliberately trimmed down. However, Rover shelved a plan to leave items like doors, roof, spare tire, and passenger seat as options.

Green paint

Series 1 Land Rovers only came painted in Sage Green. A darker green arrived in 1949. The list of paint choices was further increased in 1954 with the addition of blue and gray.

Two wheelbase choices

It was obvious that the Land Rover was capable of carrying more than the short bodywork permitted on the initial 80-inch wheelbase, so a longer chassis was developed and made available in 1953. It was 21 inches longer than the SWB chassis (which by then had grown to 86 inches). Three years later, they were both stretched another two inches.

Aluminum bodywork

Shortages of steel in the post-war period forced Rover to adopt aluminum for its bodywork. Although it was more expensive, it was the ideal material—lightweight and easily formed by hand.

Jeep-inspired chassis

The tough, steel, ladder-frame chassis complete with leaf-sprung rigid axles was clearly developed from the Willys Jeep.

Choice of body styles

Most early Land Rovers were custom made, but there were two basic body styles. The first—and by far the more popular—was an extremely simple pickup with half-doors. The station wagon body with curvaceous paneling was more utilitarian, but not as popular as the pickup.

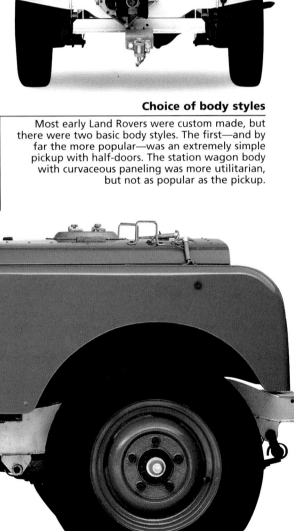

Specifications

1955 Land Rover Series 1

ENGINE

Type: In-line four-cylinder

Construction: Cast-iron block and head

Valve gear: Two valves per cylinder with intake valve mounted over exhaust valve

Bore and stroke: 3.06 in. x 4.13 in.

Displacement: 1,997 cc

Compression ratio: 6.7:1

Induction system: Single Solex carburetor

Maximum power: 52 bhp at 4,000 rpm

Maximum torque: 101 lb-ft at 1,500 rpm

Top speed: 60 mph

0-60 mph: Not quoted

TRANSMISSION

Four-speed manual with two-speed transfer box

BODY/CHASSIS

Separate chassis with aluminum two-door open body

SPECIAL FEATURES

If the Series 1 can't drive out of a compromising situation, this winch will allow it to pull itself out.

This truck is equipped with these unusual windshield-mounted pop-up turn signals.

RUNNING GEAR

Steering: Recirculating ball

Front suspension: Live axle with semi-elliptic leaf springs and telescopic shock absorbers

Rear suspension: Live axle with semi-elliptic leaf springs and telescopic shock absorbers

Brakes: Drums (front and rear)

Wheels: Steel, 16-in. dia.

Tires: 6.00 x 16

DIMENSIONS

Length: 140.8 in.   **Width:** 62.5 in.

Height: 76.0 in.   **Wheelbase:** 86.0 in.

Track: 50.0 in. (front and rear)

Weight: 2,968 lbs.

Lincoln **CONTINENTAL**

Ford's luxury division revealed one of its largest cars ever for 1958. The following year, the Continental returned as a separate Lincoln sub series offered in coupe, convertible, town car and limousine forms. Priced at just over $7,000, it was, not surprisingly, rare and exclusive.

"...unparalleled level of opulence."

"It's apt to describe this car as huge! The Mark IV is longer and wider than just about any of its contemporaries. Although it has 350 bhp on tap, this Continental is more of a cruiser than muscle car, but it still remains effortless to drive and extremely smooth on the open road. The power steering is very light and taking corners at speed can produce some interesting results. The cabin has an unparalleled level of opulence."

Dominating the interior are the jumbo-sized steering wheel and unique instruments.

1958 Lincoln issues its largest car yet for public consumption. It is offered in Capri and Premiere series and both are powered by a 375-bhp, 430-cubic inch V8. In a recession year, sales are a modest 17,134. A similar, separate machine, the Continental Mk III, priced much economically than its predecessor is also offered; 12,500 are sold.

The first Continental arrived for 1940 as an upmarket Zephyr.

1959 Continental Mk IV becomes part of the Lincoln line with its own range of models. It is priced above the Capri and Premiere. Power in the 430-cubic inch V8 drops to 350 bhp. Production reaches 15,780.

A much smaller and neater Continental debuts for 1961.

1960 The 131-inch wheelbase Lincolns make their final appearance this year. Production falls yet again to below 15,000. A new, smaller Continental bows for 1961.

UNDER THE SKIN

On a huge scale

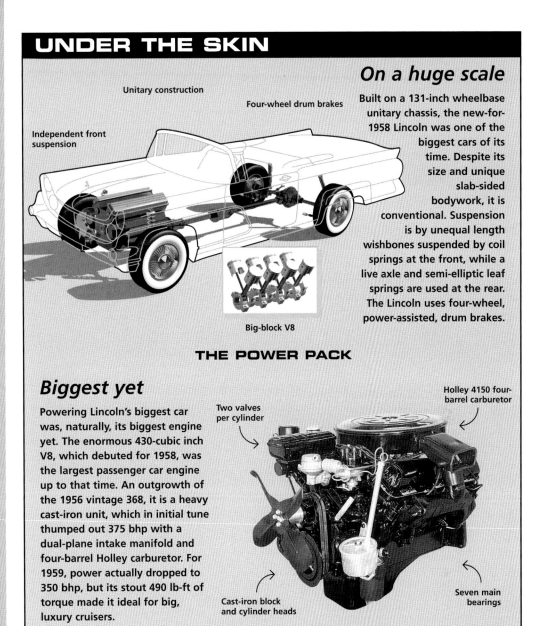

Unitary construction

Four-wheel drum brakes

Independent front suspension

Big-block V8

Built on a 131-inch wheelbase unitary chassis, the new-for-1958 Lincoln was one of the biggest cars of its time. Despite its size and unique slab-sided bodywork, it is conventional. Suspension is by unequal length wishbones suspended by coil springs at the front, while a live axle and semi-elliptic leaf springs are used at the rear. The Lincoln uses four-wheel, power-assisted, drum brakes.

THE POWER PACK

Biggest yet

Powering Lincoln's biggest car was, naturally, its biggest engine yet. The enormous 430-cubic inch V8, which debuted for 1958, was the largest passenger car engine up to that time. An outgrowth of the 1956 vintage 368, it is a heavy cast-iron unit, which in initial tune thumped out 375 bhp with a dual-plane intake manifold and four-barrel Holley carburetor. For 1959, power actually dropped to 350 bhp, but its stout 490 lb-ft of torque made it ideal for big, luxury cruisers.

Two valves per cylinder

Holley 4150 four-barrel carburetor

Cast-iron block and cylinder heads

Seven main bearings

Slow seller

Making its debut on the eve of a recession, these big Lincolns were never built in large numbers. Among Continental Mk IVs, the convertible is the most valuable—only 2,195 were built. Good examples are highly sought after by collectors today.

Despite its huge size, the Mk IV has surprisingly clean lines.

Lincoln CONTINENTAL

At 227 inches long and weighing 5,192 lbs., the Continental Mk IV was no lightweight. In fact, it was so big that owners in certain parts of the country were required to place clearance lights on their cars for use on the road.

Power top

The Lincoln's power-operated soft top retracts behind the rear seats and is hidden under a metal tonneau cover, giving it a neat top-down appearence. An unusual option was available in 1958. If the car was parked outside with its top down and it started to rain, the top would automatically raise. Ford had many problems with this option which resulted in its ultimate demise in 1959.

Monster big-block V8

Weighing more than 5,000 lbs., the Mk IV needed a massive engine to move it around. Nestling between the fenders is a monster 430-cubic inch V8, producing 350 bhp and an earth-moving 490 lb-ft of torque.

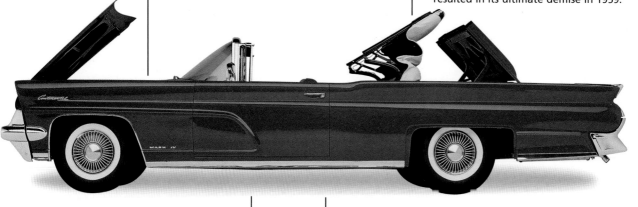

Automatic transmission

By 1959, most buyers expected automatic transmissions. Thus, the Mk IV came with a Ford Turbo-drive three-speed automatic operated with the column-shifter.

Unitary construction

A surprising feature for 1958-1960 Continentals and Lincolns was the adoption of unitary construction, making them stiffer and stronger than rival luxury cars.

Breezway rear window

With the top up, the 'Breezway' rear window gives a distinctive inverted profile. This style feature allows a smaller window, plus it reduces glare from sunlight and helps to keep the interior cool.

Independent front suspension

The Mk IV uses typical 1950s Detroit suspension at the front, with unequal length wishbones, coil springs and telescopic shocks. Air suspension was offered for 1958, but few buyers chose it.

Panoramic windshield

First seen on the 1953 Cadillac Eldorado, the panoramic windshield was a feature of most U.S.-built cars by 1959. These provide excellent forward vision due to moving the A-pillars further back.

Specifications

1959 Lincoln Continental Mk IV

ENGINE

Type: V8

Construction: Cast-iron block and heads

Valve gear: Two valves per cylinder operated by a single camshaft with pushrods and rockers

Bore and stroke: 4.30 in. x 3.70 in.

Displacement: 430 c.i.

Compression ratio: 10.0:1

Induction system: Holley 4150 four-barrel carburetor

Maximum power: 350 bhp at 4,400 rpm

Maximum torque: 490 lb-ft at 2,800 rpm

Top speed: 118 mph

0-60 mph: 10.4 sec.

TRANSMISSION

Turbo-drive three-speed automatic

BODY/CHASSIS

Unitary monocoque construction steel coupe body

SPECIAL FEATURES

A 'Breezway' power window allowed open air driving for the rear passengers.

Compared to rival 1959 luxury cars, the fins on the Mk IV are quite modest.

RUNNING GEAR

Steering: Recirculating ball

Front suspension: Unequal length wishbones with coil springs and telescopic shock absorbers

Rear suspension: Live axle with semi-elliptic leaf springs and telescopic shock absorbers

Brakes: Drums (front and rear)

Wheels: Steel disc, 14-in. dia.

Tires: 9.50 x 15 in.

DIMENSIONS

Length: 227.1 in.   **Width:** 80.1 in.

Height: 56.7 in.   **Wheelbase:** 131.0 in

Track: 61.0 in. (front and rear)

Weight: 5,192 lbs.

Mercedes-Benz 300SL

Created from Mercedes-Benz's first Le Mans-winning racing car, the 300SL 'Gullwing' was a race car built for the road. In the mid-1950s, it gave a few lucky drivers 1990s levels of performance.

"...spectacular and rare."

"Few have ever seen, let alone driven, one of the most coveted cars Mercedes Benz ever produced. Those lucky souls don't think about the astronomical price this 300SL would bring, they just enjoy this spectacular and rare automobile. It's actually fast enough to keep up with many modern sports cars. The transmission has synchros on all four gears and is easy to use, although the clutch is heavy. The ride is firm, like a sports cars should be, but definitely not old fashioned."

The cabin of the Gullwing was not a nice place to be on a hot day—it didn't have opening windows. Owners opened their doors in traffic for fresh air.

Milestones

1952 Mercedes builds its first postwar racer, the 300SL coupe. With a spaceframe chassis, Gullwing doors and 172 bhp from its six-cylinder engine, it leads its first event, the 1952 Mille Miglia, but finishes second before winning Le Mans and the Carrera Panamericana.

The 300SL: successful in racing.

1954 The street-legal version of the 300SL is introduced at the New York Motor Show.

1955 Production gets fully underway and the 300SL—with fuel injection replacing carburetors—is faster than the racer. It is also more than twice as expensive as a Chevrolet Corvette in the U.S.

1957 The Gullwing is discontinued after 1,400 have been built and the open roadster appears at the Geneva show. The chassis has been redesigned to allow conventional doors and the swing-axle rear suspension has been improved. Its top speed is up to 150 mph.

1961 Disc brakes with servo assistance are added to the car, vastly increasing stopping power. Production ends in 1963.

UNDER THE SKIN

Spaceframe

The 300SL has almost a full spaceframe chassis made from a network of small tubes. It is a lightweight yet strong design, but it means the chassis sides are too high for conventional doors, hence the lift-up Gullwing type. The swing-axle rear suspension makes for tricky handling at the limit as does the all-drum brake setup.

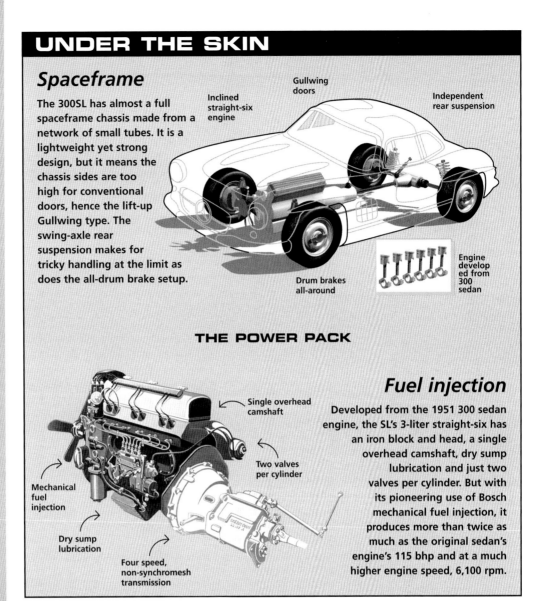

Inclined straight-six engine

Gullwing doors

Independent rear suspension

Drum brakes all-around

Engine developed from 300 sedan

THE POWER PACK

Single overhead camshaft

Two valves per cylinder

Mechanical fuel injection

Dry sump lubrication

Four speed, non-synchromesh transmission

Fuel injection

Developed from the 1951 300 sedan engine, the SL's 3-liter straight-six has an iron block and head, a single overhead camshaft, dry sump lubrication and just two valves per cylinder. But with its pioneering use of Bosch mechanical fuel injection, it produces more than twice as much as the original sedan's engine's 115 bhp and at a much higher engine speed, 6,100 rpm.

Open top fun

Although the Gullwing is more highly valued, the Roadster is by far the nicer car to drive. It had much more power, revised rear suspension for more predictable handling and a much less claustrophobic cabin than the cramped Gullwing.

Although not as desirable, the 300SL Roadster is an easier car to live with.

Mercedes-Benz **300SL**

The dramatic looks of the world's first postwar supercar were dictated by the racing car chassis under the body which made the Gullwing doors essential.

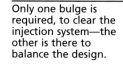

Hood bulges
Only one bulge is required, to clear the injection system—the other is there to balance the design.

Tilting steering wheel
Getting in and out of the 300SL could be difficult because of the high sills, so the steering wheel tilts to make room.

Wheel arch 'eyebrows'
These were purely a styling feature (the early racing coupes didn't have them) intended to appeal to the American market where most 300SLs were sold.

Deep side sills
Deep sill panels are necessary to cover up the sides of the spaceframe chassis.

Finned brake drums
The 300SL is stopped by massive alloy brake drums which are finned to help cooling. They were still not very effective and were eventually replaced by discs on the Roadsters.

Air extractors
To get a good flow of air through the cabin, twin extractors are incorporated into the rear of the roof.

Alloy doors

To ease the strain on the roof-mounted hinges, the doors are made from alloy rather than steel. It also helps save weight overall, as do the alloy hood and trunk lid.

Flush fitting door handles

The door handles are almost too small to notice. The end is pushed in to reveal the whole handle. Handles like these inspired the designers of the Fiat Barchetta in the 1990s.

Sedan engine

Apart from its pioneering use of fuel injection, the specification of the 300SL's engine was quite ordinary due to its sedan origins.

Specifications
1955 Mercedes 300SL

ENGINE
Type: Straight-six
Construction: Cast-iron block and head
Valve gear: Two valves per cylinder operated by single overhead camshaft
Bore and stroke: 3.35 in. x 3.46 in.
Displacement: 2,996 cc
Compression ratio: 8.5:1
Induction system: Bosch mechanical fuel injection
Maximum power: 240 bhp at 6,100 rpm
Maximum torque: 216 lb-ft at 4,800 rpm
Top speed: 165 mph*
0-60 mph: 9.0 sec.

TRANSMISSION
Four-speed manual

BODY/CHASSIS
Steel and alloy two-door coupe with steel spaceframe chassis

SPECIAL FEATURES

Engines in early cars tended to overheat so these large vents were added to allow hot engine-bay air to escape.

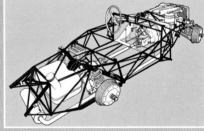

Spaceframe chassis was made light and strong, and was based on that of SL racers.

RUNNING GEAR
Steering: Recirculating ball
Front suspension: Twin wishbones with coil springs and telescopic shocks
Rear suspension: Swinging half axles with coil springs and telescopic shocks
Brakes: Drums all around
Wheels: Steel discs 5 in. x 15 in.
Tires: Crossply 6.7 in. x 15 in.

DIMENSIONS
Length: 178 in.   **Width:** 70 in.
Height: 49.7 in.   **Wheelbase:** 94 in.
Track: 54.5 in. (front), 56.5 in. (rear)
Weight: 2,850 lbs.

GERMANY 1955-1963

Mercedes-Benz 190SL

Whereas the exotic gull-winged Mercedes-Benz 300SL tempted only those lucky few able to afford it, the 190SL was a lower-priced sports car with broader appeal, but its styling emulated the far more expensive 300SL.

"...unruffled performance."

"Although it is styled to look as fast as the legendary 300SL, the four-cylinder 190SL falls well behind its big brother in the performance stakes. It was still a reasonably fast car in its day, however, and far more sophisticated than its rivals. The all-independent suspension provides reassuring roadholding and unruffled performance. The four-speed trans-mission is super slick and a pleasure to use. The car gives the impression that it would drive forever."

The 190SL's interior has real 1950s style without being too flamboyant.

1954 The 190SL makes its U.S. debut alongside the 300SL at the New York Motor Show in February. The show car is built with racing accessories.

The 190SL was replaced by the next-generation six-cylinder 230SL in 1963.

1955 Production of the 190SL finally gets underway in May.

Despite a strong resemblance to the 300SL, the 190SL shared little with its big brother.

1956 Chrome-plated trim is added to the fender moldings above the wheelwells and along the rocker panels. In all, more than 100 changes were made this year.

1963 Production comes to an end after 25,881 cars have been built.

UNDER THE SKIN

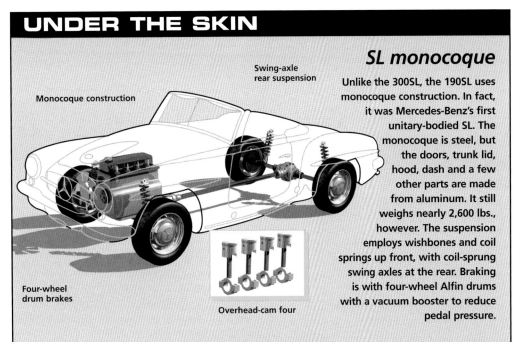

Monocoque construction

Swing-axle rear suspension

Four-wheel drum brakes

Overhead-cam four

SL monocoque

Unlike the 300SL, the 190SL uses monocoque construction. In fact, it was Mercedes-Benz's first unitary-bodied SL. The monocoque is steel, but the doors, trunk lid, hood, dash and a few other parts are made from aluminum. It still weighs nearly 2,600 lbs., however. The suspension employs wishbones and coil springs up front, with coil-sprung swing axles at the rear. Braking is with four-wheel Alfin drums with a vacuum booster to reduce pedal pressure.

THE POWER PACK

Tuned sedan four

In its day, the 1,897-cc four-cylinder engine had a very high power output for its size. The single overhead camshaft operates two valves per cylinder. It is an oversquare unit capable of revving to 6,000 rpm—very high for a 1950s engine. Two Solex sidedraft twin-choke carburetors feed the engine with fuel, and a Bosch coil and distributor take care of the ignition. A raised compression ratio of 8.5:1 (the engine uses 7.5:1 in sedan tune) helps to produce an output of 120 bhp at a high 5,700 rpm.

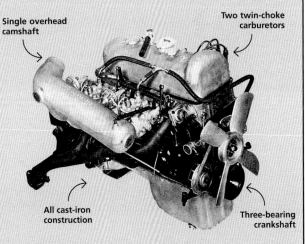

Single overhead camshaft

Two twin-choke carburetors

All cast-iron construction

Three-bearing crankshaft

Sports tourer

Although overshadowed by the 300SL, the 190SL still commands high prices today. In fact, it costs more than the later, more roadable and popular 'Pagoda-roof' SL. Although it is slow by modern standards, the 190SL is still enjoyable to drive.

The post-1956 190SL has chrome trim above the wheel wells.

Mercedes-Benz 190SL

Great looks and amazing build quality make the Mercedes-Benz 190SL a superb classic car buy, even if it is more of a boulevard cruiser than an all-out, high-performance sports car.

Supercar styling

The 190SL was sold on its looks. The strong resemblance to the exotic 300SL supercar helped sales tremendously. It outsold the more expensive car by nearly ten to one.

Four-cylinder engine

Despite its sporty looks, the 190SL uses only a 1.9-liter four-cylinder engine to move its 2,550 lbs. It gives 120 bhp. An aftermarket company, Judson, offered an aftermarket supercharger to boost power further.

Wishbone front suspension

Like most post-war sports cars, the 190SL uses double-wishbone front suspension with coil springs and telescopic shock absorbers.

Swing axle rear suspension

The rear end comprises a swing axle with a low center pivot. This ensures a lower roll center and reduces the likelihood of the outside wheel 'jacking up.' It is an effective system, giving good handling.

Hard or soft top

The 190SL was sold as a Roadster (with soft-top only) or a Coupe (with hard-top only), but they are rarely described that way. Most were sold as Roadsters and sold with the optional hardtop. The differences between the two cars are minimal.

Unitary build

The 190SL uses a steel monocoque but with a few aluminum parts to reduce weight.

Specifications

1956 Mercedes-Benz 190SL

ENGINE

Type: In-line four-cylinder

Construction: Cast-iron block and head

Valve gear: Two valves per cylinder operated by a single overhead camshaft

Bore and stroke: 3.35 in. x 3.29 in.

Displacement: 1,897 cc

Compression ratio: 8.5:1

Induction system: Two Solex twin-choke carburetors

Maximum power: 120 bhp at 5,700 rpm

Maximum torque: 105 lb-ft at 3,200 rpm

Top speed: 106 mph

0-60 mph: 11.2 sec.

TRANSMISSION

Four-speed manual

BODY/CHASSIS

Unitary monocoque construction with steel roadster body

SPECIAL FEATURES

These distinctive wheelwell blisters are also a feature on the 300SL.

The 190SL is a simple two-seater. The space behind the seats is best used for extra luggage.

RUNNING GEAR

Steering: Recirculating ball

Front suspension: Double wishbones with coil springs and telescopic shock absorbers

Rear suspension: Low-pivot swing axle with coil springs and telescopic shock absorbers

Brakes: Alfin drums (front and rear)

Wheels: Pressed steel, 5 x 13 in.

Tires: 6.40 x 13 in.

DIMENSIONS

Length: 166.1 in.   **Width:** 68.5 in.

Height: 52.0 in.   **Wheelbase:** 94.5 in.

Track: 56.2 in. (front), 58.1 in. (rear)

Weight: 2,550 lbs.

Mercury MONTCLAIR

When most people think of Mercury customs, the 1949-1951 models come to mind. However, this unusual and individual 1955 Montclair illustrates that the later Mercurys have just as much potential for customizing into one-of-a-kind vehicles.

"...a comfortable ride."

"The blue dashboard and white tuck-and-roll upholstery evoke a feeling of spaciousness. Take your place on the comfortable bench seat and start the motor. On the highway the torquey V8 enables the Mercury to do better than just keep up with the traffic and the automatic transmission is perfectly suited to laid-back cruising. The air suspension also results in a more comfortable ride than that felt in many modern cars."

This 1955 Montclair has a number of period touches, like the tuck-and-roll upholstery.

Milestones

1954 Mercury introduces its revolutionary Y-block V8 engine. Created in response to the modern GM V8s, it features overhead valves and produces 161 bhp, making for the fastest accelerating Mercurys yet seen.

Earlier model Mercurys are popular cars to customize.

1955 Retaining the basic 1952 bodyshell, this year's Mercury has more angular styling and greater expanses of chrome. A new Montclair is introduced as the top-of-the-range model.

Mercurys were entirely designed for the 1957 model year. This is a top-of-the-line Turnpike Cruiser.

1956 Having proved a success, the 1955 model receives a minor styling update. The Montclair returns and a four-door model is added to the range. An all-new Mercury debuts for 1957.

UNDER THE SKIN

Updated

In Detroit during the 1950s most cars featured a separate chassis and the 1955 Mercury was no exception. This car has been modified with an independent front suspension and a live rear axle taken from a 1981 Camaro. It also has airbags in place of the standard coil springs, and power front disc brakes are an additional safety feature.

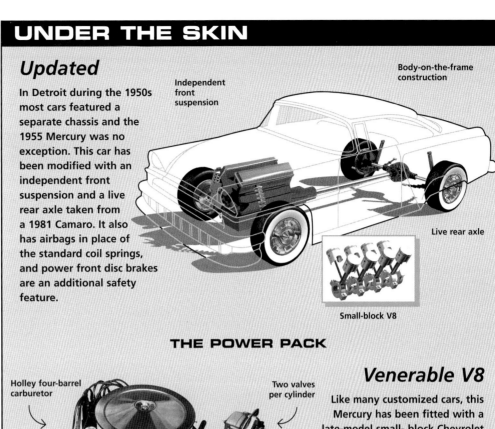

Independent front suspension

Body-on-the-frame construction

Live rear axle

Small-block V8

THE POWER PACK

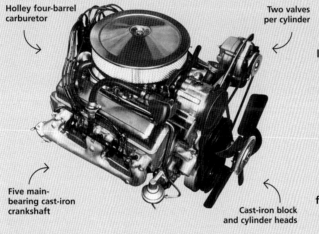

Holley four-barrel carburetor

Two valves per cylinder

Five main-bearing cast-iron crankshaft

Cast-iron block and cylinder heads

Venerable V8

Like many customized cars, this Mercury has been fitted with a late-model small- block Chevrolet V8. This particular unit, displacing 350 cubic inches, was taken from a 1983 C10 pickup. It is of cast-iron construction, with two valves per cylinder, and features a five main- bearing crankshaft. It has been fitted with an Edelbrock intake manifold and a 750-cfm Holley four-barrel carburetor. With these modifications it has a power output of 210 bhp at 4,000 rpm.

Top model

In 1955 the Montclair Sun Valley hardtop coupe was the top-of-the-range Mercury. Today, most of these cars are restored to stock specifications and, therefore, a custom version makes an interesting alternative to the popular 1949-1951 Mercurys.

The Montclair makes an interesting choice for a modern custom.

Mercury MONTCLAIR

The Montclair Sun Valley was eye-catching when it first appeared in the mid-1950s. And with its chopped roof and custom paint, this customized Mercury continues to make a statement wherever it goes.

Chevrolet V8 engine

For practicality and power output this Mercury has a small-block Chevrolet V8 installed in place of the original Y-block engine.

Tuck-and-roll upholstery

Despite the engine and running gear this car has a number of period custom features, including the 1950s-style tuck-and-roll upholstery.

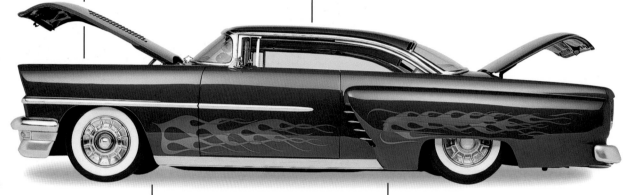

Modern running gear

A Camaro front subframe and suspension have been grafted onto the original chassis. The Salisbury rear axle was also taken from the same Camaro.

Smoothed body

Like most lead sleds the body has been smoothed out, with the headlights and taillights frenched into the body. The door handles and exterior badging have also been removed.

Air suspension

Air bags on the rear suspension give a smooth ride and also allow the car to be raised for driving or lowered for show purposes.

Modified grill

Although not obvious at first, the original bumper/grill has been reworked with additional chromed teeth.

Custom paint

As this car is driven regularly, the body has been coated in tough PPG blue acrylic urethane metallic paint. In true 1950s style, flames have been added below the beltline.

Specifications

1955 Mercury Montclair

ENGINE

Type: V8

Construction: Cast-iron block and heads

Valve gear: Two valves per cylinder operated by pushrods and rockers

Bore and stroke: 4 in. x 3.48 in.

Displacement: 350 c.i.

Compression ratio: 9.5:1

Induction system: Single Holley four-barrel carburetor

Maximum power: 210 bhp at 4,000 rpm

Maximum torque: 285 lb-ft at 2,800 rpm

Top speed: 120 mph

0-60 mph: 9.3 sec.

TRANSMISSION

Three-speed GM TurboHydramatic

BODY/CHASSIS

Separate chassis with two-door steel hardtop body

SPECIAL FEATURES

In popular lead sled style, even the radio antenna has been frenched into the bodywork.

This model even features a pair of fuzzy dice hanging from the rear-view mirror—a very period custom accessory.

RUNNING GEAR

Steering: Recirculating ball

Front suspension: Independent with unequal length wishbones, air bags, front stabilizer bar and telescopic shocks

Rear suspension: Live rear axle with airbags and telescopic shocks

Brakes: Power discs, 9.5-in. dia. (front), drums, 9-in. dia. (rear)

Wheels: Steel discs, 15-in. dia. (with 1957 Cadillac hub caps)

Tires: G78 x 15 Whitewalls

DIMENSIONS

Length: 198.6 in.   **Width:** 82.7 in.

Height: 51.8 in.   **Wheelbase:** 119 in.

Track: 62.5 in (front and rear)

Weight: 3,558 lbs.

MG TF

The TF was the last of MG's traditional 'upright' sports cars. A holdover from the great pre-war sports cars, it was out of date when it was launched but appealed to hard-core sports car enthusiasts.

"...sporty by nature."

"With your legs straight out and the large-diameter steering wheel in your chest, you're in the classic sports car driving position. The pushrod four is a willing power unit with a raspy exhaust note. It pulls well but the TF is not particularly fast. Where it comes into its own is on twisty roads. Here, the sporty by nature TF can easily lose any contemporary sedan and many sports cars that may have been riding its bumper along the straightaways."

The twin-cowl dashboard is distinctive with its centrally mounted octagonal instruments.

Milestones

1953 MG replaces the TD with the new TF model. It has crisper, more modern styling with integral headlights in the fenders, unlike the TD's separate units. The 1,250-cc XPAG four-cylinder engine is carried over from the earlier TD.

The MG T-series ran from the 1930s up to the mid-1950s.

1954 A larger engine is introduced. A bored-out version of the XPAG unit displaces 1,466 cc and is known as the XPEG. Power increases from 57 to 65 bhp. An MG TF-based streamlined car, the EX 179 breaks many top speed records at the Bonneville Salt Flats.

The TF was replaced by the more modern MGA.

1955 Production of the TF comes to an end after 9,600 vehicles have been built. The new MGA takes its place.

UNDER THE SKIN

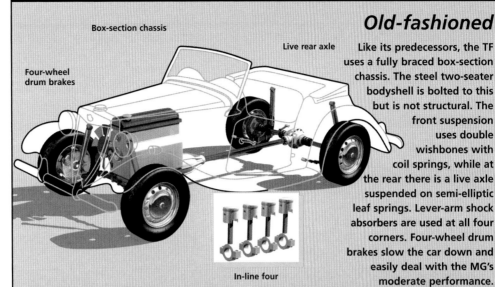

Box-section chassis

Four-wheel drum brakes

Live rear axle

In-line four

Old-fashioned

Like its predecessors, the TF uses a fully braced box-section chassis. The steel two-seater bodyshell is bolted to this but is not structural. The front suspension uses double wishbones with coil springs, while at the rear there is a live axle suspended on semi-elliptic leaf springs. Lever-arm shock absorbers are used at all four corners. Four-wheel drum brakes slow the car down and easily deal with the MG's moderate performance.

THE POWER PACK

Little four

The TF started out with the 1,250-cc XPAG four-cylinder engine used in its predecessor, the TD. It is a simple all-cast-iron, overhead-valve engine with two valves per cylinder operated by pushrods and rockers. In 1954, the engine was overbored to give a capacity of 1,466 cc. This took power from 57 to 65 bhp and torque from 65 lb-ft to 76 lb-ft. Fuel is supplied by two SU carburetors, and the engine runs a relatively high (for its time) compression ratio of 8.0:1.

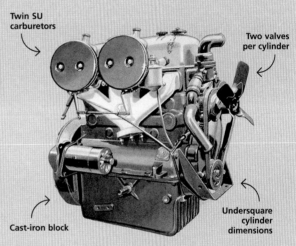

Twin SU carburetors

Two valves per cylinder

Undersquare cylinder dimensions

Cast-iron block

Big bore

The TF is perhaps the most collectable of the MG T-series models and much more usable than the pre-war cars. Although both TF derivatives look the same, the 1500 is more desirable than its smaller-engined relative because it is faster and more relaxing to drive.

The TF has lower, sleeker lines than the earlier T-series MGs.

179

MG TF

Most of the car culture in the U.S. was fascinated by street rods and lead sleds in the 1950. However, a small number of auto enthusiasts realized that the tiny, underpowered MG T-series could be real fun taking turns at high speeds.

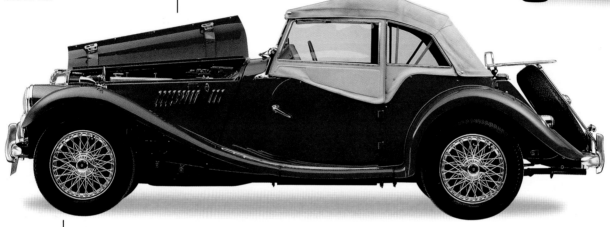

Four-cylinder engine
The XPAG engine was carried over from the MG TD. The overhead-valve unit was overbored in 1954 and renamed the XPEG.

Wire wheels
Although steel wheels were stock equipment in Europe with wire wheels as an option, in the U.S. the smarter wires were fitted as standard.

Classic MG cockpit
With its large, sprung steering wheel and octagonal gauges, the TF's cabin is undoubtedly traditional MG in style.

Sleeker styling

The TF was subtly restyled over the previous TD. It has a shorter grill and lower hood. The headlights are faired in to the wide-swept fenders too, further enhancing the car's lower lines.

Upright shape

Despite the styling changes, the TF is not very aerodynamic. This is just one reason for the car's low top speed.

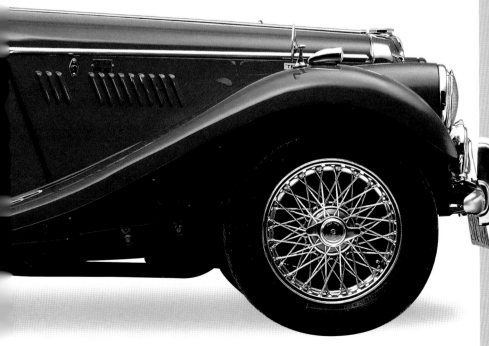

Specifications

1954 MG TF 1500

ENGINE

Type: In-line four-cylinder

Construction: Cast-iron block and head

Valve gear: Two valves per cylinder operated by a single camshaft via pushrods and rockers.

Bore and stroke: 2.83 in. x 3.54 in.

Displacement: 1,466 cc

Compression ratio: 8.0:1

Induction system: Two SU carburetors

Maximum power: 65 bhp at 5,500 rpm

Maximum torque: 76 lb-ft at 3,000 rpm

Top speed: 88 mph

0-60 mph: 16.3 sec.

TRANSMISSION

Four-speed manual

BODY/CHASSIS

Steel chassis with two-seater sports body

SPECIAL FEATURES

The TF's grill was becoming quite a rare feature when it was launched in 1953. The integral headlights distinguish the TF from earlier T-series MGs.

The TF's windshield can be folded flat. This reduces drag but means the driver is unprotected from the wind.

RUNNING GEAR

Steering: Rack-and-pinion

Front suspension: Double wishbones with coil springs and Armstrong lever-arm type shock absorbers

Rear suspension: Live axle with semi-elliptic leaf springs and Armstrong lever-arm type shock absorbers

Brakes: Drums (front and rear)

Wheels: Knock-on wire, 15-in. dia.

Tires: 5.50 x 15 in.

DIMENSIONS

Length: 147.0 in.   **Width:** 59.8 in.

Height: 52.5 in.   **Wheelbase:** 94.0 in.

Track: 48.2 in (front), 50.8 in. (rear)

Weight: 2,015 lbs.

MGA

The first post-war MG, the MGA, had a slippery aerodynamic body based on a Le Mans racer. It was also reasonably simple, reliable, and affordable with good handling.

"...slide the back."

"The big sprung steering wheel and features like the floor-mounted dip switch tell you the car is old, but once you're on the move the heavy steering lightens up and develops the kind of feel a rack-and-pinion system should. There's adequate power from the ordinary pushrod engine and the ride is better than you expect, but mid-corner bumps catch it out and send you skittering across the road. Particularly with the Twin Cam engine there's enough power to slide the back end through corners."

Traditional British sports car interior includes large, easy-to-read Smiths gauges and large-diameter sprung steering wheel.

*econd MGA prototype was
onverted into a record
reaker, but proved unsuitable.*

*MC campaigned the MGA in
llies but was overshadowed
v the Austin-Healey 3000.*

UNDER THE SKIN

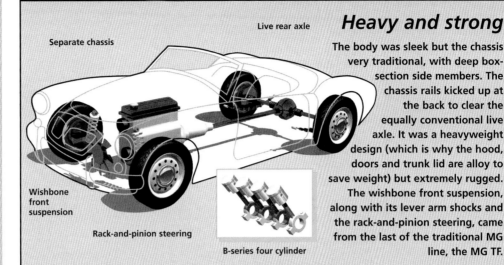

Separate chassis

Live rear axle

Wishbone
front
suspension

Rack-and-pinion steering

B-series four cylinder

Heavy and strong

The body was sleek but the chassis very traditional, with deep box-section side members. The chassis rails kicked up at the back to clear the equally conventional live axle. It was a heavyweight design (which is why the hood, doors and trunk lid are alloy to save weight) but extremely rugged. The wishbone front suspension, along with its lever arm shocks and the rack-and-pinion steering, came from the last of the traditional MG line, the MG TF.

THE POWER PACK

Pushrod power

As MG was part of BMC (British Motor Corporation) the MGA used the BMC B-series engine, a cast-iron overhead-valve pushrod engine with three main bearings and, originally in the MGA, a displacement of just 1,489 cc. Power for the pushrod B-series ranged from 68 bhp for the initial 1,489-cc unit to 86 bhp in the final 1,622-cc form. It was a non-crossflow design with carburetors and exhaust on the same side. The engine was strong and reliable. With the twin-cam, alloy head, power was hiked to 108 bhp.

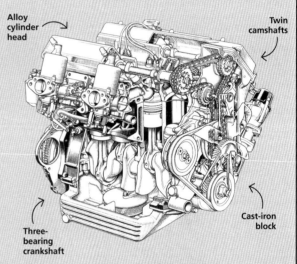

Alloy
cylinder
head

Twin
camshafts

Cast-iron
block

Three-
bearing
crankshaft

Twin Cam

Rarest and most desirable of all MGAs is the Twin Cam, with a B-series block and a new alloy twin-cam head giving 108 bhp. Early engines were unreliable if not serviced properly and sales never took off—but now a 'sorted' Twin Cam is very desirable.

The MGA Twin Cam is desirable despite the stories of its unreliability.

MGA

The MGA could hardly fail. It had all the ingredients of the older upright models that came before it—like the TA, TD and TF—but with a body which looked incredibly modern in the mid-1950s.

B-series engine
The MGA's predecessor had a 1,466-cc engine which was replaced for the MGA by the B-series engine, originally in 1,489-cc form.

Optional heater
There is little that is luxurious about the early MGA: even the crude Smiths heater was an option.

Optional four-wheel discs
Early MGAs have drum brakes all around, the Twin Cam has front discs, as did all MGAs from 1959. Toward the end of production you could order four-wheel Dunlop disc brakes if you specified the center lock wire wheels.

Optional axle ratio
If you wanted better acceleration from your MGA you could order a lower rear axle final drive ratio (4.55:1 compared with 4.10:1).

Alloy body panels
To help reduce weight, the hood, fenders, doors and trunk are all made of aluminum instead of heavy steel.

Live axle
Virtually all sports cars from the 1950s had live rear axles with semi-elliptic leaf springs. This arrangement worked well in the MGA.

No door handles
With car theft almost unheard of in the mid-1950s, it was possible to build a car with no external door handles. You simply put your hand through the sliding side window and opened the interior handle. It was also cheaper and gave a cleaner look to the door.

Wire or disc wheels
The MGA could be ordered with either center lock wire wheels or the more modern looking perforated steel discs.

Rack-and-pinion steering
Many 1950s British sports cars used advanced (for its time) rack-and-pinion steering.

Different grill

Early MGAs, like this one, have a sloping radiator grill, but for the last of the line, the MkII, the grill bars are inset almost vertically.

Specifications
1959 MGA MkI

ENGINE
Type: In-line four cylinder
Construction: Cast-iron block and head
Valve gear: Two in-line valves per cylinder operated by single block-mounted camshaft via pushrods and rockers
Bore and stroke: 2.96 in. x 3.50 in.
Displacement: 1,588 cc
Compression ratio: 8.9:1
Induction system: Two SU H4 carburetors
Maximum power: 80 bhp at 5,600 rpm
Maximum torque: 95 lb-ft at 4,000 rpm
Top speed: 103 mph
0-60 mph: 13.7 sec.

TRANSMISSION
Four-speed manual

BODY/CHASSIS
Separate box-section chassis with steel and alloy two-seater roadster or coupe body

SPECIAL FEATURES

MkI MGAs have upright rear lights mounted on small fender plinths. The MkII is recognizable by its stylish horizontally-mounted rear taillights.

The MGA always relied on twin SU carburetors, giving the engine extra fuel to produce more power over the B-series-powered sedans.

RUNNING GEAR
Steering: Rack-and-pinion
Front suspension: Double wishbones with coil springs and lever arm shocks
Rear suspension: Live axle with semi-elliptic leaf springs and lever arm shocks
Brakes: Discs front, drums rear
Wheels: Center lock wire spoke or steel discs, 16-in. dia.
Tires: 5.60 in. x 16 in., crossply

DIMENSIONS
Length: 156 in. **Width:** 58 in.
Height: 50 in. **Wheelbase:** 94 in.
Track: 47.5 in. (front), 48.2 in. (rear)
Weight: 1,985 lbs.

Morgan PLUS FOUR

With a switch to the Triumph TR2 engine, Morgan produced a sports car capable of a genuine 100 mph with handling to match. It also retained the classic looks and vintage feel of its predecessors.

"...works like a charm."

"The Morgan has a hard, bone-jarring ride. But there's another side to its character. Get the car on a smooth road and the stiff setup works like a charm. The handling is wonderful—just a flick of the extremely high-geared steering is all that is required to redirect the car. The Morgan magic starts to take shape, when you add the speed and handling to a feeling that you're going faster than you really are."

The inside of a Morgan has the appearance of a much older car.

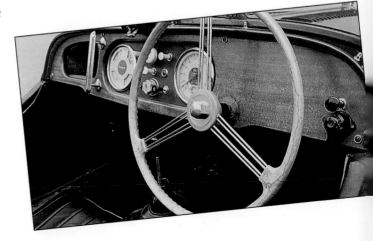

Milestones

1954 Significant revisions to the Plus Four see the traditional flat radiator grill replaced by a more modern-looking style and the exposed mudguards changed to enclosed front fenders with faired-in headlamps. The 1,991-cc engine from the Triumph TR2 sports car is fitted.

The 1936 4/4 was the first of the four-wheeled Morgans.

1955 Power output rises as Morgan gets hold of the revised Vanguard-derived engine fitted to the TR2. This has 0 bhp produced at 4,800 rpm.

The coupe Plus Four Plus also uses Triumph TR engines.

1959 The Plus Four is available with front disc brakes.

1969 Production of all Plus Fours ends when Triumph announces that it is no longer supplying four-cylinder engines. Morgan continues with the Ford-engined 4/4.

UNDER THE SKIN

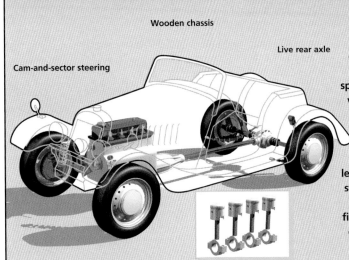

Wooden chassis

Live rear axle

Cam-and-sector steering

Inline four

Ancient design

The Morgan has a separate chassis frame with a live rear axle on semi-elliptic leaf springs. The body is based on a wooden frame, and the front suspension design dates back to before World War I, with a system of sliding pillars. The springs were lengthened to go along with a stiffer chassis frame when the Triumph TR2 engine was fitted. Steering was by a quick cam-and-sector with just two turns lock to lock.

THE POWER PACK

Standard power

Morgan never built its own engines—for the Plus Four it used the same engine found in the Triumph TR2. A 2-liter all-iron four-cylinder, it has removable wet cylinder liners rather than a bored block. The rest of the engine is straight-forward, with a single block-mounted camshaft working two inline line valves per cylinder through pushrods and rockers. It has a non-crossflow head with the intake and exhaust on the same side of the head, but it still responds well to tuning and is extremely tough and reliable. Over the years, displacement increased from 1,991 to 2,138 cc.

TR4 engine

By 1962, there was the larger 2,138-cc version of the engine used in Triumph's TR4. That gave more power and plenty more torque at 128 lb-ft to help performance, while the front disc brakes first seen in 1959 greatly help stopping power.

To enable the car to carry a family, Morgan built a four-seat version.

187

Morgan PLUS FOUR

The classic Morgan styling changed a little for the Plus Four from 1954 onward. Headlamp pods were faired into the bodywork, inboard of the fenders, and there was no longer a fully exposed radiator housing.

Four-cylinder engine

Morgan had a tradition of using engines produced by the Standard company, beginning with the 1,267-cc overhead-valve four, which it fitted to the 4/4 in 1939. This was continued after the war and led to the 2.1-liter four being used. The 1,991-cc engine was a development of that design, seen first in the Triumph TR2.

Drum brakes

Girling supplied the brakes for the Morgan. These are hydraulically operated 9-inch diameter drums on all four wheels.

Cutaway doors

The Plus Four has cutaway doors to allow room for the driver's elbow to move in a very tight cockpit. No conventional windows were fitted to the Morgan; it uses detachable side screens.

Wooden frame

Just as much a part of the Morgan as its separate chassis is the old form of body construction, in which panels were attached to a wood frame. This method continues to this day, although wood preservative is now used to make the structure last longer.

ressed-steel wheels

Vith a car as determinedly old-fashioned s the Morgan, you might expect the aditional center-lock, quick release, vire-spoke wheels. But bolt-on, pressed-eel wheels came standard.

Specifications

Morgan Plus Four

ENGINE
Type: Inline four cylinder

Construction: Cast-iron block and head

Valve gear: Two valves per cylinder operated by a single block-mounted cam with pushrods and rockers

Bore and stroke: 3.32 in. x 3.67 in.

Displacement: 1,991 cc

Compression ratio: 8.5:1

Induction system: Two SU carburetors

Maximum power: 90 bhp at 4,800 rpm

Maximum torque: 117 lb-ft at 3,000 rpm

Top speed: 102 mph

0-60 mph: 9.9 sec.

TRANSMISSION
Moss four-speed manual

BODY/CHASSIS
Separate steel ladder frame with wood framed, alloy-paneled two-door convertible body

SPECIAL FEATURES

In a throwback to vintage times, twin spare wheels are carried at the rear.

The front suspension dates back to pre-World War I times, although it was strengthened considerably.

RUNNING GEAR
Steering: Cam-and-sector

Front suspension: Sliding pillars with coil springs and telescopic shock absorbers

Rear suspension: Live axle with semi-elliptic leaf springs and lever arm shock absorbers

Brakes: Girling drums, 9.0-in. dia. (front and rear)

Wheels: Pressed-steel disc, 16-in. dia.

Tires: 5.25-16

DIMENSIONS
Length: 144.0 in.   **Width:** 56.0 in.

Height: 52.0 in.   **Wheelbase:** 96.0 in.

Track: 47.0 in. (front and rear)

Weight: 1,880 lbs.

Morris **MINOR**

Germany had its VW Beetle, but Great Britain had the Morris Minor. As a true people's car, it was well-designed, dependable and affordable. For years, it was a best-seller and still has a passionate following today.

"...way above the norm."

"In its day, the Minor was a revelation to drive, and it still has the potential to surprise you. No other economy car had such a balanced chassis, which, to this day, is fun to drive and at the same time offers an uncommonly good ride. The MM's sidevalve engine is its Achilles' heel, thanks to lazy response and poor refinement. Later Minors, with the pushrod, overhead-valve A-series engines, had much more throttle response."

Morris kept things clean and simple inside, but it suited the Minor's character perfectly.

Milestones

1948 Alec Issigonis' **dazzling** new Minor is launched in two-door sedan and convertible forms to rave reviews.

Later models are still plentiful, but the first MM is now a rarity.

1952 Following the merger of Austin and Morris to form BMC, the old sidevalve engine is replaced by Austin's 803-cc overhead-valve unit.

1953 The first Traveller station wagon is completed.

1956 The Minor 1000 arrives, with a 948-cc engine, more suitable transmission and an updated interior.

The convertible was as much of a hit as the sedan and is now the most collectible Minor.

1971 After more than two decades, often as Britain's best-selling car, the Minor is finally withdrawn from sales.

UNDER THE SKIN

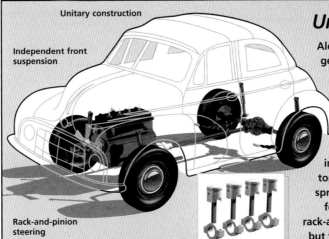

Unitary construction
Independent front suspension
Rack-and-pinion steering
In-line four

Unitary masterpiece

Alec Issigonis was the engineering genius behind the Minor. In many ways it was truly revolutionary, yet it all made perfect sense. Issigonis even wanted front-wheel drive, though he had to relent in the end. There's a unitary body/chassis with independent front suspension by torsion bars and a traditional leaf-sprung hypoid rear axle. Unusually for this class, the steering is crisp rack-and-pinion. Some changes came, but the Minor always remained true to its original engineering ideals.

THE POWER PACK

Morris cedes to Austin

Designer Alec Issigonis would have liked to use a new flat-four engine in the Minor, but economics forced Morris to depend on its pre-war Series E sidevalve 918-cc engine, which was underpowered (at 28 bhp) and lethargic. When Morris and Austin merged, it was only natural that Austin's superior A30 overhead-valve 803-cc engine should be substituted. It revs much better and gives a faster top speed. That engine grew to 948 cc and 37 bhp in 1956 (in the definitive Minor 1000), and finally to 1,098 cc and 48 bhp in 1962.

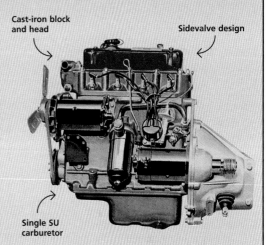

Cast-iron block and head
Sidevalve design
Single SU carburetor

Tourer or woody

The pick of the Minor family is the convertible version, called the Tourer, although the 'woody' Traveller station wagon is highly prized. The Tourer has a typical 1950s English charm about it and a well-designed soft top. In general, the earlier the model the more precious it is, so MM Tourers are the most highly collectible of all Morris Minors.

Wooden panels on the Traveller help make it a collector's favorite.

Morris **MINOR**

The chubby styling of the Minor became very familiar on British roads as the population took to the charms of this competent little car. It offered a level of driving pleasure unseen before in its class.

Unibody constructio

In 1948, just about every car ha a separate chassis. The Min was way ahead of its time adopting unitary constructio The floor was produced in single pressing, cutting costs an keeping weight down. It wa rigid, too, as proven by th convertible which didn't nee very much body reinforcemen

Sidevalve engine

The first Minors used an outdated Morris sidevalve engine to keep costs down. Issigonis had developed new flat-four sidevalve engines, but these were shelved. A more satisfying Austin A30 overhead-valve engine arrived in 1952.

Correct proportions

One of the Minor's main selling points was that it looked right, even though Morris' boss called the prototype a 'poached egg.' One famous story relates how Issigonis, at the eleventh hour, sawed a prototype in half along its length, widening the shell by 4 inches until, in the charming words of an official press release, 'proportion was propitiated and harmony satisfied.'

Basic trim

The Minor was deliberately sparsely equipped. Only the driver's door has a lock, for example, and the rear windows are fixed in position. Inside, the dashboard is plain painted metal.

Low-set headlights

In an age when many cars still had separate headlights, the faired-in, very low-set lights were a startling detail. They give the body a smooth, air-formed look. They were raised after 1950.

Specifications

1950 Morris Minor MM

ENGINE

Type: In-line four-cylinder

Construction: Cast-iron block and head

Valve gear: Two side-mounted valves per cylinder

Bore and stroke: 2.24 in. x 3.54 in.

Displacement: 918 cc

Compression ratio: 6.7:1

Induction system: Single SU carburetor

Maximum power: 28 bhp at 4,400 rpm

Maximum torque: 39 lb-ft at 2,400 rpm

Top speed: 62 mph

0-60 mph: 52.0 sec.

TRANSMISSION

Four-speed manual

BODY/CHASSIS

Unitary monocoque construction with steel two-door sedan body

SPECIAL FEATURES

Trafficators, as they were called, were fitted on British cars, although the U.S market got flashing directional lights.

The split windshield reflects the era when curved glass was still a technical challenge to manufacture.

RUNNING GEAR

Steering: Rack-and-pinion

Front suspension: Wishbones with torsion bars and shock absorbers

Rear suspension: Live axle with semi-elliptic leaf springs and shock absorbers

Brakes: Drums (front and rear)

Wheels: Steel, 14-in. dia.

Tires: 5.00 x 14

DIMENSIONS

Length: 148.0 in.   **Width:** 61.0 in.

Height: 57.0in.   **Wheelbase:** 86.0 in.

Track: 50.5 in. (front), 50.5 in. (rear)

Weight: 1,745 lbs.

NASH-HEALEY

Before Donald Healey forged his alliance with Austin to form Austin-Healey, he worked with the Nash company here in the U.S. Using Nash mechanical components, Healey built this interesting sports car for the U.S. market.

"...feeling of control."

"Compared to other cars of the day, the Nash-Healey was a revelation. Even today, its qualities shine through. The car was widely praised for its handling and especially its ride, which is extraordinarily good for a sports car. Thanks to Healey's input, it handles well with a great feeling of control, and it's certainly fast enough to be called a sports car. In truth, though, it was built more for the boulevard than the race track."

The large-diameter steering wheel dominates the simple fascia.

Milestones

1949 Nash-Kelvinator president George Mason and Donald Healey meet on board the Queen Elizabeth liner and find common ground to build a Nash-Healey sports car.

1950 A prototype is shown and a racer takes ninth place at the Mille Miglia and fourth at Le Mans.

Pinin Farina was commissioned for the 1952 restyle.

1951 The Nash-Healey is launched in the U.S. at the Chicago Auto Show and is sold through Nash dealers.

The Nash-Healey had some success in racing.

1952 Pinin Farina restyles the roadster and builds the bodywork.

1954 Production ends after 506 cars have been built.

UNDER THE SKIN

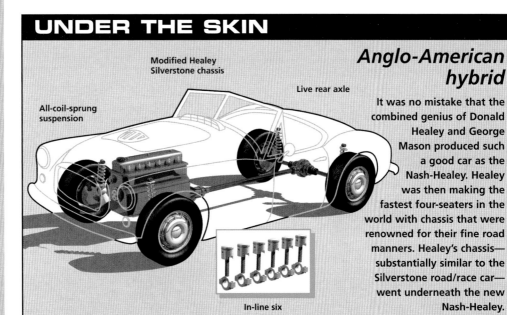

Modified Healey Silverstone chassis

Live rear axle

All-coil-sprung suspension

In-line six

Anglo-American hybrid

It was no mistake that the combined genius of Donald Healey and George Mason produced such a good car as the Nash-Healey. Healey was then making the fastest four-seaters in the world with chassis that were renowned for their fine road manners. Healey's chassis— substantially similar to the Silverstone road/race car— went underneath the new Nash-Healey.

THE POWER PACK

Dual Jetfire power

The Nash-Healey uses as many Nash mechanical components as possible, including the engine. The so-called Dual Jetfire straight six with a capacity of 3,848 cc came from the Ambassador. It is uprated with an aluminum cylinder head, hotter camshaft, higher compression ratio and twin SU carburetors. In 1952, a larger version of the engine arrived. With a still higher compression ratio and twin Carter carburetors in place of SUs, the new engine had 10 extra horsepower.

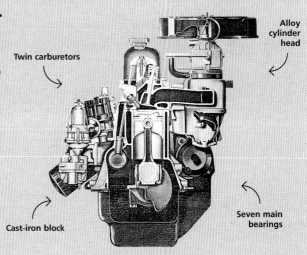

Twin carburetors

Alloy cylinder head

Cast-iron block

Seven main bearings

'Farina' Nash

The original Nash-Healey had rather slab-sided bodywork by Healey and only 104 were made before a restyled version appeared with bodywork by Pinin Farina. This is by far the more handsome car and has the more powerful 135-bhp engine.

The Farina-styled, Nash-Healey is seen by many as the best-looking version.

NASH-HEALEY

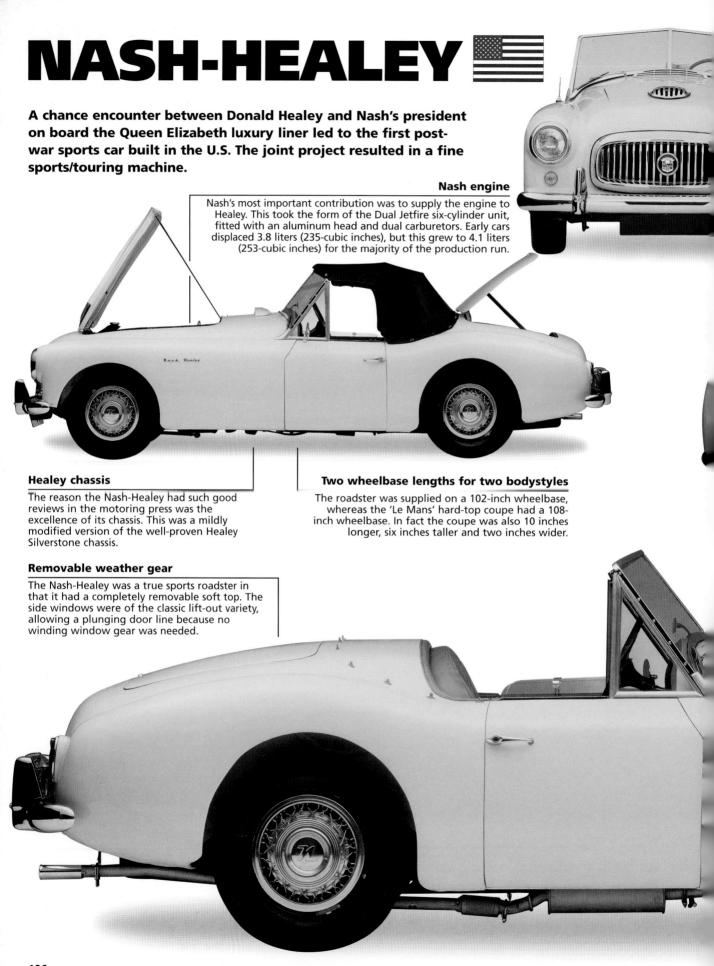

A chance encounter between Donald Healey and Nash's president on board the Queen Elizabeth luxury liner led to the first post-war sports car built in the U.S. The joint project resulted in a fine sports/touring machine.

Nash engine

Nash's most important contribution was to supply the engine to Healey. This took the form of the Dual Jetfire six-cylinder unit, fitted with an aluminum head and dual carburetors. Early cars displaced 3.8 liters (235-cubic inches), but this grew to 4.1 liters (253-cubic inches) for the majority of the production run.

Healey chassis

The reason the Nash-Healey had such good reviews in the motoring press was the excellence of its chassis. This was a mildly modified version of the well-proven Healey Silverstone chassis.

Two wheelbase lengths for two bodystyles

The roadster was supplied on a 102-inch wheelbase, whereas the 'Le Mans' hard-top coupe had a 108-inch wheelbase. In fact the coupe was also 10 inches longer, six inches taller and two inches wider.

Removable weather gear

The Nash-Healey was a true sports roadster in that it had a completely removable soft top. The side windows were of the classic lift-out variety, allowing a plunging door line because no winding window gear was needed.

196

Three-seater cabin

The original Healey-designed body was wide enough for the company to advertise that there was seating for three. The later Pinin Farina body could fit only two passengers.

Simple grill

The grill adorning the original Healey-designed body was a lot fussier than the later and simpler two-bar grill of the Farina-designed car.

Pinin Farina styling

Replacing the Healey body shown here was a very smart new open body by Italian stylist Pinin Farina. This was only natural since Farina was already restyling the regular Nash lineup. The new shape had a leaner, crisper fender line and hood, with swept-up fins at the rear, typical of the Italian design house.

Specifications

1951 Nash-Healey

ENGINE

Type: In-line six-cylinder

Construction: Cast-iron cylinder block and aluminum head

Valve gear: Two valves per cylinder operated by single camshaft via pushrods and rockers

Bore and stroke: 3.37 in. x 4.37 in.

Displacement: 3,848 cc

Compression ratio: 8.0:1

Induction system: Two Carter carburetors

Maximum power: 125 bhp at 4,000 rpm

Maximum torque: 215 lb-ft at 2,500 rpm

Top speed: 105 mph

0-60 mph: 11.5 sec.

TRANSMISSION

Three-speed manual with dual overdrive

BODY/CHASSIS

Separate chassis with steel two-door coupe or roadster body

SPECIAL FEATURES

The bulky chromed hubcaps feature a fake wire wheel pattern.

The 'toothy' Healey-designed grill was less successful than the later Pinin Farina-designed front end.

RUNNING GEAR

Steering: Walking beam

Front suspension: Trailing link with coil springs, telescopic shock absorbers and anti-roll bar

Rear suspension: Live axle with coil springs, track bar and telescopic shock absorbers

Brakes: Drums, (front and rear)

Wheels: Steel, 15-in. dia.

Tires: 6.40 x 15

DIMENSIONS

Length: 170.8 in.   **Width:** 64.0 in.

Height: 48.7 in.   **Wheelbase:** 102.0 in.

Track: 53.0 in. (front), 54.9 in. (rear)

Weight: 2,690 lbs.

Oldsmobile 88

Compared to rival designs, the 1954-1956 Oldsmobile 88, with its relatively clean lines and panoramic front and rear windows, is one of the most attractive cars of its period.

"...as fast as a modern sedan."

"When you climb inside a car that is well over 40 years old, the last thing you expect is high performance. But, thanks to its J-2 Rocket powerplant with 312 bhp, the Oldsmobile 88 flies along. Despite its size and weight, the 88 can accelerate as fast as a modern-day performance sedan and has all the torque you'd expect from a classic V8 engine. Lowering the suspension all around has certainly helped to reduce body roll around the bends."

Base model 88s were fairly glitzy inside and two-tone was the order of the day.

Milestones

1954 New 88 series launched on a 122-inch wheelbase in standard and Super 88 forms. A number of body styles are available: two and four-door sedan, Holiday two-door hardtop coupe and convertible.

The convertible body style was available from the start.

1955 A substantial facelift for 1955 introduces bold oval grill and extra two-tone paintwork options. A new two-door Holiday hardtop sedan joins the range.

By the end of the 1950s, the Oldsmobile range had much crisper styling.

1956 Another styling update adds 'gaping mouth' front grill and different shaped chrome side accents on the body.

1957 New Golden Rocket models replace the existing line-up.

UNDER THE SKIN

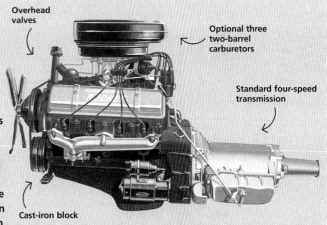

All-steel body

371-cubic inch V8 engine

Separate chassis

J-2 Rocket V8

Low technology from Lansing

The 88 series is typical for its era, boasting a coil-sprung front and leaf-sprung rear suspension with four-wheel drum brakes. Compared to the 1949-1953 88s, the 1954-1956 88 series has a longer (122-inch) wheelbase and a larger (324-cubic inch) engine. The owner of this car has fitted a 1937 La Salle three-speed transmission, although the car was originally delivered from the factory with a four-speed manual.

THE POWER PACK

More power for the infamous 'Rocket'

Based on the familiar Olds Rocket V8, the 1954 engine was bored out to 324-cubic inches and could develop between 170 and 185 bhp. This was increased to 185-202 bhp in 1955 and 230-240 bhp in 1956. The owner of this 88 has installed a 1957 371-cubic inch J-2 engine which, with its three two-barrel carburetor induction system, can produce more than 300 bhp in stock form.

Overhead valves

Optional three two-barrel carburetors

Standard four-speed transmission

Cast-iron block

Open air

The most desirable of the 1954-1956 Oldsmobiles is the convertible. It has all the luxury and style of the sedans and hardtops, but gives the added benefit of wind-in-the-hair driving. Between 1954 and 1956, Olds built nearly 50,000 convertibles.

Classic 1950s style and a convertible top combine to make a great cruising car.

Oldsmobile 88

Between 1954 and 1957, Oldsmobile set a new production record, manufacturing some 583,000 cars in 1955 alone. Here's an example of a modified 1956.

Pre-war transmission

The owner has opted to fit a vintage-style transmission from a 1937 La Salle—a prewar 'junior' Cadillac.

J2 power

This car has been fitted with a 1957 371-cubic inch engine and features the J-2 option with three two-barrel carburetors. The engine has been tuned to deliver 312 bhp.

Lowered suspension

The suspension on this car has been lowered. At the front end, 1957 coil springs were added and cut, while lowering blocks have been mounted on the rear leaf springs.

Chrome wheels

The full chrome 7 inch x 15 inch wheels are shod with Remington tires front and rear.

Hardtop coupe style

Undoubtedly the most elegant of all the Oldsmobile 88 body variations, the Holiday hardtop coupe was also the most popular.

Thunderbird paint

Coating the body in 1990 Thunderbird Bright Red enamel paint produces a strikingly different effect and is well suited to the handsome lines on this 1956 88.

Wraparound windows

For its time, the 88 was a styling sensation, featuring sleek lines and fully wraparound glass both front and rear. The so-called Panoramic wraparound treatment was pioneered by the 1953 Oldsmobile Ninety-Eight Fiesta.

Specifications
1956 Oldsmobile 88 Holiday hardtop coupe

ENGINE

Type: V8

Construction: Cast-iron cylinder block and cylinder heads

Valve gear: Two valves per cylinder operated by single camshaft via pushrods and rockers

Bore and stroke: 4.0 in. x 3.69 in.

Displacement: 371 c.i.

Compression ratio: 8.4:1

Induction system: Three two-barrel carburetors

Maximum power: 312 bhp at 4,600 rpm

Maximum torque: 410 lb-ft at 2,800 rpm

Top speed: 121 mph

0-60 mph: 8.7 sec.

TRANSMISSION

1937 La Salle three-speed manual

BODY/CHASSIS

Steel chassis with two-door hardtop coupe body

SPECIAL FEATURES

The grill of the 1956 Oldsmobile was unique to that year, with a big divider and horizontal bars.

Outer space was a popular theme among stylists in the 1950s which is evident on this 88's taillights.

RUNNING GEAR

Steering: Recirculating ball

Front suspension: Independent with coil springs

Rear suspension: Live axle with semi-elliptic leaf springs

Brakes: Drums, front and rear

Wheels: Pressed steel, 15-in. dia.

Tires: Remington G-78 (front), L-78 (rear)

DIMENSIONS

Length: 203.4 in.

Width: 77 in.

Height: 60 in.

Wheelbase: 122 in.

Track: 59 in. (front), 58 in. (rear)

Curb weight: 3,771 lbs.

Plymouth FURY

Plymouth was once America's number three make, and in the golden years of the late 1950s, the name was carried by cars such as the Fury—a high-performance luxury car with great styling.

"...great pulling power."

"A number of road testers described the Fury as having many of the qualities of a sports car, and they weren't dreaming. For a start, there's the engine. In 1958 Golden Commando guise, it has 305 bhp and is capable of clean and very quick takeoffs. There's great pulling power from just above idle, too. Combined with the superbly smooth-acting, if slightly heavy, TorqueFlite automatic transmission, this was one of the best drives in Detroit."

Classic 1950s style, notably the full-width front bench, defines the Fury's cabin.

Milestones

1956 The Fury name is first used on a Plymouth.

1957 As the range-topping model in the stunning new 1957 lineup, the Fury hardtop coupe gives buyers the luxury of performance and style in equal measure.

1957 was the first year torsion bars were used on the Fury.

1958 A mild facelift includes quad headlights, a revised grill and new taillights. A new Golden Commando V8 is offered with optional fuel injection. The Fury is also offered as a sedan.

Dodge's version of the Fury was the D500.

1959 A controversial restyle extends the tailfins and adds bigger bumpers.

1960 All-new unibody Plymouths replace the old lineup.

UNDER THE SKIN

Low and lean

Deserving its reputation for being Detroit's best-handling car in 1957, the Plymouth Fury relied on a relatively low center of gravity. All 1957-1959 Plymouths retained the old separate chassis layout. Plymouth switched to a more modern 'Torsion Air Ride' longitudinal torsion-bar front suspension, which was quite adventurous for Detroit in 1957.

Separate chassis

Longitudinal torsion-bar front suspension

Live rear axle

Cast-iron V8

One year only 350

The Fury was always fitted with the biggest and most powerful engine in Plymouth's powerplant armory—the name chosen to describe these big V8s was 'wedgehead.' For 1957, there was an all-new range of engines at Plymouth and the Fury got a unique, optional new 318-cubic inch V8 with 290 bhp on tap. The following year, the engine size and output remained the same, but the big news was the optional availability of a larger 350-cubic inch Golden Commando unit with 305 bhp. Even more desirable, but ultra-rare because of the high sticker price, was fuel injection, which added an extra 10 bhp.

THE POWER PACK

Class of '58

While the 1957 Fury is undoubtedly the most cleanly styled of the 1957-1959 models, the most desirable model in collector terms is the rarer 1958 car. It came with the option of a more powerful engine. A few models came with fuel injection.

The 1958 model is the most sought after, but examples are ultra rare.

Plymouth FURY

Living up to its name, the Fury was a full-size coupe that could outperform and outhandle many contemporary sports cars. This was due to fairly advanced engineering by 1957 Detroit standards.

Torsion-bar front suspension

The Fury was available with a suspension unlike GM's or Ford's. Torsion-bar springing was first applied to the 1957 DeSoto. This 1958 Fury uses the same system.

Golden Commando power

While the Fury stopped short of the one-horsepower-per-cubic-inch claim of its DeSoto and Chrysler stablemates, it was not far off. For 1958, the 350-cubic inch motor pumped out 305 bhp or, with fuel injection, 315 bhp.

Long, low and lean

The long, wide stance of the Fury is not just due to style. It significantly lowers the center of gravity, making the Fury one of the best-handling cars of its day.

Slimline roofline

The arching shape of the coupe roofline is one of the best styling features. It enhances the sporty feel of the car and, together with the wraparound front and rear windows, contributes toward excellent all-around visibility.

Tailfins

1957 was the biggest year yet for tailfins, and Virgil Exner's contribution made the Fury one of the year's tailfin stars. Although they were claimed to add directional stability at speed, the real reason for their existence is, of course, cosmetic.

Specifications

1958 Plymouth Fury

ENGINE
Type: V8

Construction: Cast-iron block and heads

Valve gear: Two valves per cylinder operated via pushrods and rockers

Bore and stroke: 4.06 in. x 3.38 in.

Displacement: 350 c.i.

Compression ratio: 10.0:1

Induction system: Dual Carter carburetors

Maximum power: 305 bhp at 5,000 rpm

Maximum torque: 370 lb-ft at 3,600 rpm

Top speed: 122 mph

0-60 mph: 8.0 sec.

TRANSMISSION
Three-speed automatic

BODY/CHASSIS
Separate chassis with two-door coupe body

SPECIAL FEATURES

The 'V' emblem on the grill signifies that a V8 engine is fitted.

The quad-headlight treatment was new for the 1958 model year.

RUNNING GEAR
Steering: Rack-and-pinion

Front suspension: Independent by upper and lower wishbones with longitudinal torsion bars and shock absorbers

Rear suspension: Live axle with semi-elliptic leaf springs and shock absorbers

Brakes: Drums (front and rear)

Wheels: Steel, 14-in. dia.

Tires: 8.00 x 14

DIMENSIONS
Length: 206.0 in.   **Width:** 78.0 in.

Height: 57.0 in.   **Wheelbase:** 118.0 in.

Track: 60.9 in. (front), 59.6 in. (rear)

Weight: 3,510 lbs.

Pontiac CHIEFTAIN

In the immediate post-war years, buyers were hungry for new cars. The straight-eight Chieftain helped GM's sole surviving companion marque achieve more than 300,000 sales during the 1949 model year.

"...smooth riding cruiser."

"With only 104 bhp from its straight-eight and weighing over 3,500 lbs., the Chieftain is definitely not a sports car. What it is, though, is a smooth-riding cruiser. Soft spring settings help smooth out the bumps without causing wallowing under normal driving conditions. Attempting high-speed cornering results in extreme body lean and the narrow tires squeal under the weight. For relaxing summer drives, this Poncho is hard to beat."

Column-mounted shifters were almost universal in most cars by 1949.

Milestones

1949 Replacing the Torpedo
line is the Chieftain. Beneath the new styling is the venerable straight-six or eight and 'Knee-Action' front suspension. Front fenders are now integrated with the body.

Only a mild facelift was made for its sophomore year in 1950.

1950 The Chieftain line is
expanded with the addition of a Super Deluxe Catalina two-door hardtop. The straight-eight's displacement is enlarged to 268.4 cubic inches and power is up to 108 bhp.

The 1953 Pontiac is longer and now has power steering.

1952 The Business Sedan and Coupes
are dropped. Korean war restrictions and a steel strike limit Pontiac's output to 271,000 units.

1953 One piece windshields
and power steering are fitted.

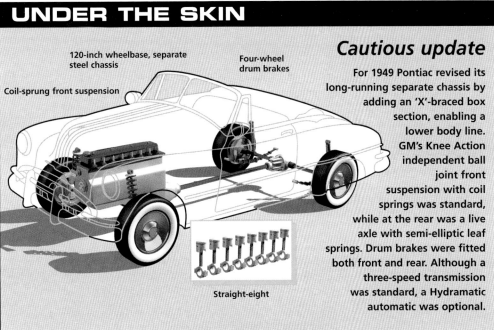

120-inch wheelbase, separate steel chassis

Coil-sprung front suspension

Four-wheel drum brakes

Straight-eight

Cautious update

For 1949 Pontiac revised its long-running separate chassis by adding an 'X'-braced box section, enabling a lower body line. GM's Knee Action independent ball joint front suspension with coil springs was standard, while at the rear was a live axle with semi-elliptic leaf springs. Drum brakes were fitted both front and rear. Although a three-speed transmission was standard, a Hydramatic automatic was optional.

THE POWER PACK

Veteran eight

Designed by Benjamin Anibal, Pontiac's straight-eight engine made its debut in 1933. By 1949 it was still powering Pontiacs, though by this stage it had been enlarged to 248.9 cubic inches. An all-cast-iron design, it was typical of L-head engines with side-valve lay-out that resulted in offset combustion chambers. The use of a long-stroke crankshaft produced 188 lb-ft of torque at 2,000 rpm. The basic engine remained in production until 1954, by which time it had 127 bhp.

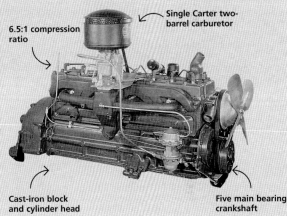

6.5:1 compression ratio

Single Carter two-barrel carburetor

Cast-iron block and cylinder head

Five main bearing crankshaft

Deluxe

For 1949 all Pontiacs got a single A-body chassis and were both longer and lower. The most expensive of all was the Deluxe Chieftain Eight convertible. The basic design continued through 1954. Today, good examples sell for serious money.

A pristine Deluxe convertible is worth up to $30,000 today.

207

Pontiac CHIEFTAIN

It took until 1949 before Pontiac offered its first new post-war cars. Longer, lower and wider than pre-war models, with cleaner, more integrated styling, they were also offered with more luxury features.

Side-valve, in-line eight

Although rival Oldsmobile® got a V8 for 1949, Pontiac stuck with its tried and tested L-head six and eight engines. Steady improvement, however, saw the power increase every year during the early 1950s as the horsepower race intensified. In 1949, it put out 104/106 bhp, but by 1954 it was up to 127.

Whitewall tires

Classy whitewall tires became increasingly popular on medium-priced cars during the 1940s. In 1952, due to the conflict in Korea, supplies of whitewalls were restricted along with supplies of copper, used on bumpers and chrome trim.

Power convertible top

Deluxe Chieftain convertibles came with a mohair-lined, power-operated top and a small glass rear window. Plexiglas windows did not become popular until the late 1950s.

Sealed beam headlights

GM had pioneered sealed beam lights in the late 1930s and these were still standard for 1949. Three years later, the famous Autotronic Eye arrived. This system dimmed the headlights automatically at oncoming traffic.

Drum brakes

Drum brakes were the industry standard in 1949. The Chieftain's were hydraulically operated and could stop the car in just over over 200 feet from 60 mph—more than adequate by contemporary standards.

Specifications

1950 Pontiac Chieftain

ENGINE

Type: In-line eight-cylinder

Construction: Cast-iron block and head

Valve gear: Two side-mounted valves per cylinder driven by a single, block-mounted camshaft with solid lifters

Bore and stroke: 3.25 in. x 3.75 in.

Displacement: 248.9 c.i.

Compression ratio: 6.5:1

Induction system: Single Carter WCD two-barrel carburetor

Maximum power: 104 bhp at 3,800 rpm

Maximum torque: 188 lb-ft at 2,000 rpm

Top speed: 86 mph

0-60 mph: 19.0 sec.

TRANSMISSION

Four-speed Hydramatic automatic

BODY/CHASSIS

Separate steel chassis with two-door convertible body

SPECIAL FEATURES

The Pontiac Indian Chief hood ornament illuminates when the headlights come on.

Rear fender skirts were dealer-installed options in 1949.

RUNNING GEAR

Steering: Worm-and-sector

Front suspension: Double wishbones with coil springs and telescopic shock absorbers

Rear suspension: Live axle with semi-elliptic leaf springs and telescopic shock absorbers

Brakes: Drums (front and rear)

Wheels: Stamped steel, 15-in. dia.

Tires: 7.10 x 15

DIMENSIONS

Length: 202.5 in. **Width:** 75.8 in.

Height: 63.3 in. **Wheelbase:** 120.0 in.

Track: 58.0 in. (front), 59.0 in. (rear)

Weight: 3,670 lbs.

Pontiac BONNEVILLE

Traditionally, Pontiacs were reliable, dependable cars that suffered from a lackluster image. By 1959, the image started to change with the announcement of a new crop of lower, sleeker, full-size cars boasting up to 345 bhp and with a 'Wide Track' ride.

"...fast, relaxed cruising."

"The driving position is much lower than previous Ponchos and the visibility is better. Tractable in traffic, with incredible lower-end power, the V8 is also capable of blasting you to 60 mph in around 8 seconds. Although it boasts a wider track suspension, the car still has a tendency to pitch and wallow over uneven surfaces. Dive under hard braking is quite pronounced, too. However, for fast, relaxed cruising, a 1959 Bonneville is tough to beat."

The jazzy interior has a full-width bench seat upholstered in three different shades of vinyl.

Milestones

1957 A limited production convertible joins the Pontiac lineup. Named Bonneville, after the famous salt flats, it has a fuel injected, 310-bhp V8 engine. Only 630 models were sold.

Bonneville got a shorter, narrower body for 1961.

1958 The Bonneville becomes a full series on bigger, redesigned Pontiacs. It shares the 122-inch wheelbase with the Chieftain and is offered in hardtop and convertible form.

Even today, the Bonneville maintains a dash of sportiness.

1959 Pontiacs are restyled with a longer, lower body. The Bonneville range is expanded to include a four-door Safari™ Wagon, Sport Coupe and Vista hardtop sedan.

1960 Minor changes include new grill and taillights and a slightly altered interior.

UNDER THE SKIN

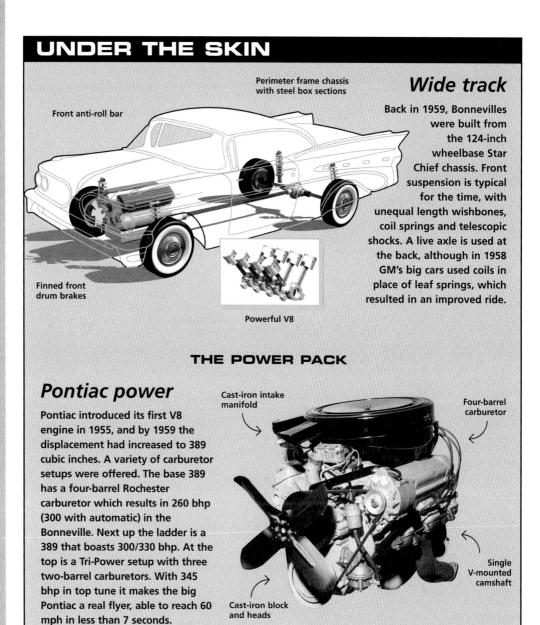

Front anti-roll bar

Perimeter frame chassis with steel box sections

Finned front drum brakes

Powerful V8

Wide track

Back in 1959, Bonnevilles were built from the 124-inch wheelbase Star Chief chassis. Front suspension is typical for the time, with unequal length wishbones, coil springs and telescopic shocks. A live axle is used at the back, although in 1958 GM's big cars used coils in place of leaf springs, which resulted in an improved ride.

THE POWER PACK

Pontiac power

Pontiac introduced its first V8 engine in 1955, and by 1959 the displacement had increased to 389 cubic inches. A variety of carburetor setups were offered. The base 389 has a four-barrel Rochester carburetor which results in 260 bhp (300 with automatic) in the Bonneville. Next up the ladder is a 389 that boasts 300/330 bhp. At the top is a Tri-Power setup with three two-barrel carburetors. With 345 bhp in top tune it makes the big Pontiac a real flyer, able to reach 60 mph in less than 7 seconds.

Cast-iron intake manifold

Four-barrel carburetor

Single V-mounted camshaft

Cast-iron block and heads

True classic

The 1959 Pontiac is one of the most attractive-looking cars of the glitzy 1950s. The most desirable are the Bonneville Sport coupe and convertible. Cars fitted with a 345-bhp Tri-Power V8 and a manual transmission have truly classic status.

The Sport Coupe is perhaps the best-looking 1959 Bonneville.

Pontiac BONNEVILLE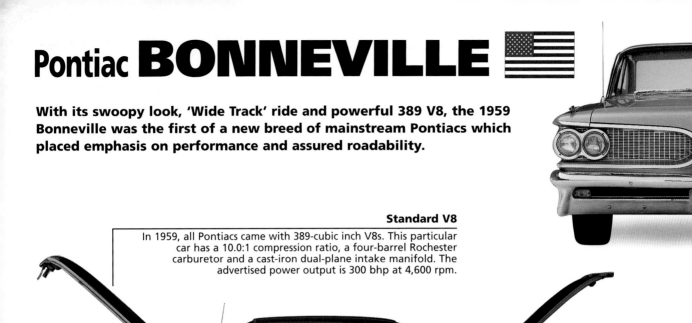

With its swoopy look, 'Wide Track' ride and powerful 389 V8, the 1959 Bonneville was the first of a new breed of mainstream Pontiacs which placed emphasis on performance and assured roadability.

Standard V8

In 1959, all Pontiacs came with 389-cubic inch V8s. This particular car has a 10.0:1 compression ratio, a four-barrel Rochester carburetor and a cast-iron dual-plane intake manifold. The advertised power output is 300 bhp at 4,600 rpm.

Wide Track

A big selling point in 1959 was the 'Wide Track' ride, which was claimed to improve handling and stability at speed. Compared to other big cars of the era, Pontiacs do feel more confident on the road.

Optional rear gearing

A variety of rear axle ratios were offered starting with a tall 3.08:1 for high-speed cruising and maximum fuel economy, through 3.23:1 and 3.64:1, and up to strip-storming 3.90:1 and 4.10:1 ratios. The last two were dealer installed.

Hardtop styling

The Bonneville Custom was the top-of-the-line series in 1959 and three different versions were available: four-door Vista hardtop, two-door Sport coupe and convertible. The sedan was by far the most popular, with 38,696 built. The hardtop coupe, seen here, was second, with 27,769 sold.

Split grill

1959 was a milestone year. It marked the first appearance of the familiar split grill. Although this feature was absent on the 1960 models, it reappeared the following year and has been a trademark of all Pontiacs since.

Smaller wheels and tires

To make the 1959 models appear even lower and longer, Pontiac switched to 14-inch wheels and tires.

Convenience items

Options available in 1959 included air-conditioning ($355), tinted glass ($35), electric antenna ($20) and a Sportable radio ($104) with a Motorola Reverbaround speaker positioned in the center of the rear seat.

Specifications

1959 Pontiac Bonneville

ENGINE

Type: V8

Construction: Cast-iron block and heads

Valve gear: Two valves per cylinder operated by a single camshaft with pushrods and rockers

Bore and stroke: 4.06 in. x 3.75 in.

Displacement: 389 c.i.

Compression ratio: 10.0:1

Induction system: Rochester four-barrel carburetor

Maximum power: 300 bhp at 4,600 rpm

Maximum torque: 450 lb-ft at 2,800 rpm

Top speed: 120 mph

0-60 mph: 8.1 sec.

TRANSMISSION

TurboHydramatic three-speed automatic

BODY/CHASSIS

Steel perimeter frame with separate hardtop two-door coupe body

SPECIAL FEATURES

Unusually, the reverse lights were mounted at the ends of the fins.

The Bonneville has optional fender skirts which are easily removed.

RUNNING GEAR

Steering: Recirculating ball

Front suspension: Unequal-length wishbones with coil springs, telescopic shock absorbers and anti-roll bar

Rear suspension: Live axle with coil springs and telescopic shock absorbers

Brakes: Drums **Tires:** 145/70 R14

Wheels: Steel disc, 7.0 x 15 in.

DIMENSIONS

Length: 220.7 in. **Width:** 75.4 in.

Height: 51.4 in. **Wheelbase:** 124.0 in.

Track: 63.7 in. (front), 64.0 in. (rear)

Weight: 4,233 lbs.

Porsche 356

Although Porsche had designed several vehicles for other manufacturers, the 356 was the first car to be built with a Porsche badge. It was Volkswagen Beetle-based and was an outstanding sports and racing car.

"...can be pushed hard."

"With its eager, smooth and free-revving engine, the 356 is a car that begs to be driven hard. Even in normal driving, the engine sees 5,000 rpm frequently. The flat-four is very flexible and will pull evenly, if not vigorously, from very low speeds in third and top gears. Lift-off oversteer on the later cars was quickly remedied, so even unskilled drivers can push the 356 on twisty roads with the power on to make the most of the traction."

With more embellishments than earlier examples, the 356B is still a real joy to drive.

Milestones

1947 Ferry Porsche starts work on the first Porsche-badged car—the 356.

1948 The prototype hits the road. It uses a mid-mounted VW engine.

The Porsche 356C was also available in a much sought-after convertible form.

1949 The Type 356 makes its motor show debut at Geneva in the spring.

The more sophisticated 911 followed in the 356's footsteps.

1951 A 356 wins its class at Le Mans.

1955 The updated 356A is introduced with Speedster and Carrera variants.

1959 The new 356B has a facelifted body and more powerful engines.

1963 The final 356C is launched. It is replaced by the 911 in 1965.

UNDER THE SKIN

Beetle-based

Like the Beetle, the 356 has a platform chassis, with a trailing arm and torsion bar front suspension and swing axles and torsion bars at the rear. Drum brakes front and rear are standard, although discs arrived on the 356C in 1963. This model also introduced ZF worm-and-peg steering.

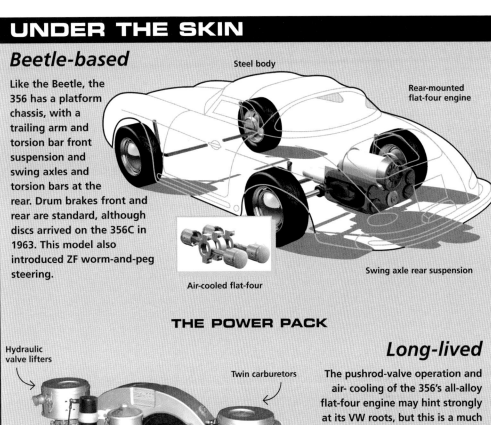

Steel body

Rear-mounted flat-four engine

Air-cooled flat-four

Swing axle rear suspension

THE POWER PACK

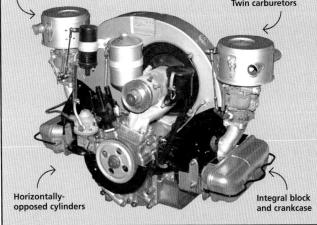

Hydraulic valve lifters

Twin carburetors

Horizontally-opposed cylinders

Integral block and crankcase

Long-lived

The pushrod-valve operation and air-cooling of the 356's all-alloy flat-four engine may hint strongly at its VW roots, but this is a much more sophisticated unit. Power rose from just 40 bhp in the early cars to 95 bhp in the final 356C 1600SC model, and the unit lived on in the entry-level 911-bodied Porsche—the 912. The ultimate engine, however, is the Carrera unit with twin overhead camshafts per cylinder bank. In 2.0-liter form it could take the 356 to 125 mph.

Speedster

Probably the most recognized of all Porsche 356 variants is the Speedster. First introduced in 1954, it was designed as a no-frills convertible. It was a slow seller, therefore not too many were built. This makes it highly desirable today.

During its four year production run, the Speedster hardly changed.

215

Porsche **356**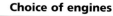

From its introduction in 1948, the 356 was improved annually. It matured from a crude little tourer to a sophisticated and competitive sports car.

Karmann-built bodywork

This car has the rare Karmann Hardtop bodywork. Introduced for the 1961 model year, it was built for only one year. It is basically a cabriolet with a welded-on hard top.

Choice of engines

The air-cooled flat-four engine comes in 1,100-, 1,300-, 1,500- and 1,600-cc versions and produces between 40 and 95 bhp in pushrod form. The quad-cam Carrera unit is highly specialized and is developed from racing practice.

Beetle-derived suspension

Although derived from the Volkswagen Beetle, the swing axle rear suspension has few components in common, particularly on later cars. Springing is by torsion bars with telescopic shock absorbers.

Worm and peg

[Th]e worm-and-peg steering was a [V]W item, and was improved by a [st]eering damper from the type A onward. On the 365C a ZF steering box was used.

[S]ynchromesh transmission

[E]arly cars have 'crash' non-synchromesh [tr]ansmissions, but a full synchro [tr]ansmission on later cars is noted for [it]s precision and 'engineered' feel [d]espite its lengthy linkage.

Drum brakes all around

Twin leading shoe hydraulic brakes are found on all 356s up until the C model of 1963, which features four-wheel discs.

Specifications

1959 Porsche 356B 1600S

ENGINE
Type: Flat-four
Construction: Alloy block and heads
Valve gear: Two valves per cylinder operated by a single camshaft via pushrods and rockers
Bore and stroke: 3.25 in. x 2.91 in.
Displacement: 1,582 cc
Compression ratio: 8.5:1
Induction system: Two Zenith carburetors
Maximum power: 75 bhp at 5,000 rpm
Maximum torque: 85 lb-ft at 3,700 rpm
Top speed: 103 mph
0-60 mph 13.0 sec.

TRANSMISSION
Four-speed manual

BODY/CHASSIS
Steel platform chassis with steel Karmann bodywork and welded-on hard top

SPECIAL FEATURES

These sport mirrors are most often seen on later 356B and C models.

By 1965, amber rear turn signals were fitted on European-specification cars.

RUNNING GEAR
Steering: Worm-and-peg
Front suspension: Torsion bars with trailing arms, telescopic shock absorbers and anti-roll bar
Rear suspension: Swing axles with torsion bars and telescopic shock absorbers
Brakes: Hydraulic drums (front and rear)
Wheels: Steel discs, 4.50 x 15 in.
Tires: Radials, 165 x 15

DIMENSIONS
Length: 155.5 in.   **Width:** 65.7 in.
Height: 50.7 in.   **Wheelbase:** 82.6 in.
Track: 51.5 in. (front and rear)
Weight: 2,059 lbs.

FRANCE 1956-1968

Renault DAUPHINE

**This was the car that Renault hoped would take the U.S. by storm.
However, despite a huge amount of pre-production testing, the small,
rear-engine car with its tiny 845-cc motor was just too fragile to last.**

"...enormous charm."

*"Forget the lack of performance, because this car has
enormous charm despite idiosyncrasies such as the
lackadaisical shifter and uninspiring driving feel. The steering
is light and direct and the small rear-mounted engine is
surprisingly smooth. Even with the rear-heavy weight distribution and crude swing axles, it doesn't suffer oversteer, and it
stays comfortable even over long distances."*

**The blend of metal and plastic is typical
of Renault cars of this era.**

Milestones

1952 Renault produces the first prototype Dauphines. They cover more than two million miles of rigorous testing before production gets underway.

The 4CV was Renault's first rear-engined, post-war car.

1956 The first Dauphines start to roll off the production line. Initial sales are strong in the U.S. where it competes against the VW Beetle.

The larger Caravelle used the same rear-engine layout.

1957 Independent Renault tuning expert Amedée Gordini improves the Dauphine's cylinder head and increases power to 38 bhp. The conversion is adopted by Renault, which produces it itself.

1968 After more than 2 million cars have been built, production of the Dauphine ends.

Nice and light

The Dauphine needed to be as light as possible given its low power output, so an advanced unitary-construction steel shell was used. Additional front and rear subframes were fitted to carry the suspension and rear-mounted engine. The front suspension is a double-wishbone setup and the rear consists of swing axles on either side of the three-speed transmission and final drive. Drum brakes are used.

Double-wishbone front suspension

Rear-mounted engine

Drum brakes front and rear

Inline four

THE POWER PACK

Detuned small engine

An inline, four-cylinder wet-liner engine is used in the Dauphine. Its cast-iron liners run in a cast-iron block instead of an alloy one like modern wet-liner engines. Topping off the block is a non-crossflow alloy head with two inline valves per cylinder actuated by a single block-mounted camshaft. The engine has a very long stroke and is detuned in standard form with just 30 bhp from its 845 cc. This allowed tuners such as Gordini to make large increases in power output with relatively minor changes. The detuned engine is very economical, however.

Gordini power

The best of the production Dauphines is the Gordini. It features modified intake and exhaust ports, and a larger 32-mm carburetor instead of 28 mm. This increases power from 30 to 38 bhp and reduces the 0-60-mph time to 28.2 seconds.

The simple and functional Dauphine sold in massive numbers.

Renault **DAUPHINE**

One of the Dauphine's greatest strengths was its style. Nothing in its class could match its smart, rounded and aerodynamic appearance. Despite problems with build quality, it reestablished the Renault name.

Sliding side windows

Although the front windows wind up and down in the usual way, the rear side windows are of the simpler sliding type to keep manufacturing costs down

Four-cylinder engine

In standard form, the 845-cc four-cylinder engine was in a deliberately low state of tune to ensure a long and reliable life. There was much more torque than power from the long-stroke engine.

Supercharged option

Many Dauphines were sold in the U.S. As an option, the Judson Research and Manufacturing Co. of Conshokocken, England offered a supercharger kit for just $165. It virtually halved the 0-60 time to 15.5 seconds.

Magnetic clutch

Dauphine drivers had the option of the Ferlec magnetic clutch to turn the car into a semi-automatic. When the shifter is moved, the magnetic system automatically comes into operation to disengage the clutch.

Wishbone front suspension

The front suspension was quite advanced, consisting of double wishbones with concentric springs and telescopic shocks. It is mounted on a subframe bolted to the body.

Rear radiator

So that the Dauphine could have trunk space under the front cover with decent capacity, the radiator is located in the rear, inside the engine bay.

Specifications

1957 Renault Dauphine

ENGINE

Type: Inline four-cylinder

Construction: Cast-iron block and alloy cylinder head

Valve gear: Two valves per cylinder operated by a single block-mounted camshaft with pushrods and rockers

Bore and stroke: 2.28 in. x 3.15 in.

Displacement: 845 cc

Compression ratio: 7.25:1

Induction system: Single Solex carburetor

Maximum power: 30 bhp at 4,200 rpm

Maximum torque: 48 lb-ft at 2,000 rpm

Top speed: 71 mph

0-60 mph: 31.6 sec.

TRANSMISSION

Three-speed manual

BODY/CHASSIS

Unitary monocoque construction with four door sedan body

SPECIAL FEATURES

The spare tire is carried under the front cover. Access is gained through a panel hidden under the license plate.

Air for the rear-mounted radiator enters through grills in front sections of the rear wheels.

RUNNING GEAR

Steering: Rack-and-pinion

Front suspension: Double wishbones with coil springs and telescopic shock absorbers

Rear suspension: Swing axles with coil springs and telescopic shock absorbers

Brakes: Drums, 8.9-in. dia. (front and rear)

Wheels: Pressed-steel disc, 15-in. dia.

Tires: 5.20 x 15

DIMENSIONS

Length: 155.0 in.   **Width:** 60.0 in.

Height: 57.0 in.   **Wheelbase:** 89.5 in.

Track: 49.5 in. (front), 48.0 in. (rear)

Weight: 1,360 lbs.

Riley **RM ROADSTER**

The combination of a twin-cam, four-cylinder engine, rack-and-pinion steering, and front A-arms produced a convertible with handling and performance that was hard to match in the 1940s.

"...relaxed, high-speed driving."

"With its heavy steering and stiff springs, the Riley has a vintage feel, but this is compensated by precise cornering and sharp handling from the stiff suspension. It has a hint of understeer and very little body roll, and roadholding is better than most of its competitors. The Riley's stability at speed and com-fortable leather-lined cabin make high-speed driving very relaxed, and there's surprisingly little buffeting from the wind with the top down."

The combination of leather and wood is a common feature in Rileys.

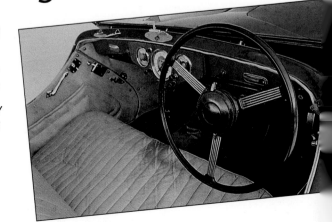

937 The 2.5-liter ngine that will power the gger Rileys throughout the 50s makes its debut.

ealey's Silverstone uses the me 2.5-liter engine as the RM.

948 Riley's new oadster appears. sentially, it is a pre-war design, beit one that had not made it to production before the war arted. Its appearance is odified to suit the U.S. market. has a bench seat and column earshift. The RMD convertible ppears at the London Motor ow but does not go into oduction until 1950.

e elegant but short-lived RMD a full four-seat convertible.

950 Production of e RMC ends after just er 500 are made and only 77 ld to the intended U.S. market.

951 After 200 cars re sold in the U.S., the MD is discontinued.

UNDER THE SKIN

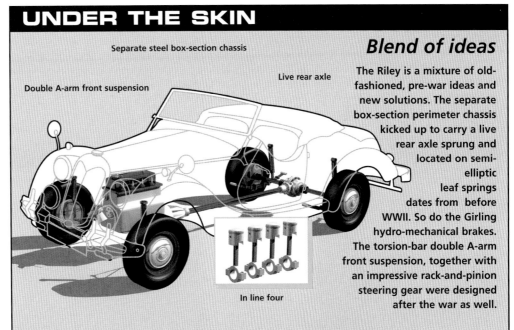

Separate steel box-section chassis

Double A-arm front suspension

Live rear axle

In line four

Blend of ideas

The Riley is a mixture of old-fashioned, pre-war ideas and new solutions. The separate box-section perimeter chassis kicked up to carry a live rear axle sprung and located on semi-elliptic leaf springs dates from before WWII. So do the Girling hydro-mechanical brakes. The torsion-bar double A-arm front suspension, together with an impressive rack-and-pinion steering gear were designed after the war as well.

THE POWER PACK

Novel design

Riley's engine design was novel and advanced for its time. Although the RM's 2.5-liter engine is big for a four-cylinder, and is all cast-iron, the valve gear and cylinder head are very cleverly designed. Two valves per cylinder are operated in hemispherical combustion chambers to give an efficient crossflow cylinder head design. The valves are opened by twin camshafts mounted high in the block rather than above the head that require very short pushrods to reach the rockers.

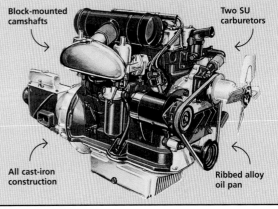

Block-mounted camshafts

Two SU carburetors

All cast-iron construction

Ribbed alloy oil pan

Classic style

The most flamboyant of the open Rileys from the 1940s is the RMC Roadster. It has a single bench seat, a column-mounted shifter, and the advantage that the top folds away completely under a cover. Because of its shape, it also has a big trunk.

The classic lines of the RMC Roadster make it a very desirable collector's car.

Riley **RM ROADSTER**

Designed by the company's own stylist, the 2.5-liter Riley looked its best as a four-door sedan, whereas the two-door RMC was designed to win buyers here in the U.S.

Twin-cam engine

Although the 2.5-liter four-cylinder is a twin-cam engine, its layout is designed simply to give a good combustion chamber shape, not high revs. The long-stroke design helps give an impressive amount of torque at only 3,000 rpm.

Rack-and-pinion steering

With its 1940s model, Riley became the first British manufacturer to go into production with a combination of double A-arm front suspension and rack-and-pinion steering, setting the standard for years to come.

Mohair hood

The Roadster was an expensive car, and Riley made sure the quality of the convertible top was high. There is no power operation, but the headliner is made from mohair and fully lined.

Drum brakes

The Riley's Girling hydro-mechanical brake system sounds antiquated, with just the front drums having hydraulic operation and a mechanical linkage for the rear drums. It works surprisingly well, though, because most of the braking force is taken by the front wheels.

V-shaped windshield

The RMC Roadster has a flat windshield because an integral part of that car's design was a windshield that folded flat. In theory, this would increase the car's top speed.

Wood-framed bodywork

Riley used very traditional methods for making their car bodies, relying on an ash wood frame over which steel panels could be fastened. It means the bodies play very little part in the overall structural stiffness of the cars.

Specifications

1950 Riley RMC Roadster

ENGINE
Type: In-line four-cylinder
Construction: Cast-iron block and head
Valve gear: Two valves per cylinder operated by two block-mounted camshafts with pushrods and rockers
Bore and stroke: 3.17 in. x 4.72 in.
Displacement: 2,443 cc
Compression ratio: 6.8:1
Induction system: Two SU carburetors
Maximum power: 100 bhp at 4,500 rpm
Maximum torque: 134 lb-ft at 3,000 rpm
Top speed: 98 mph
0-60 mph: 19.0 sec.

TRANSMISSION
Four-speed manual

BODY/CHASSIS
Separate steel box-section perimeter chassis frame with wood-framed steel body.

SPECIAL FEATURES

The unusual stalked rear lights make the rear of the RMC easily recognizable.

The distinctive sweep on the top of the grill is a feature of all Rileys.

RUNNING GEAR
Steering: Rack-and-pinion
Front suspension: Double A-arms with longitudinal torsion bars and telescopic shock absorbers
Rear suspension: Live axle with semi-elliptic leaf springs and hydraulic shock absorbers
Brakes: Drums, 12.0-inch dia. (front and rear)
Wheels: Pressed steel disc, 6 x 16 in.
Tires: Crossply, 6.00 x 16

DIMENSIONS
Length: 186.0 in.   **Width:** 63.5 in.
Height: 55.0 in.   **Wheelbase:** 119.0 in.
Track: 52.3 in. (front and rear)
Weight: 3,052 lbs.

Rolls-Royce SILVER CLOUD

Touted as 'the best car in the world,' the Silver Cloud is a pivotal model: the first to have its bodywork built by Rolls and the last to have a separate chassis. In terms of elegance and presence it has no peers.

"...fine, traditional values."

"Stepping into any Rolls-Royce is a special experience but to discover what these cars are really about, make it a Silver Cloud. The cabin is a haven of calm in a faddish world, a reminder of the traditional values of good taste and fine materials such as Connolly leather and wood veneer. The driving experience also comes from a different age: a fine ride and near-silent running. The steering may lack feel, but there's ample performance."

The Rolls' cabin is unequaled for elegance, luxury and fine quality workmanship.

Milestones

Milestones

1955 Rolls-Royce launches its replacement for the Silver Dawn, the elegant new Silver Cloud; sister company Bentley produces a near-identical S-type model.

1956 Power steering and air conditioning, become popular options.

The ultra-exclusive Phantom VI limousine is based on the Cloud.

1957 A long-wheelbase (127-inch) chassis is also offered, and the engine is uprated.

Replacing the Cloud for 1965 was the Silver Shadow sedan.

1959 A Silver Cloud arrives with a V8 engine.

1962 Silver Cloud III has double headlights and a more powerful V8 engine.

1965 The new Silver Shadow replaces the Silver Cloud.

UNDER THE SKIN

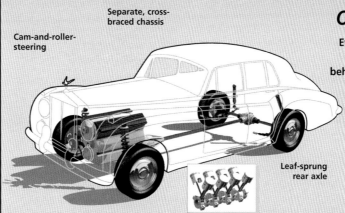

Separate, cross-braced chassis

Cam-and-roller-steering

Leaf-sprung rear axle

Modern V8

Out of the past

Even by the standards of 1955, Rolls-Royce was running way behind the pace of technological development. Its philosophy was a resolutely unhurried application of any new developments. The chassis is a separate cross-braced twin-rail device, in box sections, and is as robust as it is archaic. There is coil-sprung independent front suspension and a leaf-sprung rear axle with gaitered leaves.

THE POWER PACK

Six or eight cylinders

When the Silver Cloud was launched, it used an in-line six-cylinder engine, but with the arrival of the Silver Cloud II in 1959, Rolls-Royce stepped into the V8 age. It introduced an all-new, all-aluminum overhead-valve engine that owes much to General Motors designs. In those days, Rolls-Royce considered itself to be above publishing power outputs for its engines—it said they were merely 'adequate'—but a good estimate would be 220 bhp. The basic design survived for almost four decades, finally bowing out in 1998.

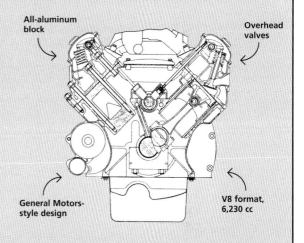

All-aluminum block

Overhead valves

General Motors-style design

V8 format, 6,230 cc

Exclusive

Given the improvements made, the Silver Cloud II is the best of the standard models. If you want exclusivity, track down one of the coachbuilt models: Mulliner's Drophead Coupe is particularly well favored, currently worth up to four times the value of a standard sedan.

The V8-engined Clouds are the best buys.

Rolls-Royce SILVER CLOUD

The Silver Cloud is regarded with great affection by Rolls-Royce enthusiasts because it is a 'true' Rolls and yet is surprisingly practical to own. It has stiff-upper-lip styling, but that is part of its appeal.

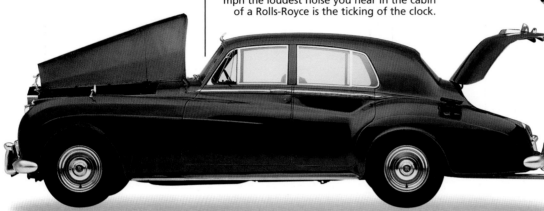

Loud clock

American advertising for the Silver Cloud picked up on an editorial comment that at 60 mph the loudest noise you hear in the cabin of a Rolls-Royce is the ticking of the clock.

Separate chassis

Apart from the phantom, which remained in ultra-limit production for royalty into the 1980s, the Silver Cloud is the last Rolls-Royce to feature a separate chassis.

GM automatic transmission

The four-speed automatic transmission used in the Silver Cloud is actually a General Motors design built under license in Britain.

Rear suspension control

The Silver Cloud retains a classic Rolls-Royce feature—a controller on the steering column that adjusts the rear shocks, changing the stiffness to suit driving conditions.

'Unified' bodywork

Unlike previous Rolls-Royces, with their coachbuilt bodies, the Silver Cloud was originally offered with a standard body design. The shell was built by Pressed Steel of Cowley near Oxford, a company that also built bodies for far humbler cars such as the Hillman Minx and Jaguar Mark VII.

Choice of wheelbase

The standard Silver Cloud has a 123-inch wheelbase but, from 1957 a long-wheelbase (127-inch) version was also offered. It has a division between the driver and rear passengers, an extra window above the rear wheel cutout and more legroom.

Optional air conditioning

Air conditioning became an option in 1956. The first system was a massive unit mounted in the trunk, but from 1959 a new system was used with most of the hardware in the passenger side wheel cutout.

Specifications

Rolls-Royce Silver Cloud II

ENGINE
Type: V8
Construction: Aluminum block and heads
Valve gear: Two valves per cylinder operated by a single camshaft via pushrods and rockers
Bore and stroke: 4.10 in. x 3.60 in.
Displacement: 6,230 cc
Compression ratio: 9.0:1
Induction system: Two SU carburetors
Maximum power: 220 bhp at 4,000 rpm
Maximum torque: 340 lb-ft at 2,200 rpm
Top speed: 112 mph
0-60 mph: 11.4 sec.

TRANSMISSION
Four-speed automatic

BODY/CHASSIS
Separate chassis with steel four-door sedan body

SPECIAL FEATURES

A very British feature is the large license plate light and trunk handle.

Single headlights were replaced by a more striking double design in 1962.

RUNNING GEAR
Steering: Cam-and-roller
Front suspension: Unequal-length wishbones with coil springs, shock absorbers and anti-roll torsion bar
Rear suspension: Rigid axle with semi-elliptic leaf springs, shock absorbers and radius arm
Brakes: Drums (front and rear)
Wheels: Steel, 15-in. dia.
Tires: 8.20 x 15 in.

DIMENSIONS
Length: 211.8 in.   **Width:** 74.8 in.
Height: 64.0 in.   **Wheelbase:** 123.0 in.
Track: 58.5 in. (front), 60.0 in. (rear)
Weight: 4,558 lbs.

Rolls-Royce PHANTOM V

In 1959, Rolls-Royce combined its new alloy V8 engine with a stretched version of the Silver Cloud II chassis to form the luxurious long-wheelbase Phantom V limousine. At the time, it was the most expensive car in the world.

"...an easier drive."

"With its power-assisted steering, the Phantom V is easier to drive than previous Rolls-Royces. To get the smooth shift that its passengers would prefer, the secret is to downshift manually even though the automatic transmission can do it for you. Acceleration is blissfully smooth, but once its speed exceeds 30 mph, it is advisable to switch to the firmer rear shock absorber setting to prevent it from bouncing. The Phantom can run over 100 mph with the V8 remaining barely audible."

The tasteful use of wood is exactly what you would expect of a Rolls-Royce.

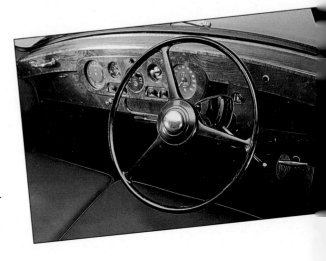

Milestones

1953 Rolls-Royce starts work on a new V8 engine design. It lasts well into the 1990s.

The Phantom III was the first Rolls-Royce to use a V12 engine.

1959 After more than six years of development, the V8 engine is finally ready for production. It is first used in the Silver Cloud II. The Phantom V limousine is also launched in the same year. It is mechanically very similar to the Silver Cloud II but is larger and heavier.

...antoms were built—and sold readily—right up to 1992.

1968 Phantom V production ends as the new long-wheelbase version of the Silver Shadow is released.

UNDER THE SKIN

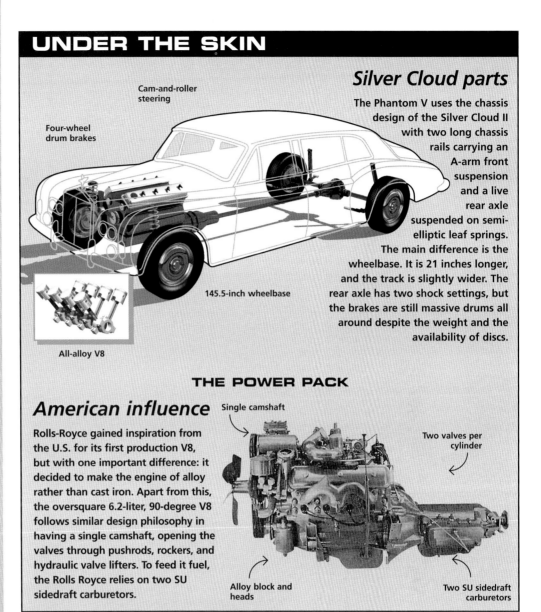

Cam-and-roller steering

Four-wheel drum brakes

145.5-inch wheelbase

All-alloy V8

Silver Cloud parts

The Phantom V uses the chassis design of the Silver Cloud II with two long chassis rails carrying an A-arm front suspension and a live rear axle suspended on semi-elliptic leaf springs. The main difference is the wheelbase. It is 21 inches longer, and the track is slightly wider. The rear axle has two shock settings, but the brakes are still massive drums all around despite the weight and the availability of discs.

THE POWER PACK

American influence

Rolls-Royce gained inspiration from the U.S. for its first production V8, but with one important difference: it decided to make the engine of alloy rather than cast iron. Apart from this, the oversquare 6.2-liter, 90-degree V8 follows similar design philosophy in having a single camshaft, opening the valves through pushrods, rockers, and hydraulic valve lifters. To feed it fuel, the Rolls Royce relies on two SU sidedraft carburetors.

Single camshaft

Two valves per cylinder

Alloy block and heads

Two SU sidedraft carburetors

Royal assent

A Phantom V was specially built for Queen Elizabeth II in 1960 to be the main State car. The principal difference is a higher roof line with a Plexiglas dome fitted for higher visibility. The passenger compartment is lit by fluorescent strip lights.

The Phantom V is so quintessentially British, even the Queen has one.

Rolls-Royce PHANTOM V

Formality, timelessness and elegance is what the Phantom V is all about. This was achieved in a shape that didn't last as long as the mainstream Silver Cloud II that was built right alongside of it.

V8 engine

Rolls-Royce wanted quiet refinement above all else with the V8 engine, which is why it settled on an unstressed 6.2-liter V8 with pushrod overhead valves giving quieter operation. The engine is all alloy, even though weight was never an issue.

Three-speed automatic

All Rolls-Royces from this period use GM's HydraMatic three-speed automatic transmission. When the later Silver Shadow was being built, the HydraMatic-based transmission was replaced by GM's superior TH400 automatic.

Occasional middle seats

When extra passengers need to be carried, two occasional seats can fold up and away from recesses in the lower part of the front seatbacks. These seats are not adjustable, but there is plenty of legroom.

Long wheelbase

The luxurious interior required the wheelbase of the Phantom V to be lengthened more than 21 inches compared with the standard Silver Cloud II Sedan.

Transmission brake

Because the handbrake could not hold the huge weight of the Phantom on any real slope, a transmission brake comes into operation when the car is parked with the ignition off and reverse gear selected.

Adjustable rear shock absorbers

Like the Silver Cloud II, the Phantom V has two-position rear shock absorbers that can be changed by using a switch on the dashboard. The Phantom V has a very soft initial setting and a harder setting that is recommended when the car is traveling over 30 mph.

Specifications

1959 Rolls-Royce Phantom V

ENGINE

Type: V8

Construction: Alloy block and heads

Valve gear: Two valves per cylinder operated by a single camshaft

Bore and stroke: 4.10 in. x 3.60 in.

Displacement: 6,230 cc

Compression ratio: 9.0:1

Induction system: Two SU HD6 sidedraft carburetors

Maximum power: Not quoted

Maximum torque: Not quoted

Top speed: 101 mph

0-60 mph: 13.8 sec.

TRANSMISSION

Three-speed automatic

BODY/CHASSIS

Separate steel chassis frame with coachbuilt limousine bodywork

SPECIAL FEATURES

Quad headlights distinguish this as a later Phantom V.

The rear doors open backward to provide easier access for passengers.

RUNNING GEAR

Steering: Cam-and-roller

Front suspension: Double A-arms with coil springs piston-type telescopic shock absorbers and anti-roll bar

Rear suspension: Live axle with semi-elliptic leaf springs, torque arms and electrically controlled shock absorbers

Brakes: Drums, 11.08-in. dia. (front and rear)

Wheels: Pressed-steel disc, 15-in. dia.

Tires: 8.90 x 15

DIMENSIONS

Length: 238.0 in.　　**Width:** 79.0 in.

Height: 69.5 in.　　**Wheelbase:** 144.0 in.

Track: 60.8 in. (front), 64.0 in. (rear)

Weight: 5,712 lbs.

Skoda FELICIA

The name Felicia conjures up images of easy-going happiness so it's no surprise that the convertible Skoda was the company's most glamorous model. It offered good looks and semi-sporty motoring at a bargain price.

"...respectable performance."

"Anyone who has struggled with the wayward handling of a rear-engined Skoda will be pleasantly surprised by the much more confident Felicia. The overhead-valve engine is not the most free-revving but delivers perfectly respectable performance. The controls may feel a little heavy, and because the suspension was designed to cope with poor roads, a bumpy ride is in order. That said, the Felicia negotiates corners in a safe fashion."

Simpler than many Western cars, the Felicia is nevertheless well trimmed inside.

Milestones

1955 Skoda launches its new people's car, the 440 sedan.

The Felicia was based on the Octavia sedan.

1958 A restyled, more powerful convertible model is released with the type number 450.

1959 The Convertible model is named Felicia, mirroring the sedan's name change to Octavia.

1961 A bigger 1,221-cc engine is available the new Felicia Super.

The new Felicia—a small, front-drive hatchback or sedan debuted during 1990.

1964 Production of the Felicia ends as Skoda turns to a new rear-engined philosophy.

UNDER THE SKIN

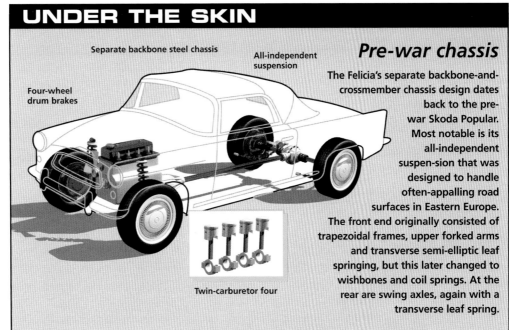

Separate backbone steel chassis

All-independent suspension

Four-wheel drum brakes

Twin-carburetor four

Pre-war chassis

The Felicia's separate backbone-and-crossmember chassis design dates back to the pre-war Skoda Popular. Most notable is its all-independent suspen-sion that was designed to handle often-appalling road surfaces in Eastern Europe. The front end originally consisted of trapezoidal frames, upper forked arms and transverse semi-elliptic leaf springing, but this later changed to wishbones and coil springs. At the rear are swing axles, again with a transverse leaf spring.

THE POWER PACK

Pre-war durability

In design, the 1.1-liter inline four-cylinder engine dates back to before the war. It is an overhead-valve unit with three main bearings and solid valve lifters. In the sedan it has a single Jikov carburetor, but for the droptop Felicia it is fitted with twin downdraft carburetors and has a higher compression ratio. Initially, the 1,089-cc engine developed 50 bhp, which later rose to 53 bhp. From 1961, a Felicia Super model was also offered, with a larger-bore (2.83 inches x 2.95 inches) 1,221-cc unit taken from Skoda's biggest model, the 1201. This engine boasts a few extra horse-power and useful additional torque.

Felicia Super

Many people think of Skodas as poor-quality economy cars, but the Felicia disproves this perception. Like all Skodas of the period, it is solidly built but also looks attractive. If you have a choice, go for the larger-engined Felicia Super.

A Felicia Super was introduced in 1961 with a 1,221-cc engine.

Skoda FELICIA

Skodas were always tough little cars, designed to cope with very poor roads. The Felicia was a rare attempt to inject some fun and allure into the marque, a factor that makes it desirable today.

Four-seater cabin

Despite its compact dimensions, the Felicia is a full four-seater with relatively generous space. The trunk is also a good size.

Choice of engine sizes

When launched, the Felicia had a 50-bhp, 1,089-cc engine. From 1961, you could also buy a Felicia Super with a 53-bhp, 1,221-cc unit that was advantageous mainly for its torquey pulling power.

Fender bulge

One of the strongest features of the body design is a bold, extended arch over each front wheel. Its character is emphasized by a chrome strip running above it.

Convertible top

Unique to the Felicia in Skoda's range was its convertible roof, which folds away elegantly behind the seats. Alternatively, you could opt to fit a removable fiberglass hardtop for an extra $150. This had the distinction of being designed by Ghia.

Restyled front end

Compared to the Octavia sedan, the Felicia looks sleeker, thanks to a restyled front end. Whereas the sedan had an old-fashioned split grill, the Felicia is much more modern with its single oval grill and attractive mesh.

Tailfins

Even the Czechs were influenced by the tailfin craze. The Felicia has small fins tacked onto what is otherwise a very curvaceous bodystyle.

Specifications

1959 Skoda Felicia

ENGINE
Type: Inline four-cylinder
Construction: Cast-iron block and head
Valve gear: Two valves per cylinder operated by a single camshaft via pushrods and rockers
Bore and stroke: 2.68 in. x 2.95 in.
Displacement: 1,089 cc
Compression ratio: 8.4:1
Induction system: Two downdraft carburetors
Maximum power: 53 bhp at 5,000 rpm
Maximum torque: 55 lb-ft at 3,500 rpm
Top speed: 83 mph
0-60 mph: 24.5 sec

TRANSMISSION
Four-speed manual

BODY/CHASSIS
Separate backbone chassis with steel two-door convertible body

SPECIAL FEATURES

All Felicia models were built as convertibles.

Fins and dagger-shaped taillights mirror Detroit cars of the period.

RUNNING GEAR
Steering: Worm-and-nut
Front suspension: Double wishbones with coil springs and shock absorbers
Rear suspension: Swing axles with semi-elliptic leaf spring and shock absorbers
Brakes: Drums (front and rear)
Wheels: Steel disc, 15-in. dia.
Tires: 5.50 x 15

DIMENSIONS
Length: 159.0 in.   **Width:** 63.0 in.
Height: 54.0 in.   **Wheelbase:** 94.5 in.
Track: 47.6 in. (front), 49.2 in. (rear)
Weight: 2,009 lbs.

CZECHOSLOVAKIA 1955-1975

Tatra **T2-603**

The big, beautiful T603 was the last of the streamlined Tatras built for Czech diplomats. Beautifully engineered, it features a 2.5-liter, air-cooled V8 that was enough to propel it to a top speed of nearly 100 mph.

"...better than you'd expect."

"With a high top gear and a slippery shape the T603 is happiest on long runs where it will cruise at high speeds. Acceleration is willing, though the column shifter requires some acclimatization. The four-wheel disc brakes are strong and the steering is very light because there is very little weight at the front of the car. In fact, the T603 corners much better than you'd expect—it stays very flat for its massive size and traction is excellent."

The front bench seat in the T603 can easily seat three people in comfort.

The Tatra T600 Tatraplan also had its engine mounted in the rear.

1936 The 100-mph T87 replaces the T77. Production continues until 1950.

1955 After a five-year break, the T603 is announced with a 2.5-liter V8. Early cars have three headlights behind one-piece glass.

Replacing the 603 was the T613. This is a T613-5 model.

1969 The 603 is fitted with disc brakes and an electronic ignition.

1975 The 613 replaces the 603 after 20,422 cars have been built.

1998 Tatra road car production comes to an end.

UNDER THE SKIN

Aerodynamic

The 603's intelligently designed and virtually handmade steel monocoque isn't as heavy as it appears to be. A large car by European standards, it can accommodate three passengers on its bench seats. The front suspension relies on trailing arms, while swing axles and coil springs are at the rear. Steering is by rack-and-pinion, and the transmission is a four-speed with a large gap between third and fourth.

Swing axle rear suspension

Flat floorpan

Lightweight V8

Four-wheel disc brakes

THE POWER PACK

Rear-mounted V8

The 603's lightweight, V8 engine is cooled by air using two scavenger blowers. The blowers automatically control the engine temperatures by a thermostat that opens shutters in the air intake below the rear bumpers. In contrast to earlier Tatra V8 engines, the camshaft is mounted in the center of the block. The addition of two carburetors boosted power from 95 bhp, as produced by the early cars first seen in 1955, to 105 bhp by the late 1960s. Like earlier Tatras, the 603's engine is mounted behind the rear axle, but despite this the handling is quite predictable.

Redesigned

The later T2-603 model is the most desirable of the Czech-built Tatras for several reasons. For one, adding two carburetors increases the power. Secondly, the redesigned front end with four lights replacing the three is more useful and attractive.

The rounded look of the 603 is sure to turn people's heads.

Tatra **T2-603**

Tatra used the rear-mounted engine design for all of its passenger cars. The most successful model was the distinctive-looking 603. It stayed in production for 20 years.

Spacious interior

Early T603s can seat six passengers with ample head and legroom. Later T2-603 models are five seaters but still have cavernous interiors.

V8 engine

The 603's 2.5-liter, V8 engine was one of the lightest in the world for its capacity and power when it appeared in 1955—it weighs just 398 lbs.

Aerodynamic styling

The 603's smooth, wind-cheating shape with its near-flat underside, shows the car's performance potential—105 mph on 105 bhp from such a large sedan is remarkable for this period. Note the split rear window: originally the 603 would have had a fin like the earlier T77 and T87 models.

Disc brakes

Early 603 models had drum brakes, but from the mid-1960s, Dunlop discs—as found on the MKII Jaguar—were fitted as standard.

Spare tire

The spare tire is stored in a special compartment at the front of the car, separate from the luggage area.

Tatra T2-603

ENGINE

Type: V8

Construction: Alloy block and head

Valve gear: Two valves per cylinder operated by a single camshaft

Bore and stroke: 3.00 in. x 2 .75 in.

Displacement: 2,472 cc

Compression ratio: 8.2:1

Induction system: Twin Jikov carburetors

Maximum power: 105 bhp at 5,000 rpm

Maximum torque: 123 lb-ft at 4,000 rpm

Top speed: 99 mph

0-60 mph: Not quoted

TRANSMISSION

Four-speed manual

BODY/CHASSIS

Unitary monocoque construction with steel four-door sedan body

SPECIAL FEATURES

The side air scoops help to cool the rear-mounted V8 engine.

The quad headlight front end is a hallmark of later T2-603 models.

RUNNING GEAR

Steering: Rack-and-pinion

Front suspension: Trailing arms, with coil springs, telescopic shock absorbers and anti-roll bar

Rear suspension: Swing axles with coil springs and telescopic shock absorbers

Brakes: Discs (front and rear)

Wheels: Steel disc, 15-in. dia.

Tires: Crossply, 6.70 x 15

DIMENSIONS

Length: 196.7 in. **Width:** 74.6 in.

Height: 61.2 in.   **Wheelbase:** 105.3 in.

Track: 58.5 in. (front) 55.1 in (rear)

Weight: 3,241lbs.

Triumph **TR2**

The first of the TRs that became popular in the U.S. featured tough mechanical components and a strong, 2-liter, four-cylinder engine. The TR2 was affordable and fast enough to become a proven race winner.

"...extremely impressive."

"Don't expect refinement; the stiff, short-travel suspension means the TR2 has a harsh ride, but this allows the car to be thrown around. The back end comes around if provoked, but it is easily caught. It is a real blast to drive. The transmission is wonderful, the engine is responsive and the acceleration is extremely impressive for such a small car in the mid-1950s."

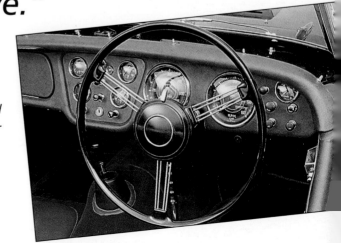

You sit up close to the large steering wheel in the cockpit of a TR2.

Milestones

1952 Standard

Triumph chairman Sir John Black decides they should build a rival to MG. The prototype, the 20TS, is quickly produced, mostly from existing components.

The TR2 was a competitive rally car in the 1950s.

1953 A heavily

revised Triumph, the TR2, is exhibited at the Geneva Show. With the help of a specially designed aerodynamic windshield, the TR2 reaches 125 mph on the Jabbeke highway in Belgium.

The TR5 was the first TR to use a six-cylinder engine.

1954 The TR2

shows its strength by finishing first and second in the British RAC Rally. A privately entered car comes in 15th overall at Le Mans.

1955 Improvements

such as front disc brakes and appearance changes prompt a name change to TR3. In all, 8,628 TR2s have been made.

UNDER THE SKIN

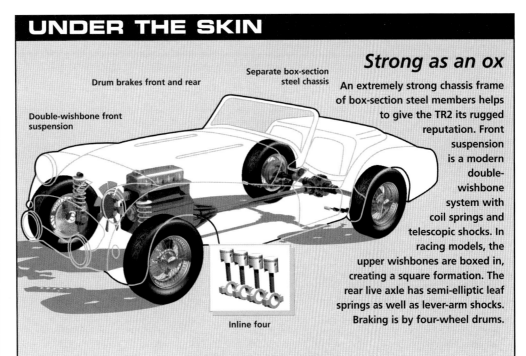

Drum brakes front and rear

Separate box-section steel chassis

Double-wishbone front suspension

Inline four

Strong as an ox

An extremely strong chassis frame of box-section steel members helps to give the TR2 its rugged reputation. Front suspension is a modern double-wishbone system with coil springs and telescopic shocks. In racing models, the upper wishbones are boxed in, creating a square formation. The rear live axle has semi-elliptic leaf springs as well as lever-arm shocks. Braking is by four-wheel drums.

THE POWER PACK

Solid design

An inline four-cylinder engine was the obvious choice for the TR2. The long-stroke 2.0-liter is all cast-iron, but rather than having a solid bored block, it has removable cast-iron wet liners for the pistons to run in, so a rebore would never be necessary. The iron head holds two valves, worked by a block-mounted camshaft with pushrods and adjustable rockers in a non-crossflow design. The exhaust and intake valves are on the same side of the head, with the angled spark plugs on the other side. To increase reliability in the competition cars, Nimonic valves capable of withstanding 600°C were used.

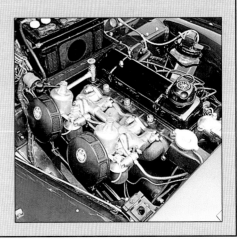

OVC 276

This car was the first to be registered by the TR competitions department. Number OVC 276 competed in four events in 1954–1955, including the Mille Miglia and a class-winning performance in the Liège-Rome-Liège rally. It was also a spare car at Le Mans.

This car has been completely restored to its original specification.

Triumph **TR2** 🇬🇧

The TR styling was inspired. It looked rugged as well as pretty, with its flowing front and rear fenders and cutaway doors. It suggested the speed and acceleration that it delivered.

Four-cylinder engine
Standard Triumph's four-cylinder engine first appeared in the Standard Vanguard sedan but was used in smaller displacement for the TR2. That was easily achieved by using narrower liners to give a .08-inch smaller bore.

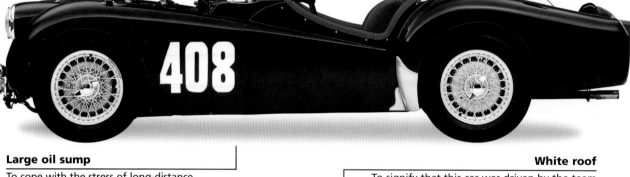

Large oil sump
To cope with the stress of long-distance events, this car has a 1.5-gallon oil pan that's cast in alloy to save weight.

White roof
To signify that this car was driven by the team leader, Ken Richardson, its roof and convertible cover are white. This made the car easily identifiable in black-and-white TV footage and photographs.

Overdrive for competition

For competition use, there was overdrive working on second, third and fourth gears, effectively giving the car seven forward gears. The change in and out of overdrive was very quick. This system appeared in the roadgoing TR3.

Quick-release tunnel

So that repairs could be performed as quickly as possible, the transmission tunnel has a quick-release mechanism on it.

Specifications

1954 Triumph TR2

ENGINE

Type: Inline four-cylinder

Construction: Cast-iron block with wet liners and cast-iron head

Valve gear: Two valves per cylinder operated by a single block-mounted camshaft with pushrods and rockers

Bore and stroke: 3.32 in. x 3.68 in.

Displacement: 1,991 cc

Compression ratio: 8.5:1

Induction system: Two SU carburetors

Maximum power: 90 bhp at 4,800 rpm

Maximum torque: 117 lb-ft at 3,000 rpm

Top speed: 103 mph

0-60 mph: 12.2 sec.

TRANSMISSION

Four-speed manual with overdrive

BODY/CHASSIS

Separate steel chassis with steel two-door convertible body

SPECIAL FEATURES

The spare wheel is located in a neat space beneath the trunk.

The decals from when the car raced and rallied for the TR factory still remain.

RUNNING GEAR

Steering: Cam-and-lever

Front suspension: Double wishbones with coil springs and telescopic shock absorbers

Rear suspension: Live axle with semi-elliptic leaf springs and lever-arm shock absorbers

Brakes: Drums (front and rear)

Wheels: Knock-on/off center-fixing wire spoke, 15-in. dia.

Tires: Michelin X, 5.50 x 15

DIMENSIONS

Length: 151.0 in. **Width:** 55.5 in.

Height: 50.0 in. **Wheelbase:** 88.0 in.

Track: 45.0 in. (front), 45.5 in. (rear)

Weight: 2,070 lbs.

Triumph **TR3**

Spurred on by MG's success, Triumph quickly developed its own light-weight, no-nonsense roadster. The initial TR2 was soon followed by the TR3, a powerful little sportster with a bargain price tag.

"...an undeniably fun car."

"Compared to other similar sports cars of its day, the TR3 is a solid, fast, traditional sports car. Its 100-bhp engine gives it a very good turn of speed and it can cruise very comfortably in overdrive top gear; the generous torque also makes driving very easy. Several strengths stand out: a pleasant close-ratio transmission and exceptional economy, with disc brakes and powerful braking. It's also an undeniably fun car to drive."

A big steering wheel and well-stocked dash are typical of 1950s sports cars.

UNDER THE SKIN

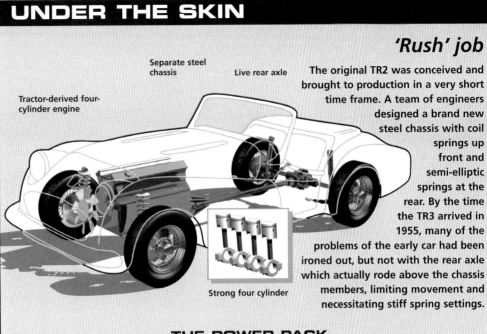

Separate steel chassis

Live rear axle

Tractor-derived four-cylinder engine

Strong four cylinder

'Rush' job

The original TR2 was conceived and brought to production in a very short time frame. A team of engineers designed a brand new steel chassis with coil springs up front and semi-elliptic springs at the rear. By the time the TR3 arrived in 1955, many of the problems of the early car had been ironed out, but not with the rear axle which actually rode above the chassis members, limiting movement and necessitating stiff spring settings.

THE POWER PACK

Vanguard engine

The 2.0-liter powerplant was a development of the Standard Vanguard sedan four-cylinder unit, itself a derivative of the parent company's Ferguson tractor engine. This pushrod overhead valve engine may have an agricultural feel but it's certainly powerful in the TR3. With twin SU carburetors it develops 95 bhp in original form and 100 bhp from early 1956. The TR engine had a reputation for robustness and reliability—100,000 miles is no problem for the sturdy four.

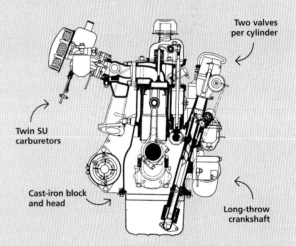

Two valves per cylinder

Twin SU carburetors

Cast-iron block and head

Long-throw crankshaft

Classic TR

In many ways the TR3 is the best of the old-fashioned TR family. It had overcome many of the crudities and inadequacies of the hastily-developed TR2, and was faster, while retaining the charm of the 'hole-in-the-wall' grill style and no external door handles.

The TR3 is considered by many as the classic TR.

Triumph **TR3**

The TR3 had the distinction of being the most cost-efficient 100-mph car on the market and that alone was enough to bring it a following. It was also rugged, well put together and extremely reliable.

Full-width grill

Unlike the grill of the earlier TR2 and TR3, the TR3A has a full-width chrome grill. It gives the front end a much cleaner look.

'Tractor' engine

The 2.0-liter four-cylinder engine's origins lay with the Ferguson agricultural tractor. While that may not have been glamorous, it certainly made the powerplant rugged and reliable, and its power output was very generous at between 95 and 100 bhp.

High ground clearance

A significant benefit of the TR3's chassis arrangement was that no significant component lay unprotected under the chassis. The TR3 frequently triumphed in competitive events because it managed to avoid being damaged.

Cut-away doors

One of the very traditional features of the TR3 was its cut-away doors. As of 1954, the doors had become 'short doors' to help them clear high sidewalks.

Simple dashboard

The interior was deliberately very simple, with bucket seats and a wood-rim steering wheel. The driver enjoyed a fine spread of six gauges with the speedometer and tachometer directly in front, and four secondary gauges in the center of the instrument panel.

Axle over chassis

Triumph engineers elected to run the axle above the rear chassis members. This limited axle travel and necessitated the use of very stiff springs at the rear.

Specifications

1957 Triumph TR3A

ENGINE
Type: In-line 4-cylinder
Construction: Cast-iron block and head
Valve gear: Two valves per cylinder operated by single camshaft via pushrods and rockers
Bore and stroke: 3.27 in. x 3.62 in.
Displacement: 1,991 cc
Compression ratio: 8.5:1
Induction system: Two SU carburetors
Maximum power: 100 bhp at 5,000 rpm
Maximum torque: 117 lb-ft at 3,000 rpm
Top speed: 106 mph
0-60 mph: 11.4 sec.

TRANSMISSION
Four-speed manual with optional triple overdrive

BODY/CHASSIS
Separate chassis with two-door sports body

SPECIAL FEATURES

The smooth glass wind deflectors are very useful in keeping the weather out when you have no wind-up windows.

A trunk-mounted luggage-rack adds extra storage space.

RUNNING GEAR
Steering: Cam-and-lever
Front suspension: Wishbones with coil springs and shock absorbers
Rear suspension: Rigid axle with semi-elliptic leaf springs and shock absorbers
Brakes: Discs (front and rear)
Wheels: Steel or wires 15 in. dia.
Tires: 5.50 in. x 15 in.

DIMENSIONS
Length: 151.0 in. **Width:** 55.5 in.
Height: 50.0 in. **Wheelbase:** 88.0 in.
Track: 45.0 in. (front), 45.5 in. (rear)
Weight: 2,200 lbs.

Volkswagen **BEETLE**

The legendary 'people's car' was commissioned by Adolf Hitler and continually modernized during its life. It has kept its distinctive shape and engine layout while more than 20 million Beetles have been produced from factories around the world.

"...was always bound to succeed"

"The Beetle's charm is immediate; the flat-four's whirring buzz is infectious and even the low-powered ones feel eager. The light gearshift is incredibly good for a car of its day, and so is the soulful but easy steering. You might expect the handling of the early swing-axled cars to be rather tricky, but it isn't, partly because there's too little power for you to get into much trouble. With a comfortable ride and effective brakes the Beetle mixture was always bound to succeed."

The no-frills interior of the Beetle shows its utilitarian design. As an affordable car for the masses, it had nothing that was unnecessary.

Ferdinand Porsche discusses the design with his son, Ferry.

UNDER THE SKIN

Simple and strong

Torsion bar suspension all around allows easy separation of the floorpan from the bodyshell without disturbing any of the running gear. For this reason, the Beetle chassis has been the most widely used base for kit cars. 1970 saw the first major departure from the original specification with MacPherson struts replacing the intrusive front transverse torsion bars. At the same time semi-trailing arms were introduced to replace the rear swing axles.

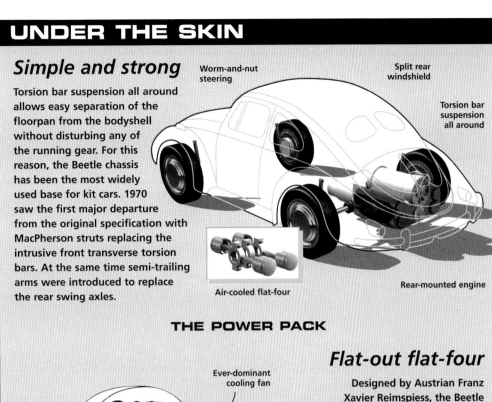

Worm-and-nut steering

Split rear windshield

Torsion bar suspension all around

Air-cooled flat-four

Rear-mounted engine

THE POWER PACK

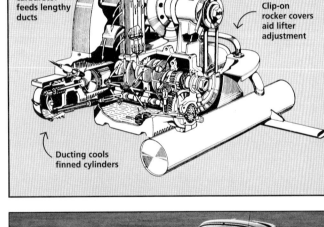

Ever-dominant cooling fan

Single carburetor feeds lengthy ducts

Clip-on rocker covers aid lifter adjustment

Ducting cools finned cylinders

Flat-out flat-four

Designed by Austrian Franz Xavier Reimspiess, the Beetle engine is an air-cooled over-square flat-four 'boxer' of simple design. Alloy is used for the cylinder block and heads, and the valves are operated by pushrods from a central camshaft. It was refined and enlarged over the years from its original 985 cc to 1,600 cc in 1971. Bulletproof and reliable, the engine was designed to withstand sustained top-speed driving on the open highways. It only has one inherent problem—carburetor icing.

Karmann bug

Among the most desirable of all Beetles are the convertibles. The first appeared as early as 1949 but those built by Karmann in the 1970s were much more luxurious and took the Beetle into the realm of status symbol, rather than 'people's car.'

The cabriolet conversion VW was sub-contracted to Karmann.

251

Volkswagen BEETLE

Simple, sturdy and robust: the Beetle was all of those things. It was practical and affordable too, and over the years its performance improved dramatically to keep it competitive for well over 30 years.

Flat-four engine

The flat-four engine was light, thanks to the use of alloy rather than cast iron, and the cylinder barrels could be detached for overhaul. Original power output was just 25 bhp.

Drum brakes

Only drum brakes were available when the Beetle was developed, but they were enlarged through the car's lifetime until eventually front disc brakes became available on the 1302 model.

Rear-mounted battery

Never intended as a performance car, no effort was made to balance the weight of the engine by mounting items like the battery at the front.

Swinging arm rear suspension

Independent rear suspension was unusual when the Beetle was created, and although the swing axle system was simple, it worked well. It only became a problem when the Beetle acquired more power.

ot air heater

ith no water
stem a heater is
rd to arrange.
rly Beetles had a
stem which fed hot
r through the sills
to the passenger
mpartment to
ep the rear
indow
frosted.

Flat windshield

Early Beetles had flat
windshields. Later cars
had more familiar
curved windows that
were less prone to
annoying reflections.

Torsion bar front suspension

The Beetle has
short trailing arms
connected to
torsion bars. This
design was space
efficient and more
than adequate,
even when its
power was steadily
increased.

Larger rear window

First designs for the
Beetle showed no rear
window at all. It entered
production after the war
with two small rear
windows. The split rear
window design was
replaced with a single
window in 1953 and
was enlarged over
the years.

Specifications
1954 VW Beetle deluxe Sedan

ENGINE

Type: Air-cooled horizontally opposed flat-four

Construction: Aluminum cylinder barrels with cast-iron liners and alloy cylinder heads

Valve gear: Two valves per cylinder operated by pushrods from a single central camshaft

Bore and stroke: 3.03 in. x 2.52 in.

Displacement: 1,192 cc

Compression ratio: 6.1:1

Induction system: One solex downdraft single-choke carburetor

Maximum power: 30 bhp at 3,400 rpm

Maximum torque: 56 lb-ft at 2,000 rpm

Top speed: 78 mph

0-60 mph: 16.1 sec.

TRANSMISSION

Four-speed manual

BODY/CHASSIS

Separate steel body on pressed-steel backbone and floor-platform chassis

SPECIAL FEATURES

Early Beetles had semaphore indicators rather than flashing indicator lights.

Volkswagen's Wolfsburg factory was built on the land of Count Von Schulenberg. The Wolfsburg badge represents the Count's coat of arms.

RUNNING GEAR

Steering: Worm-and-nut

Front suspension: Double torsion bars with radius arms

Rear suspension: Swing axle with torsion bar and radius arms

Brakes: Drums, 9-in. dia. (front), 9-in. dia. (rear)

Wheels: Pressed steel 15-in. (front and rear)

DIMENSIONS

Length: 165 in.   **Width:** 61 in.

Height: 61 in.   **Wheelbase:** 94.5 in.

Track: 51.1 in. (front), 49.2 in. (rear)

Weight: 1,629 lbs.

Index